LIFE IN CHRIST

LIFE IN CHRIST

Lessons from Our Lord's
Miracles and Parables

The Miracles of Our Lord

Volume 1

Charles H. Spurgeon

We love hearing from our readers. Please contact us
at www.anekopress.com/questions-comments with
any questions, comments, or suggestions.

Cover Design: Natalia Hawthorne, BookCoverLabs.com
Cover Painting: Matt Philleo
eBook Icon: Icons Vector/Shutterstock
Editors: Heather Thomas and Sheila Wilkinson

Printed in the United States of America
Aneko Press – *Our Readers Matter*™
www.anekopress.com
Aneko Press, Life Sentence Publishing, and our logos are trademarks of
Life Sentence Publishing, Inc.
203 E. Birch Street
P.O. Box 652
Abbotsford, WI 54405

RELIGION / Christian Life / Spiritual Growth
Paperback ISBN: 978-1-62245-390-0
eBook ISBN: 978-1-62245-391-7
10 9 8 7 6 5 4 3 2
Available where books are sold

Contents

Chapter 1

Our Lord's Question to the Blind Men

And when Jesus departed from there, two blind men fol-
lowed him, crying out and saying, Thou Son of David, have
mercy on us. And when he was come into the house, the blind
men came to him; and Jesus said unto them, Believe ye that
I am able to do this? They said unto him, Yes, Lord. Then he
touched their eyes, saying, According to your faith be it unto
you. And their eyes were opened; and Jesus straitly charged
them, saying, See that no one knows it. (Matthew 9:27-30)

In our own streets, we may occasionally meet a blind beggar, but they fill the streets of the Middle Eastern cities. Inflammation of the eye is the scourge of Egypt and Syria. Volney (1759-1820) declared that in Cairo, out of a hundred people he met, twenty were completely blind, ten were blind in one eye, and twenty others suffered some form of disease in their eyes to varying degrees. The problem is immense in the Middle and Far East, and things were probably worse in our Savior's time. We ought to be grateful that leprosy, afflictions of the eye, and other forms of disease have been held in check among us in modern times to the point that the plague, which devastated our city (London) two hundred years ago, is now unknown, and our hospitals are no longer crowded with lepers.

Today, blindness is often prevented, frequently cured, and no longer a leading cause of poverty in this country. Because there were so many blind people in our Savior's day, many flocked to him, and we read about him healing them. Mercy met misery on its own battlefield. Where human sorrow was most obvious, divine power displayed compassion.

Today, though, it is a very common thing for men to be blind spiritually. This fact causes me to have great hope that our Lord Jesus will act in the same way and display his power in the midst of our abundant evil. I trust that some who read these words long to obtain spiritual sight and see Jesus like the two blind men in Matthew, because to see Jesus is to see everlasting life. To those who feel their spiritual blindness and yearn for the light of God and of pardon – the light of love and peace, the light of holiness and purity – our eager desire is that the darkness may be lifted, and the divine light may find a passage into your soul's inner gloom to cause the night of your sinful nature to pass away forever.

It is a very common thing for men to be blind spiritually.

Oh, that the moment of light may be at hand for many of you who are "inwardly blind." The possibility of immediate illumination is the blessing I urge you to consider. I know that truth can dwell in the memory for years and at some point produce fruit. But our prayer is for immediate results, considering the nature of the light we're talking about. In the beginning, *God said, Let there be light, and there was light* (Genesis 1:3). And when Jesus, the Son of God, walked as a man on earth, all he did was touch the eyes of the blind, and immediately they received sight. If only that was the norm today!

Men who were led by the hand to Jesus or groped their way along the wall to find him were touched by his finger and went home without a guide, rejoicing that Jesus Christ had opened their eyes. Jesus is still able to perform such miracles. And, depending upon the Holy Spirit, we will preach his Word and watch for the signs to follow, expecting to see them at once. Why shouldn't those who read this and are blinded by sin be blessed with the light of heaven? This is our heart's inmost desire, and to this end we direct our efforts. With that said, let's look at the text and allow ourselves to be affected by the truths which it will present to us.

The Seekers

First, we must look at the seekers themselves – the two blind men. There's something about them worthy of imitation by all who desire to be saved.

The two blind men were in downright earnest. The words which describe their appeal to Christ are *crying out*. This doesn't mean simply speaking, because it says, *crying out and saying. Crying out* implies earnest, energetic, pathetic begging and pleading. Their tones and actions indicated that their desire was a deep, passionate craving. Imagine yourselves in such a case and how starved for blessed light you would be if for years you had been forced to live in what Milton called "the ever-during dark." They hungered and thirsted after sight.

We can't hope for salvation until we seek it with the same sense of need. Few display such a strong sense of earnestness about being saved, but many demonstrate this type of passion regarding their money, their health, or their children. They're quick to show their passion for politics and business, but the moment you bring up matters of true godliness, they're as cool as the Arctic snows. How can this be? Do you expect to be saved while you're half asleep? Do you expect to find pardon and grace while you continue in lethargic indifference? If so, you are sadly mistaken, for *life is given unto the kingdom of the heavens, and the valiant take hold of it* (Matthew 11:12).

The soul's eternal destiny is no small matter, and salvation by the precious blood of Christ is not something to take lightly.

Death and eternity, judgment and hell are not things to play with. The soul's eternal destiny is no small matter, and salvation by the precious blood of Christ is not something to take lightly. Men aren't saved from eternity in hell by a careless nod or a wink. A mumbled "Our Father" or a hasty "Lord, have mercy upon me" will not suffice. These blind men would have remained blind if they hadn't cried out in earnest to have their eyes opened. So, many today continue in their sins, because they don't act with a strong sense of urgency to escape. These men were fully awake. Are you? Can you, with a sincere heart, join with me in these two verses?

Jesus, who now art passing by,
> Our Prophet, Priest, and King thou art:
Hear a poor unbeliever's cry,
> And heal the blindness of my heart:

Urging my passionate request,
> Thy pardoning mercy I implore,
Whoe'er rebuke I will not rest,
> Till thou my spirit's sight restore.
> (John Wesley)

Perseverance in Prayer

The blind men were persevering in their devoted pursuit of Christ. How did they manage to follow the movements of the Lord? We don't know. It must have been very difficult, because they were blind, but they probably asked others which way the Master had gone and kept their ears open to every sound.

They likely asked, "Where is he? Where's Jesus? Lead us, guide us. We must find him." We don't know how far our Lord had gone, but we do know they followed as far as he went. They persevered so bravely that when they reached the house where he was, they didn't stay outside until he came out again. They pressed into the room where he sat. Their quest for sight was so persistent that their pleas attracted his attention. He paused and listened while they said, *Thou Son of David, have mercy on us.*

In this way, their perseverance prevailed: no man will be lost who knows the art of persistent prayer. If we resolve to never leave the gate of mercy until the gatekeeper opens to us, our persistence will cause him to open the door. If we grab onto the angel of the Lord and hang on saying, "I won't let go until you bless me," we will emerge from the wrestling more than a conqueror.

A mouth open in unceasing prayer will result in open eyes that see faith clearly. So, pray in the darkness, even if there seems to be no hope of light. When God, who is light, moves a poor sinner to plead and cry out with the commitment to continue until the blessing comes, he doesn't even consider disregarding that poor crying heart. Perseverance in prayer is a sure sign that the day of opening the eyes of the blind is near.

The blind men had a definite objective in their prayers. They knew what they wanted. They weren't like children crying for nothing or greedy misers crying for everything. They wanted their sight and they knew it. Many blind souls are unaware of their blindness, so when they pray, they ask for anything except the one thing they need.

> **Many so-called prayers are made up of nice words and pretty, pious sentences, but they are not prayer.**

Many so-called prayers are made up of nice words and pretty, pious sentences, but they are not prayer. To those who are saved, prayer is communion with God. To those seeking salvation, it's asking for what you want and expecting to receive it through the name of Jesus. But what sort of prayer is it when there's no sense of need, no direct asking, and no intelligent pleading? Have you in precise words asked the Lord to save you? Have you expressed your need for a new heart, your need for being washed in the blood of Christ, and your need for being made God's child and adopted into his family? There is no praying until a man knows what he's praying for and determines to pray for it, as if he cares about nothing else.

If someone is filled with passion and insistence and makes his requests known, he is sure to succeed in his pleading. With a strong arm, he draws the bow of desire and places a sharp arrow of passionate longing upon the string. Then, with clarity of sight, he takes deliberate aim. Because of his diligence, we can expect him to hit the very center of the target. Pray for light, life, forgiveness, and salvation; pray with all your soul. As surely as Christ is in heaven, he will give these good gifts to you. He has never refused a single one.

Mercy

In their prayers, these blind men honored Christ, because they said, *Thou Son of David, have mercy on us.* The religious leaders of the land refused to recognize our Lord as being of the royal seed, but these blind men proclaimed Jesus as the Son of David. They were blind, but they could see a great deal more than some with clear vision. They saw that the Nazarene was the Messiah, sent from God to restore the kingdom to Israel.

Because they knew the Messiah was prophesied to open blind eyes, they believed Jesus the Messiah could open their blind eyes. So they appealed to him to perform what he had the power to do. In this way, they recognized him as Messiah and honored him with a real, practical faith. The prayer which crowns the Son of David will always reach the throne of God.

Pray. Glorify Christ Jesus in your prayers. Plead the merit of his life and death and give him glorious titles, because your soul has a deep love and reverence for him. Prayers that adore Jesus carry in them the force and swiftness of eagles' wings. They ascend to God, because the elements of heavenly power are abundant in them. Prayer that makes little of Christ is prayer that God will make little of, but prayer that glorifies the Redeemer rises like a perfumed pillar of incense from the Most Holy Place, and the Lord himself smells the sweet fragrance.

These two blind men also confessed their unworthiness. *Thou Son of David, have mercy on us.* Their only appeal was for mercy. They said nothing about their worthiness. They didn't attempt to gain favor because of their past sufferings, their perseverance, or their plans for the future. Their appeal was *Have mercy on us.* He who demands a blessing from God as if he is entitled to it will never receive it.

We must plead with God as a condemned criminal appeals to his king and asks for a royal pardon to free him from the consequences of his actions. As a beggar pleads for money in the street by appealing to man's generosity, so must we appeal to the Most High. We ask for his compassion and direct our requests to his lovingkindness and tender mercy in this way, "O God, if you choose to destroy me, I deserve it. If you never look on me with a kind expression, I can't complain. But save me, a sinner, Lord, for mercy's sake. I have no claim upon you whatsoever, but because you are full of grace, look on a poor blind soul that eagerly looks to you."

I can't put fine words together. I've never studied speech. In fact, my heart loathes the very thought of intentionally speaking with fine words when souls are in danger of eternal separation from God. No, I work to speak straight to your hearts and consciences, and if there is anyone with faith to receive, God will bless them with fresh revelation.

"And what kind of listening is that?" you ask.

The way in which a man says, "As far as I understand that the preacher delivers God's Word, I will follow him and do what he tells the seeking sinner to do. I will pray and plead tonight, and I will persevere in my requests before God; I will use all my effort to glorify the name of Jesus while I confess my own unworthiness. I will crave mercy at the hands of the Son of David." Happy is the preacher who knows this will be the result of his labor.

Belief

Notice the question that Jesus asked them. They had pursued the Lord to have their eyes opened. They both stood before him whom they couldn't see, but who could see them and could reveal himself to them by the words he spoke. He questioned them, not so he could know them, but so they could know themselves. He asked one question: *Believe ye that I am able to do this?*

The answer to that question was the only thing which stood between them and sight. Their answer determined if they left that room as seeing men or blind. I believe that this same question stands between every seeking sinner and Christ. *Believest thou that I am able to do this?* And if any man can answer as these blind men did, *Yes, Lord,* he will receive the same reply, *According to your faith be it unto you.*

Let's look at this important question with serious attention. It concerned their faith. *Believe ye that I am able to do this?* He didn't ask what their character had been in the past, because when men come to Christ, the past is forgiven them. He didn't ask if they had tried other methods to open their eyes, because whether they had or not, they were still blind. He didn't even ask them if they thought another physician might have a miraculous cure for them. He didn't ask any of these things, because curious questions and idle speculations are never suggested by the Lord Jesus.

His inquiries were all meant to reach one point – faith. Did they believe that he, the Son of David, could heal them? Why does our Lord, not only in his ministry but also in the teaching of the apostles, always place such importance upon faith? Why is faith so essential? It's because of its power to receive. A bank won't make a man rich, but without a place for his money, how could a man acquire wealth?

Faith by itself couldn't contribute a penny to salvation, but it's the bank which holds Christ within itself. It holds all the treasures of divine love. If a man is thirsty, a rope and bucket alone aren't much use to him. But if there's a well nearby, he needs the bucket and rope to lift the water. Faith is the bucket with which men have the ability to draw water out of the wells of salvation and drink to their heart's content. At some time, you may have paused at the water cooler to have a drink but realized you couldn't when the cups were gone. The water was there, but you couldn't get it. It might have been tempting to drink directly from the spigot, but you really wanted a little cup. Faith is that little cup, which we hold up to the flowing stream of Christ's grace. We fill it, then we drink and are refreshed. This example illustrates the importance of faith.

Laying a cable under the sea from England to America would have seemed useless to our ancestors, and it would be useless now if science hadn't taught us how to speak across great distances through the illustration of lightning. Yet, the cable became important, because the best inventions of telegraphy would have been useless for transatlantic communication without a connecting wire between the two continents. Faith is like the cable. It's the connecting link between our souls and God, and God's living message flashes through it to our souls. Faith is sometimes weak like a thin thread, but it's still a precious thing, because it's the beginning of great things.

Years ago, men wanted to build a suspension bridge over a navigable river, which flowed through a mighty chasm. They proposed to hang an iron bridge from cliff to cliff but puzzled over how to start. They shot an arrow from one side to the other, and it carried a tiny thread across the ravine.

That almost-invisible thread was enough to begin with. The connection was established. Then they used the thread to draw a piece of twine across; they used the twine to pull a small rope across, and they used the rope to carry a cable across. Soon, iron chains crossed with the other supplies needed to build the bridge.

In the same way, faith is often very weak. But even in that case, it's of great value, because it serves as a pathway for communication between the soul and the Lord Jesus Christ. If we believe in him, a link forms between him and us. Our sinfulness rests on his grace, our weakness hangs on his strength, and our nothingness hides in his abundance. But if we don't believe, we remain separated from Jesus, and no heavenly blessing can flow to us.

> Our sinfulness rests on his grace, our weakness hangs on his strength, and our nothingness hides in his abundance.

To every seeking sinner, the question I have to ask in my Master's name has to do with faith and nothing else. It doesn't matter if you're rich or poor, if you come from high society or live in the country, or if you earned a doctorate or possess an eighth-grade education. We have the same gospel to deliver to every man, woman, and child, and we must place the emphasis on the same point – *Believest thou?* If you believe, you will be saved. But if you don't believe, it's impossible for you to share in the blessings of God's grace.

The next question concerned their faith *in Jesus*. He asked, *Believe ye that I am able to do this?* We could ask a sinner whose eyes have been opened, "Do you believe you can save yourself?"

His answer would be, "No, I don't, because I know better. My own ability is dead."

We might then ask him, "Do you believe ordinances and sacraments can save you?"

If he's intelligent and has been awakened, he'll reply, "I know better. I've tried them, but by themselves they are nothing but arrogance."

He is correct; nothing remains of us which hope can build upon, even for an hour. But when we look only to Jesus, our focus passes from ourselves to him, and we can hear him say, *Believe ye that I am able to do this?*

When we speak about the Lord Jesus Christ, we aren't simply talking about a historical person. We speak of one who is above all others.

He is the Son of the Most High God, and yet he came to earth as a baby in Bethlehem and grew up as other children do. He became a man in physical form and wisdom and lived here for thirty years or more, doing good.

In the end, this glorious God in human flesh died, *the just for the unjust, that he might bring us to God* (1 Peter 3:18). He stood in our place to bear our punishment. He did this so the payment for our sin would be acceptable in God's sight; as a just man, Jesus became the justifier for all who believe. He died and was buried, but the grave could only hold him for a short time. Early in the morning on the third day he rose from the dead and conquered sin and death.

Jesus remained on earth in his risen form long enough for many to bear witness of his resurrection. No event in history is as authenticated as the resurrection of Christ. He was seen by individuals, small groups, and by more than five hundred brethren at once. After that, he ascended into heaven as his disciples watched.

Do you believe that I am able to save you?

Now he is seated at the right hand of God. The same man who died upon the cross is on the throne in the highest heavens as Lord of all, and every angel delights to worship him.

The one question he is asking you through my lips is this: "Do you believe that I am able to save you? – that I, the Christ of God who now dwells in heaven, am able to save you?" Everything depends upon your answer to that question. I know what it should be. Surely, if he is God, nothing is impossible or even difficult for him. If he laid down his life to make payment on your behalf, and God accepted that payment by permitting him to rise from the dead, then his blood is able to cleanse you and me. Your answer should be: "Yes, Lord Jesus, I believe that you are able to do this."

Now consider the importance of another word of the Matthew text: *Believe ye that I am able to do* **this**? It would have been useless for these blind men to say, "We believe that you can raise the dead."

"No," says Christ, "the matter at hand is the opening of your eyes. *Believe ye that I am able to do* **this**?"

They might have replied, "Good Master, we believe that you stopped the woman's issue of blood when she touched thy garment" (Luke 8:43).

"No," he says, "that's not the question. Your eyes need to be dealt with. You want sight, and the question about your faith is *believe ye that I am able to do* **this?**"

Some can believe for other people, but you must answer the question for yourself, "Do you believe that Christ is able to save *you – even you?* Is he able to do *this?*"

You may be living a life full of sin. Maybe you've crowded a great deal of wickedness into a short space, and it's taken a toll on you. As you look back on your life, you realize that you've never known another man or woman who threw their lives away more foolishly than you.

So, do you desire to be saved? Can you say from your heart that you do? After you've answered that question, answer this one: Do you believe that Jesus Christ is able to do *this* – to blot out all your sins, to renew your heart, and to save you right now?

You might believe he is able to forgive sin, but do you believe that he is able to forgive your sin? Your sin is the sin in question; do you believe? Don't worry about others right now, but consider yourself. *Believest thou that he is able to do* **this?** *This* – this sin of yours, this misspent life – is Jesus able to cope with *this?* Everything depends on your answer to that question.

Faith is pointless if you only believe in the Lord's power over others but declare that you have no confidence in him for yourself. You must believe that he is able to do whatever concerns you; or you are, for all practical purposes, an unbeliever.

I know many have never embraced the vices of the world. I am thankful that you have been kept from this difficult path. But I know some of you almost wish that you had been such open sinners, so the change in you would be as obvious as the change you see in some of them.

Don't indulge such an unwise wish but listen while I ask you the same question. You're a "good person" who has obeyed every outward duty but has neglected God. The problem with good people is that they think repentance is impossible for them, because they've been consumed by self-righteousness to the point that they don't know how to cut out the gangrene.

The Lord Jesus Christ can save you from your self-righteousness as easily as he can save someone else from his guilty habits. Do you believe that he is able to do *this*? Do you believe God is able to accomplish *this* work in your life? This question requires a yes or no answer.

The Lord Jesus Christ can save you from your self-righteousness.

You might cry, "But my heart is so hard." Do you believe he can soften it? Suppose it's as hard as granite. Don't you believe that the Christ of God can turn it into wax? Suppose your heart is as volatile as the wind and waves of the sea. Can you believe that he can make you stable-minded and place you firmly upon the Rock of Ages forever?

If you believe in him, he will do this for you because of your faith. However, everybody can embrace Christ's power for others, but they have tremendous difficulty embracing it for themselves. Each man is accountable for himself. You must be willing to be honest with yourself. Jesus asks each one, "Do you believe that I am able to do *this*?"

Someone might say, "It would be the most surprising thing that the Lord Jesus ever did if he saved me tonight." Do you believe he can do it? Will you trust him to do it now?

"But it would be such a strange thing, such a miracle!" The Lord Jesus works strange things. It's his way. He's always been a miracle-worker. Can you believe he's able to do this for you, which is needed in order to save you?

The power which faith has is wonderful – power over the Lord Jesus himself. I've often experienced, in a little way, how confidence will master me. It's common to be conquered by the trustfulness of a tiny child. The child's simple request was too full of trust to be refused. Have you ever been grasped by a blind man at a street crossing who said to you, "Sir, would you take me across the road?" Then, perhaps, he said somewhat cunningly, "I can tell by the tone of your voice that you are kind. I feel I can trust you." At times like this, you felt that you were in for it, and you couldn't let him go.

When a soul says to Jesus, "I know you can save me, my Lord. I know you can, so I trust in you." He won't dismiss you. He won't even wish to do so, because he said, *he that comes to me I will in no wise cast out* (John 6:37).

Sometimes I tell a story to illustrate this point. It shows how faith wins everywhere. Many years ago, my garden happened to be surrounded by a hedge. It was green but provided poor protection. A neighbor's dog was very fond of visiting my garden. Since he never improved my flowers, I never gave him a friendly welcome.

I walked along one evening and saw him doing mischief. I threw a stick at him and told him to go home. How did the creature reply to me? He turned around, wagged his tail, and happily picked up my stick. He brought it to me and laid it at my feet. Did I strike him? No, I'm not a monster. He and I were friends immediately, because he trusted me and conquered me.

As simple as that story is, it's the same philosophy as a sinner's faith in Christ. As the dog mastered the man by confiding in him, a poor guilty sinner masters the Lord himself by trusting him and saying, "Lord, I'm a poor dog of a sinner, and you have every right to drive me away, but I believe you're too good for that. I believe you can save me, and I trust myself in your hands. Whether I'm lost or saved, I trust myself to you."

You will never be lost if you trust in this way. He who trusts himself with Jesus has already answered the question, "Do you believe that I am able to do this?" There's nothing left but for him to go on his way and rejoice, because the Lord has opened his eyes and saved him.

A Reasonable Question

Believe ye that I am able to do this? Let me show that this was a reasonable question for Christ to ask and equally reasonable for me to emphasize. Our Lord Jesus could have said, "If you don't believe that I'm able to do this, why did you follow me? Why did you follow me and not somebody else? You followed me down the streets and into this house. Why have you done this if you don't believe I'm able to open your eyes?"

A large number of you attend a place of worship. You like to be there but why, if you don't believe Jesus? What do you go there for? Do you go to seek a Savior who can't save you? Are you like a fool who seeks after one you can't trust? I've never heard of a sick man who runs after a doctor in whom he has no confidence. Do you attend places of worship without having any faith in Jesus? Then why do you attend?

Again, these blind men prayed to Jesus to open their eyes, but why did they pray? If they didn't believe Jesus could heal them, their prayers were a joke. Would you ask a man to do something you knew he couldn't do? Prayer must always be measured by the quantity of faith we put into it.

Some of you have been in the habit of praying since you were little children. You seldom go to bed without repeating the prayers your mother taught you. Why do you do that if you don't believe that Jesus Christ can save you? Why ask him to do what you don't believe he can do? What strange inconsistency – to pray without faith!

These two blind men called Jesus Christ the *Son of David*. Why did they confess his Messiahship? Most of you do the same. I suppose that out of our congregation few doubt the deity of Christ. You believe in the Word of God. You don't doubt that it's inspired. You believe that Jesus Christ lived, died, and now dwells in glory.

However, if you don't believe he's able to save you, what's the point of saying he's God? God, and not able? A dying, bleeding, atoning sacrifice, and not able to save? If this is your case, your public profession of faith in Christ Jesus is not your true one. If you were to write out your standing in Christ, it would go something like this, "I don't believe in Jesus Christ as the Son of God, or that he made a full payment for sin, and I don't believe that he is able to save me." Wouldn't that be closer to reality?

He is worthy of your trust, and your trust is all he asks of you.

Consider how often you listen to the teaching of the Word, pray for help and guidance, and profess to be a believer in the Word of God. How is it possible that you don't believe in Jesus? He must be able to save you.

More than twenty-seven years ago, I put my trust in Jesus. From my first-hand experience, I can say that in every hour of darkness, in every season of depression, in every time of trial, I've found him faithful and true. So, I trust him with my soul. If I had a thousand souls, I would trust them with him. If I had as many souls as there are sands upon the seashore, I wouldn't ask for a second Savior. I would put them

14

all into his precious hand, which was pierced with the nail, so he could hold us securely forever.

He is worthy of your trust, and your trust is all he asks of you. He is able and willing, because he died for you. He only asks you to believe that he is able to save you and wants you to trust yourself to him.

Notice the answer these blind men gave to his question. They said to him, *Yes, Lord.* I've been pressing you with the same question, and I repeat it again. Do you believe Christ is able to save you and that he is able to do this even with all your uniqueness?

Now for your answer. How many of you will say, *Yes, Lord*? I'm tempted to ask you to say it out loud, but I'll beg you to say it within your secret souls, *Yes, Lord.* May God the Holy Spirit help you say it *unmistakably* without any holding back or mental reservation, "Yes, Lord. Blind eyes, dumb tongue, cold heart – I believe you are able to change them all, and I give myself to you to be renewed by your divine grace." Say it and mean it. Say it with conviction, clearly, and with your whole heart, "Yes, Lord."

The two men replied immediately. The question was barely out of Christ's mouth, and they gave the answer, *Yes, Lord.* There's nothing like a quick answer when you ask a man, *Believe ye that I am able to do this?* If he stops, rubs his head, and finally says, " Y-yes," doesn't such a *yes* sound more like *no*?

The best yes in the world is the one that comes immediately. "Yes Lord, as bad as I am, I believe you can save me, because I know your precious blood can take away every stain. I have lived a life of sin and only professed religion. I've lived as a hypocrite to the point that I don't feel like I belong in the church or in the world. I realize that I'm actually the opposite of what I should be. Yet, I believe that if Christ died for sinners, then he must be able to save the worst of them. I come to God through him, and I believe he is able to save even me." That's the kind of answer I desire from each of you. May the Spirit of God produce it!

Finally, we come to our Lord's response to their answer. He said, *According to your faith be it unto you.* This was the same as saying, if you believe in me, there is light for your blind eyes. They received true sight for true faith. If you believe with firm conviction, you won't have only one eye opened or both eyes half opened, but you will have complete sight in both eyes.

Firmly grounded faith will clear away every speck and make your vision strong and clear. If your answer is quick, his answer will also be quick. The Lord's power just kept in step with their faith. If their faith was true, his cure was true. If their faith was complete, his cure was complete. And if their faith said yes, immediately, he gave them sight immediately.

If you take a long time to say yes, it will take a long time to get peace. But if you say, "I will receive it, because I believe it's true, and Jesus must be able to save me. I will give myself up to him." If your response is immediate, you will have instantaneous peace. Yes, you who are burdened will find rest.

You will wonder where the burden has gone and look around and find that it has vanished, because you have looked to the Crucified One and trusted all your sins to him. The bad habits you've been trying to conquer, which have forged fresh chains to bind you, will fall off you like spiders' webs. If you can trust Jesus to break them and surrender yourself to him to be renewed by him, it will be done and done immediately. And heaven's eternal arches will ring with shouts of sovereign grace.

I've presented you with everything you need to make the right decision. My only hope is that the Holy Spirit will lead you to seek like the blind men sought and to trust as they trusted.

Some people are diligent in finding reasons why they shouldn't be saved. I have battled with some of these, and they always end up saying, "Yes, that's true, but . . ." Then we try to chop that *but* to pieces, but after a while they find another and say, "Yes, I now see that point, but . . ." So, they fortify their position of unbelief with *buts.*

If anybody desired to give you a thousand pounds, can you tell me any reason why he shouldn't? I think if he came to you and presented you with a check for that amount, you wouldn't obsess over reasons you shouldn't accept the check. You wouldn't keep on saying, "I would like the money, but . . ." No, if there was any reason why you shouldn't have it, you'd let someone else figure it out. You wouldn't waste your energy, trying to find reasons against taking the money. After all, you aren't supposed to be your own enemy.

Yet, when it comes to eternal life, which is infinitely more precious than all the treasures of this world, men act like fools and say, "I really want it, and Christ is able to do it, but . . ." To argue against yourself is total foolishness.

If a man were in Newgate Prison, condemned to die, and scheduled to be hanged in the morning, when the sheriff came and said, "There's a free pardon for you," do you think that man would object?

Would he cry, "I would like another half hour to consider my case, so I can figure out some reason why I shouldn't be pardoned?" No, he would jump at the opportunity.

I pray that you would also jump at the opportunity for pardon, and that the Lord would make you feel such a sense of danger and guilt that you promptly cry, "I do believe; I will believe in Jesus."

> **Sinners aren't half as sensible as sparrows.**

Sinners aren't half as sensible as sparrows. David said, *I watch and am as a sparrow alone upon the house top* (Psalm 102:7). Well, have you noticed the sparrow? He keeps his eyes open, and the moment he sees a grain of wheat or anything to eat down in the road, he flies to get it. I've never seen him wait for an invitation, much less someone to beg and plead with him to come and eat.

He sees the food and says to himself, "Here's a hungry sparrow, and there's a piece of bread. Those two things go well together; there's no good reason to keep them apart." Down he flies and eats up all he can find as fast as he finds it. Oh, if you only had half the sense of the sparrow, you would say, "Here's a guilty sinner, and there's a precious Savior. These two things go well together, there's no good reason to keep them apart. I believe in Jesus and Jesus is mine."

I pray that you may find Jesus right now. I pray that you would look to Jesus Christ and believe. Faith is only a look, a look of simple trust. Faith is dependence, a believing that he is able to do this and trusting him to do it right now. God bless every one of you, and may we meet in heaven for Christ's sake. Amen.

Chapter 2

The Plain Man's Pathway to Peace

*And when Jesus departed from there, two blind men fol-
lowed him, crying out and saying, Thou Son of David, have
mercy on us. And when he was come into the house, the blind
men came to him; and Jesus said unto them, Believe ye that
I am able to do this? They said unto him, Yes, Lord. Then he
touched their eyes, saying, According to your faith be it unto
you. And their eyes were opened; and Jesus straitly charged
them, saying, See that no one knows it.* (Matthew 9:27-30)

I'm not going to elaborate on this incident or draw illustrations from
it. However, I'm going to direct your attention to one single point in
it – extreme simplicity. The Bible includes other cases of blind men, and
we have various accounts associated with them. In one account, Jesus
made clay, applied it to the blind man's eyes, and sent him to wash at
the pool of Siloam. But in Matthew 9, the cure was simple. The men
are blind, they cry to Jesus, they come to Jesus, they confess their faith,
and they receive their sight immediately.

In many other accounts of miracles performed by Christ, circumstances were difficult. In one case, four men let a man who suffered from
palsy down through the roof to where Jesus was (Luke 5:17-25). In a
second account, a woman came behind him in the crowd and touched
the hem of his garment. When he discovered her, he asked who had

touched him (Mark 5:25-34). Then we read of Lazarus who had been dead four days, and the situation seemed impossible until Jesus commanded him to come out of the tomb (John 11:1-45).

But everything in the Matthew 9 account is straightforward and simple. These blind men are conscious of their blindness and confident that Christ can give them sight. They cry to him, come to him, believe he is able to open their eyes, and they receive their sight immediately.

In their case, we see some simple elements: a sense of blindness, a desire for sight, prayer, their coming to Christ, an open declaration of faith, and then the cure. The whole matter in a nutshell. No details suggest anxiety. The whole interaction is simplicity itself, and that's the point we'll consider in detail.

Some conversions are as uncomplicated as this biblical account of Jesus opening of the eyes of these blind men. We should never doubt the reality of the work of grace in these conversions, because of how easily they occur and the lack of dramatic details surrounding the conversion. We should never presume that a conversion is a less genuine work of the Holy Spirit, because it's simple. May the Holy Spirit grant us wisdom as we dig into this text.

Coming to Christ in the Midst of Difficulty

I must acknowledge it's an undisputed fact that many people must overcome great difficulties when coming to Christ. We must admit that most don't come as simply and quickly as these blind men came. We each know people who came to Christ through a process of struggle, effort, disappointment, long waiting, and a kind of desperation that almost forced them to come. Perhaps our own stories are among these.

Entire biographies are written to explain in great detail the struggles of those who have believed before us. You've probably read John Bunyan's description of how the pilgrims came to the wicket gate. They were directed by Evangelist to a light and a gate. They went that way according to his direction.

A young man in Edinburgh was anxious to speak to others about their souls. One morning, he spoke to an old woman. He began by saying to her, "Here you are with your burden."

"Aye," she said.

He asked her, "Did you ever feel a spiritual burden?"

"Yes," she said, resting a bit, "I felt the spiritual burden years ago, before you were born, and I got rid of it, too. But I didn't go the same way that Bunyan's pilgrim did."

Our young friend was surprised to hear her say that and thought she might be following unsound doctrine, so he begged her to explain.

"No," she said, "when I became concerned for the condition of my soul, I heard a true gospel minister, who encouraged me to look to the cross of Christ. I lost my load of sin there, and I didn't hear one of those watered-down preachers like Bunyan's Evangelist."

"How," said our young friend, "did you determine that?"

"Why, that Evangelist, when he met the man with the burden on his back, said to him, 'Do you see that wicket gate?' 'No,' said he, 'I don't.' 'Do you see that light?' 'I think I do.' Why, he shouldn't have spoken about wicket gates or lights. He should have said, 'Do you see Jesus Christ hanging on the cross? Look to him, and your burden will fall off your shoulder.' He sent that man 'round the wrong way when he sent him to the wicket gate, and a lot of good it did him, for he was likely to end up choked in the slough of despond. I looked at once to the cross and away went my burden."

"What," said the young man, "did you never go through the slough of despond?"

"Ah," she replied, "more times than I care to tell. But since the first time I heard the preacher say, 'Look to Christ,' I looked to him. I've been through the slough of despond since then, but it's much easier to go through that slough with your burden off than it is with your burden on."

> We must be done with self in all forms and keep our eyes only on Jesus if we want to be at peace.

And so, it is. Blessed are they whose eyes are only and always on the Crucified. The older I grow the more sure I am of this – that we must be done with self in all forms and keep our eyes only on Jesus if we want to be at peace. Was John Bunyan wrong? Certainly not. He described things as they generally are. Was the old woman wrong? No, she was perfectly right. She described things as they ought to be, and as I wish they always were. Still, our experiences are not always what they should be, and much of what Christians experience cannot be considered Christian experiences.

Regretfully, I must admit that a large number of people, before they come to the cross and lose their burden, go 'round and 'round, trying this plan and that plan, instead of coming directly to Christ as they are and look to him to find light and life immediately. So, why is it that some take so long to come to Christ?

In some cases, ignorance is the problem. Perhaps there's no other subject men are more ignorant of than the gospel. Isn't it preached in hundreds of places? Yes, thank God, it is. It's illustrated in books without number, but still men don't come. Neither hearing or reading alone can cause a man to discover the gospel. The Holy Spirit must teach them, or men will remain in ignorance as to the simplicity of salvation by faith.

Men are in the dark and don't know the way, so they run here and there to find a Savior who is already there and ready to bless them. *But what does it say? The word is near thee, even in thy mouth and in thy heart: that is, the word of faith, which we preach, that if thou shalt confess with thy mouth the Lord Jesus and shalt believe in thine heart that God has raised him from the dead, thou shalt be saved* (Romans 10:8-9).

In order for salvation to be of grace, it must be received only by faith and not through the works of the law, nor by the work of a priest or by any rites, rituals, or ceremonies whatsoever.

Many times, men are hindered by prejudice. People are brought up in the belief that salvation must be through ceremonies, and to some degree or other it is obtained by their works. Numbers of people have learned a sort of half-and-half gospel, part law and part grace, and they are in a thick fog about salvation. They know redemption has something to do with Christ, but it's a mixture with them. They don't quite see that it's all Christ or no Christ.

They think that we are saved by grace, but they don't see that salvation must be of grace from top to bottom. They fail to see that in

22

order for salvation to be of grace, it must be received only by faith and not through the works of the law, nor by the work of a priest or by any rites, rituals, or ceremonies whatsoever.

Being brought up to believe that there is something they must do, they struggle a long time to break the chains of slavery and enter into the blessed sunlight of the Word, where the child of God sees Christ and finds liberty. Believe and live is a foreign concept to a soul that is persuaded its own works have some ability to win eternal life.

With many, the hindrance lies in downright bad teaching. The teaching that is all too common today is dangerous. The modern-day church service makes no distinction between saint and sinner. The teaching is like one-size-fits-all clothing, which is made to fit everyone, but really fits nobody. They offer prayers to satisfy saints or sinners but appease neither. The words may be beautiful and grand, but they give people a false sense of security to believe that they're somewhere between being saved and being lost but not actually lost. Certainly, they aren't quite saints but a sort of Samaritan who fears the Lord, serves other gods, and hopes to be saved by a combination of grace and works.

It's hard to bring men to grace alone and faith alone. They want to stand with one foot on the sea and the other foot on the land. Much of today's teaching attempts to build them up in the thought that there's something they are able to do themselves to accomplish salvation. Because of this, they don't learn within their own souls that they must be saved by Christ and not by themselves.

We must also consider the natural pride of the human heart. We don't like to be saved by charity; we want to have a part in it. When we are confronted with the truth, we are driven away from self-confidence, but we hang on by our teeth if we can't find a hold by any other means. With awful desperation, we trust in ourselves. We will cling by our eyelashes to the illusion of self-confidence. We won't give up carnal confidence if there is any way possible to hold on to it.

Then, with our pride, opposition to God enters. The human heart doesn't love God, and it often displays its opposition by opposing him about the plan of salvation. *For the prudence of the flesh is death, but the prudence of the Spirit, life and peace, because the prudence of the flesh is enmity against God; for it does not subject itself to the law of God, neither indeed can it* (Romans 8:6-7). The enmity of the unrenewed heart is not displayed by actual open sin in all cases. Since open sin is so overt in our society, in a sense it has become moral. Because mankind has become so comfortable in his "acceptable sin," he hates God's plan of grace alone. This is where pride and opposition to God join forces.

Men are so fortified in their position that they hate that the Scripture mentions divine sovereignty or teaches, *I will have mercy on whom I will have mercy, and I will have compassion on whom I will have compassion* (Romans 9:15). They embrace talk of the rights of fallen men and how a loving God wouldn't punish anyone. Then, when it comes to sovereignty and God's demonstration of his grace according to his own perfect will, they can't endure it.

If they tolerate God at all, it won't be on the throne. If they acknowledge his existence, it's not as King of kings and Lord of lords who acts according to his will and has a right to pardon whom he desires. If they reject the Savior, he will leave them to perish in their guilt. Ah, these are the hearts who don't love God as God, as revealed in Scripture. They make themselves a god of their own desires and cry: *These are thy gods, O Israel* (Exodus 32:8).

In some instances, the struggle of the heart in accepting Christ arises from a singularity of mental conformation. Such instances should be looked at as exceptions and not the rule. For instance, take the case of John Bunyan. If you read *Grace Abounding*, you'll find that for five years or more, he was tempted by Satan, tempted by his own self, and the victim of fearful despair. He took a very long time before he could come to the cross and find peace.

However, don't think that because we struggle in a similar way, you or I will ever turn into John Bunyans. We may dabble, but we are guaranteed to never write a *Pilgrim's Progress*. We might imitate him in his poverty, but we aren't likely to mirror him in his genius. A man with such an imagination and full of wondrous dreams is not born every day.

When a man does come to Christ, his gift doesn't always bear the fruit of a restful life. When Bunyan's imagination had been purified and sanctified, its masterly productions were seen in his marvelous allegories. But before he was renewed and reconciled to God, his mind, as unique as it was, would have been a curse. That marvelous gift would have brought him intense despair if it hadn't been controlled by the Holy Spirit.

Do you understand how eyes accustomed to pitch darkness could barely withstand exposure to the light? Bunyan was not the rule, but the exception. Now, you may be an odd person. I can sympathize with you, because I'm odd myself, but be cautious about forming the belief that everybody else must be odd, too.

If you and I happened to go the long way around to reach salvation, we must not think that everybody should follow our bad example. Let's just be thankful that some people's minds are less twisted and gnarled than ours and not set up our experience as a standard for other people. We know that obstacles may become apparent when we present the gospel to those who possess an extraordinary quality of mind or a spirit of depression. These unique qualities may make the people who possess them peculiar as long as they live.

Others don't come to Christ because of assaults from Satan. Remember the story of the child whose father brought him to Jesus, but *as he was yet a coming, the demon threw him down into convulsions* (Luke 9:42). The evil spirit knew his time was short, and he would soon be cast away from his victim, so he threw him to the ground, made him thrash around in a seizure, and left him half dead. Satan does this with many men. He torments them with all the brutality of his fiendish nature, because he fears that they're about to escape from his service, and he will no longer be able to control them. As Isaac Watts said, "He worries whom he can't devour, with a malicious joy."

We've described those who come to Christ through Satan's attacks, those who come in simplicity, and those who must battle through pride and opposition. Now, we'll turn our attention to those who are not ignorant, have been well instructed, and readily see the light. These instances are cause for great rejoicing.

Simple Obedience

Many come to Christ through much difficulty, but it's not necessary to come this way. I mention this, because I've known Christian men distressed deep within their hearts, because they fear that they came to Christ too easily. As they looked back, they've imagined that they couldn't possibly have been converted at all, because their conversion wasn't accompanied by the agony and torment of mind that others speak of.

First, I'll say that it's very hard to see how feelings of despair can be essential to salvation. Take a moment and look at the argument from the opposite perspective. Is it possible for unbelief to help a soul to faith? Isn't it clear that the anguish, which many experience before they come to Christ, comes directly from unbelief? They don't trust. They say they can't trust, so they're like the troubled sea which can't rest. Their mind is tossed to and fro and tormented by their unbelief. Is this a foundation for holy trust?

I realize that he laid down his life in my place, so I trust him with my whole heart.

It would be the oddest thing in the world if unbelief prepared a soul for faith. If I sowed the ground with thistle seed, is it possible it would be more ready for good corn? Is deadly poison an assistance to health? I don't understand this thought process.

It seems far better for the soul to believe the Word of God immediately and more likely to be a genuine work when the soul that is convinced of sin eagerly accepts the Savior. This is God's way of salvation. He demands that I trust his dear Son who died for sinners. I recognize that Christ is worthy of trust because he is the Son of God. So his sacrifice must be able to pay for my sin. I realize that he laid down his life in my place, so I trust him with my whole heart.

God invites me to trust him, and I do trust him without any question. If Jesus Christ satisfies God, he certainly satisfies me. I come and trust myself with him. Doesn't this response have everything needed? Does it make any sense that raging and despair have anything to do with saving faith? I don't see it.

Some have wrestled with the most awful thoughts. They've falsely believed that God couldn't possibly forgive them. They've imagined that even if he could pardon them, he wouldn't, because they weren't his elect or his redeemed. Though they've seen the gospel presented in love, they still question if they would actually find rest if they did come. *Come unto me, all ye that labour and are heavy laden, and I will give you rest* (Matthew 11:28). They invent suspicions and assumptions, some of which amount to blasphemy against the character of God and the person of his Christ.

I have no doubt that these people have been forgiven according to the riches of divine grace, but their sinful thoughts didn't help them obtain that pardon. My own dark thoughts of God left many scars upon my spirit but were washed away with all my other sins. When I look back at those things, I know there was never any good in them. I can't see any benefit they could have been to anybody. Is it possible to take a bath in ink in order to remove a stain? Can our sin be removed by our sinning more? Sin cannot possibly aid grace, and the sin of unbelief cannot help towards faith.

Again, much of this struggling and tumult within, which some have experienced, is the work of the devil. Is it necessary to salvation for a man to be under the influence of Satan? Does Christ need the devil to come in and help him? Is it helpful for those who seek Christ to see the black fingers of the devil at work with the lily hands of the Redeemer? Impossible. That's not my judgment of the work of Satan, and I don't believe it will be yours.

If you were never driven to blasphemy or despair by Satan, thank God. You wouldn't have gained anything by it, but you would have been a serious loser. No man should imagine that if he had been the prey of tormenting suggestions, his conversion would bear more marks of legitimate truth. No mistake can be more groundless. The devil can't be of any service to any of you. He will do you damage and nothing but damage. Every blow he strikes hurts and does not heal.

Even when Mr. Bunyan wrote of Christian fighting with Apollyon, he said that though he won the victory, he gained nothing. *And they had a king over them, who is the angel of the bottomless pit, whose name in Hebrew tongue is Abaddon, and in Greek, Apollyon meaning destroyer* (Revelation 9:11). A man would be better off to take a detour of many miles over hedge and ditch than to come into conflict with Apollyon a single time.

Everything necessary for conversion is found in simply coming to Jesus without delay. When it comes to the battle, we must face it if it comes but certainly not look for it. It's easy to see how Satanic temptation hinders and keeps men in bondage when they could be living in liberty but difficult to see any good that it could accomplish.

> **Everything necessary for conversion is found in simply coming to Jesus without delay.**

Many instances prove that all this doubting, fearing, despairing, and being tormented of Satan are not essential for legitimate salvation. Countless Christians have come without hesitation to Christ, as these two blind men did, and to this day know little about those things. I know many believers who would tell you that they've ministered to and prayed with those who come to Christ with difficulty, but they've felt, "We don't know anything about all this from our own experience." They were taught the way of God from childhood and trained by godly parents. When they came under the influences of the Holy Spirit early in life, they heard that Jesus Christ could save them. They knew that they wanted to be saved, and they just went to him. It was almost as naturally as when they went to their mother or their father when they were in need. They trusted the Savior and found peace immediately.

Several of the honored leaders who attend our church came to the Lord in this simple manner. Only yesterday, I was pleased when I saw several who confessed faith in Jesus, who had no trace of terrible burns and scars associated with their salvation experience. They heard the gospel, saw their need for salvation, accepted it on the spot, and entered immediately into peace and joy. Now, we aren't saying that there are only a few such conversions, but we proclaim boldly that we know of countless such instances. Thousands of God's most honored servants walk before him in holiness and are notably useful, and whose experience was as simple as ABC. Their whole story might be summed up in this verse:

> I came to Jesus, as I was,
>   Weary and worn and sad;
> I found in him a resting-place,
>   And he has made me glad.

(Horatius Bonar)

I will even say that many whose lives provide the most evidence that they are renewed by grace can't tell you the date their conversion took place but only the circumstances that surrounded it. We don't doubt their conversion, because their lives prove its truth.

You may have many trees in your garden that you've forgotten when they were planted. However, if you get plenty of fruit from them, you're not concerned about an exact date.

I know several people who don't know their own age. I was talking to one the other day who thought she was ten years older than I found out to be the truth. I didn't tell her she wasn't alive, because she didn't know her birthday. If I had suggested that, she would have laughed at me. Yet, some believe that they must not be saved, because they don't know the date of their conversion. If you trust the Savior, and he is all your salvation and all your desire, and if the entirety of your life is affected by your faith, such that you bring forth the fruits of the Spirit, you don't need to worry about times and seasons.

Thousands in the fold of Jesus can proclaim that they are in it, but the date they passed through the gate is totally unknown to them. Thousands came to Christ, not in the darkness of the night but in the brightness of the day. These can't describe weariness, struggle, and despair, but they can sing of free grace and dying love. They came joyously home to their Father's house. The sadness of repentance was sweetened with the delight of faith, which came simultaneously with repentance to their hearts. I know these things to be so.

Here's the simple truth. Many young people are brought to the Savior without any of the torment that afflicts some of us. Another group may come in a similar fashion, unencumbered by the cares of this life. They live simply – in a childlike way. We should all wish to belong to that group. Some professors might be offended to be placed in that group, but I would glory in it. Too many of the doubting, critical people love to complicate life and are great fools for their efforts.

The childlike ones drink the milk, while these folks analyze it. To some minds the hardest thing in the world is to believe a self-evident truth. If they can, they will always complicate the point and puzzle themselves, or they're not happy. In fact, they are never sure until they're uncertain and never at ease until they're disturbed. Blessed are those who believe that God can't lie and are quite sure it must be true if God has said it. These cast themselves upon Christ whether they sink or swim. If Christ's salvation is God's way of saving man, it must be the right way, and they accept it. Many have come to Christ in this way.

Now, we'll take this a step further – the essentials of salvation are all accomplished in the simple, pleasant, happy way of coming to Jesus just as you are. So, what are the essentials? The first is repentance. Some dear souls may feel no remorse, but they hate the sin they once loved. They may not understand the fear of hell, but they feel the burden of sin, which is a great deal better.

They've never stood shivering under the gallows, because, to them, the crime is more dreadful than the punishment. The Holy Spirit has taught them to love righteousness and seek after holiness, and this is the essence of repentance. Those who come to Christ in this way, with simplicity of heart, have certainly obtained true faith. They don't rest in their own tears but in Christ's blood. Their confidence doesn't come from their own emotions but from Christ's suffering. They stand firm in the certainty that Christ has come to save all those who trust him. They demonstrate faith of the purest kind.

These who believe in simplicity of faith also possess love. Faith works in love, and they show it. They often seem to have more love when they first believe than those who come so burdened and full of despair. Because their minds are calm and quiet, they see the beauty of the Savior clearly, and they burn with love for him. They immediately begin to serve him, while others wait for their wounds to heal and try to make their broken bones rejoice.

I don't want to seem unsympathetic to a painful experience, but I want to show that simply coming to Christ as the blind men came and believing that he could give them sight isn't one bit inferior to experiencing despair. Both possess all the essentials of salvation.

Next, notice that the gospel command never implies the same kind of experience, which some have experienced. Are we commanded to preach to men, "Be dragged around by the devil, and you will be saved"? No. We proclaim, "Believe in the Lord Jesus Christ, and you will be saved." So, what's my responsibility in this? To say to you, "Despair, and you will be saved"? No. It's to remind you that Scripture proclaims, *Believe on the Lord Jesus Christ, and thou shalt be saved* (Acts 16:31).

Should we say, "Torture yourself, mangle your heart, scourge your spirit, and grind your soul to powder in desperation"? No. Believe in the infinite goodness and mercy of God in the person of his dear Son and come and trust him. That's the gospel command. It's put into various forms. Here's another example: *Look unto me, and be ye saved, all the ends of the earth; for I am God, and there is no one else* (Isaiah 45:22).

If I came to you and said, "Tear your eyes out," that wouldn't be the gospel, would it? No. It says, *Look unto me.* The gospel doesn't say, "Cry your eyes out." And it doesn't say, "Blind your eyes with a hot iron." No, it says, *Look, look, look.* It's the very opposite of anything like remorse, despair, and blasphemous thought. It's just *look.*

Let's look at it from another perspective. We are told to take of the water of life freely; we are asked to drink of the eternal spring of love and life. *And let him that is thirsty come; and whosoever will, let him take of the water of life freely* (Revelation 22:17). What are we told to do? To make this water of life scalding hot? No. We are to drink it as it freely flows out of the fountain. Are we commanded to make it drip a drop at a time and lie under it, desiring but not able to obtain a mouthful of water? Nothing of the sort. We are to step down to the fountain, drink, and be content, for it will quench our thirst.

What's the gospel again? Isn't it to eat the bread of heaven? *Why do ye spend money for that which is not bread? and your labour for that which does not satisfy? Hearken diligently unto me, and eat ye that which is good, and let your soul delight itself in fatness* (Isaiah 55:2). We are to encourage people to come in to the gospel banquet. And what are they supposed to do when they come? Silently watch others eat? Stand and wait until they feel hungrier? Try forty days of fasting like Dr. Henry Tanner did? Nothing of the sort.

You might think this is the gospel by the way some people preach and act, but it's not. You are to feast on Christ at once. You don't need to fast until you turn yourself into a living skeleton and then come to Christ. I'm not sent with that type of message, but this is my word of good news:

> Ho, every one that thirsts, come ye to the waters, and he that
> has no money; come ye, buy, and eat; come, buy wine and
> milk without money and without price. Why do ye spend
> money for that which is not bread? and your labour for that
> which does not satisfy? Hearken diligently unto me, and eat
> ye that which is good, and let your soul delight itself in fat-
> ness. (Isaiah 55:1-2)

Freely take what God freely gives, and simply trust the Savior. Isn't that the gospel? So, is it reasonable to say that you can't trust Christ because you don't feel this or that? I assure you that I've known many who came to Christ just as they were and never experienced those horrible feelings. Come as you are. Don't try to make righteousness out of your unrighteousness, confidence out of your unbelief, or Christ out of your blasphemies, and don't foolishly imagine that despair produces hope. It's impossible.

You are to leave self behind and accept your position as hidden in Christ where you will be safe. *For ye are dead and your life is hid with the Christ in God* (Colossians 3:3). As the blind man said, when Christ asked him, *Believe ye that I am able to do this?* Your response should be the same, *Yes, Lord.* Trust yourself to your Savior, and he is your Savior.

I'll conclude with a final observation: people who are privileged to come to Jesus Christ softly, pleasantly, and happily are not losers. They simply have less to tell. When it requires a long series of trials to drive a man out of himself, and at last he comes to Christ like a wrecked vessel tugged into port, he has a lot to talk and write about. Perhaps, he thinks it's interesting to be able to share where he came from. And if he can share it to God's glory, it's quite reasonable that he should. Many of these stories are found in biographies, because they excite interest and make a life worth writing about, but you should never conclude that all godly lives are the same.

Happy are those whose lives couldn't be written, because they were so uneventful. Some of the most blessed lives don't get written about, because there's nothing very noteworthy about them. But I say this: when those blind men came to Christ just as they were and said they believed he could open their eyes, he opened their eyes. Isn't there as much of Christ in their story as there could possibly be?

The men themselves are almost unspoken of, but the healing Master is where our attention is drawn. More details about the men's lives might even take away the prominence Christ should have. There he stands, the blessed, glorious One who opens the eyes of the two blind men. There he stands alone, and his name is glorious!

There was a woman who spent all she had on physicians, but instead of getting better, she grew worse. She could have had a long story to share of the various doctors she had visited. However, the recounting of her many disappointments would not have glorified the Lord Jesus one bit more than when these two blind men said, "We heard of him, we went to him,

> Let Christ be first, last, and everything in between.

and he opened our eyes. We never spent a penny on doctors. We went straight to Jesus just as we were, and all he said to us was, 'Do you think that I can do it?' and we said, 'Yes, we believe you can.' He opened our eyes, and it was all done."

If my experience ever stands in my Master's light, I'll do away with my best experience. Let Christ be first, last, and everything in between. Don't you agree? If you come to Christ immediately with nothing unique surrounding the experience, if you're a nobody coming to the blessed Everybody, if you're nothing coming to him who is the All in all, if you're a lump of sin and misery, a great vacuum, and nothing but emptiness that never needs be thought of again, if you will come and lose yourselves in his infinitely glorious grace, that is all that is needed. It seems to me that you won't lose anything by the fact that there's nothing sensational in your experience. There will be a huge sensation of the loss of self, but it's immediately replaced with salvation in Jesus – glory be to his name.

You might think that those who come gently lack evidence of their experience after the fact. Someone once said to me, "I almost wish sometimes that I had been an overt sinner, so I could see the change in my character. But, since I've been morally grounded from my childhood, it's sometimes hard for me to see a definite change."

Let me tell you, friends, that dramatic evidence isn't much help in times of darkness, for the devil says to that man, "You haven't changed your life. You changed your actions, but your heart is still the same. You turned from a bold, honest sinner into a hypocritical, wavering professor. That's all you've done. You gave up open, blatant sin, because your strong passions declined, or you thought you would try another way of sinning. Now you're only making a false profession and still not living how you should."

Very little comfort is gained, no matter what type of conversion we experience, when the archenemy becomes our accuser. In reality, it comes to this: you can never place any confidence in how you came to Christ. Your confidence must always rest in him, whether you came to him flying, running, or walking. If you get to Jesus, you're all right. It's not how you come; it's that you come to him.

Have you come to Jesus? If you've come and doubt whether you've really come, come over again. Never argue with Satan about whether you're a Christian. If he says you are a sinner, reply to him, "So I am, but Jesus Christ came into the world to save sinners, and I will begin again." He's an old lawyer and very cunning. He knows how to baffle us, because we don't understand things as well as he does.

He has spent thousands of years perfecting his skill to make Christians doubt their faith in Christ, and he understands it well. Never answer him. Refer him to the one who speaks for you. Tell him you have an Advocate on high who will answer him. Tell him you will turn to Christ again. If you never went to Jesus before, you will go now. And if you've been before, you will go again. That's the way to end the quarrel. As to evidence, it's fine in theory, but when trials and temptation come, wise men let evidence go. The best evidence a man can have that he is saved is that he still clings to Christ.

Lastly, some may think that those who lack a spectacular testimony lack usefulness, because they won't be able to sympathize with those who are deeply troubled and who must battle despair when they are coming to Christ. Well, there are more than enough of us who can sympathize with those difficult cases, and I don't know that anyone can sympathize with everyone in every respect.

> **The best evidence a man can have that he is saved is that he still clings to Christ.**

One day I told a man who had considerable property that his poor minister had a large family and could barely keep a coat on his back. I said I was confused about how some Christian men who profited under the ministry of that man didn't supply his needs. He answered that he thought it was a good thing for ministers to be poor, because then they could sympathize with the poor. I acknowledged his response and reminded him that there ought to be one or two who aren't poor to sympathize with those who are rich.

I would give to the poor pastor; then he would have the power to sympathize with both classes. The man didn't seem to see my argument, but I think there's a good deal of truth in it. Believers who have had painful experiences can be a blessing as they sympathize with those who have been through that pain. But don't you think it's an equal blessing to have others who, because they haven't gone through that experience, can sympathize with those who haven't gone through it?

We also need some who can say, "Don't be troubled, because the great dog of hell didn't howl at you. If you entered the gate calmly and quietly, and Christ has received you, don't be upset or consider yourself lacking; I came to Jesus the same way." That type of testimony is just as necessary to comfort those who come to Christ in that way. So, if you lose the power to sympathize one way, you will gain the power to sympathize in another, and there will be no great loss after all.

To sum all this up, I wish that every man, woman, and child would come to trust the Lord Jesus Christ. This salvation is unequal to any other so-called redemption. Christ took human sin upon himself and suffered in the sinner's place. All we have to do is accept what Christ has done and trust ourselves wholly to him. He who refuses this plan of salvation deserves to perish, and so he must. Was there ever so sweet, so undeniable, and so plain a gospel? It's a joy to preach it. Will you receive it? Will you yield to be nothing and have Jesus to be all in all?

I pray that none of us reject this perfect way of grace, this open way, this safe way. Come, wait no longer. *The Spirit and the bride say, Come* (Revelation 22:17). Lord, draw them by the love of Jesus. Amen.

Chapter 3

Men as Trees

*And he came to Bethsaida, and they bring a blind man unto
him and beseech him to touch him. So, taking the blind man
by the hand, he led him out of the town; and spitting into
his eyes and putting his hands upon them, he asked him if
he saw anything. And looking, he said, I see men; I see that
they walk as trees. After that, he put his hands again upon
his eyes and caused him to see; and he was whole and saw
everyone, far away and clearly.* (Mark 8:22-25)

Our Savior often healed the sick with a touch, because he wanted
us to understand that the infirmities of fallen humanity can only
be removed through contact with his own blessed humanity. He had,
however, other lessons to teach, so he also utilized other methods of
healing the sick.

The use of various methods was wise for more than one reason. Had
our Lord performed all his miracles in the same way, men would have
attached importance to the method he used to perform the miracle and
would have viewed it superstitiously rather than of the divine power by
which he accomplished the miracle. This may be one reason our Master
presents us with great variety in the miracles he performed. They always
contain the same goodness and display the same wisdom and power.
Yet, he's careful to make each one distinct from all the others, so we

can see the unmistakable goodness of God, and we realize our Savior doesn't lack ways to heal and has no need to repeat himself.

Sin entangles our carnal natures and holds us to what is seen and forget the unseen. The Lord Jesus changes his outward manner of working to emphasize that he's not bound to any method of healing, which is nothing by itself. He wants us to understand that if he chose to heal by touch, he could also heal with a word. If he cured with a word, he could eliminate the word and work by his will. He wants us to grasp that a glance of his eye is as effective as a touch of his hand. Even without being visibly present, his invisible presence can work the miracle while he remains at a distance.

In this miracle of the blind man at Bethesda, our Savior deviated from his usual practice not only in the method of healing but also in the type of cure. In most of his miracles, our Savior restored the person in one step. When we read about the deaf and mute man, Jesus not only opened the man's mouth, but he gave him clear speech even though the man had never heard a sound before. So, he received the gift of language and the power to make articulate sounds at the same time.

In other cases, the fever left the patient at once, the leprosy was healed on the spot, and the issue of blood was stopped. But here, Jesus took a more leisurely approach and only gave part of the blessing at first. He paused and let his patient consider how much he had received and how much was withheld. Then, through a second act, Jesus finished the good work.

Perhaps our Lord's action in this case was motivated not only by his desire to make each miracle unique, but also so men would realize he had more than one way of effecting miracles. It may have been determined by the particular type of disease.

Jesus wouldn't have healed some sicknesses by degrees because it seemed necessary to deal a decisive blow and end them. The casting out of a devil, for instance, must be accomplished entirely, or it's not accomplished at all, and a leper is still a leper if a single spot remains. Jesus could, however, heal blindness by degrees to give an initial glimmer and then expose the eyes to the full light of day. Perhaps, this was a gentler approach to allow the optic nerve to grow accustomed to the light.

Since the eye symbolizes understanding, it's quite fitting to heal the human understanding by degrees. The will must be changed immediately. The affections must be turned instantly. Most of what makes up the human nature must experience a distinct and complete change. But the understanding is influenced and changed over a long period of time.

The heart of stone cannot be gradually softened but must be instantaneously made into a heart of flesh; this is not necessary with the understanding. Our understanding is often brought into proper balance and order in a gradual way. At first, the soul might receive a limited understanding of truth and rest there in relative safety. After some time, it may come to embrace and understand more of the mind of the Spirit. Men can remain in that degree of light without serious consequence although not without loss. This stage could be described as seeing but not seeing afar. The ultimate restoration of the understanding may be reserved for when more growth has taken place.

This spiritual sight may never be given to us in absolute perfectness until we enter into the light for which spiritual eyes are necessary – that place where they need no candle or light of the sun, because the Lord God will give them light. *And there be no night there; and they need no lamp neither light of the sun; for the Lord God shall give them light; and they shall reign for ever and ever* (Revelation 22:5).

This miracle paints a picture of the progressive healing of a darkened understanding. It can't be used as a picture of the restoration of a willful sinner from the error of his way or the turning of the unrestrained and depraved from the filthiness of their lives. It's a picture of the darkened soul gradually illuminated by the Holy Spirit and brought by Jesus Christ into the light of his kingdom.

Picture this Case

This account paints a picture of a common class today. Many come to us who have been spiritually blind for the previous part of their lives. They've been mere formal churchgoers or those who embrace the ritual of religion.

This person has a darkened understanding. He isn't possessed with a demon, for a man possessed with a demon raves and rages; he is dangerous to society and must be bound with chains, watched, and guarded because he's a danger to himself and others.

The blind person in Mark 8 is perfectly harmless. He has no desire to injure others and isn't likely to be violent towards himself. He's sober, steady, honest, and kind; his spiritual condition is cause for our pity but not our fear. When these unenlightened people associate with the Lord's people, they don't rave and rage against the saints but respect them and love their company. They aren't haters of the cross of Christ but are even lovers of it in their poor blind way.

They don't persecute, slander, or make fun of believers, nor do they intentionally pursue lives of wickedness. On the contrary, although they can't see the things of God, they feel their way along the paths of morality in an admirable manner. In some ways, they might even serve as examples to those who can see.

This blind person isn't polluted with a contagious disease, foul and loathsome like leprosy. A leper must be put away to a place reserved for him, because he contaminates everyone he comes in contact with.

That isn't the case with this blind man who comes to the Savior. He's blind, but he doesn't make others blind. If he associates with other blind people, he doesn't increase their blindness. If he is brought in contact with those who can see, he doesn't injure their sight in any way. They might even gain some benefit from coming in contact with him, because they're led to be thankful for the eyesight they possess when they think about the darkness which envelopes him.

This isn't the case of a person immersed in a life of lustful perversion or sinful behavior. This man would not be a bad influence on your children or lead your son or your daughter into sin. The unenlightened people we're talking about are loved in our families, because they don't spread false doctrines or set bad examples. Even when they talk of spiritual things, they make us pity them, because they know so little. They cause us to be grateful to God, because he opened our eyes to see the wondrous things of his Word.

They don't hate God or live lives steeped in sin. No, these people aren't at a disadvantage in any way, except when it comes to the understanding of the mind's eye. Their understanding is what is darkened.

In all the other aspects, these people I'm picturing here are hopeful if not healthy.

They aren't deaf; they are happy to hear the gospel and eager to do what it says. However, they don't understand it. They receive the letter but only a small degree of the Spirit. At the same time, they do hear and are on their way to getting a greater bless- ing, for *faith comes by hearing, and the ear to hear by the word of God* (Romans 10:17).

These people aren't dumb either. They can speak, and they even pray to an extent, but their prayer can barely be considered spiritual, even though they have a kind of enthusiasm about it that we shouldn't disregard. They've attended a place of worship from childhood and never neglected the outward forms of religion.

> They've attended a place of worship from childhood and never neglected the outward forms of religion. Unfortunately, they are still blind!

Unfortunately, they are still blind! They hear and pray without hesitation, so they aren't absolutely deaf or dumb. They're also capable in other ways. Their hand isn't withered, as in the case of the one whom Christ met in the synagogue. *And when he was departed from there, he went into their synagogue; and, behold, there was a man who had his hand withered* (Matthew 12:9-10).

Neither are they afflicted by intense depression of spirit like that daughter of Abraham who had been bent over for many years.

> *And, behold, there was a woman who had a spirit of infir- mity eighteen years and was bowed together and could in no wise lift herself up. And when Jesus saw her, he called her and said unto her, Woman, thou art loosed from thine infir- mity. And he laid his hands on her, and immediately she was made straight and glorified God.* (Luke 13:11-13)

These people are cheerful and diligent in the ways of the Lord. If the cause of God wants assistance, they're ready to assist. Though their spiritual eyes see dimly, and they can't enter the full understanding of spiritual things, they are often the first to volunteer for any good cause. They don't volunteer because they thoroughly understand the spiritual nature of the action, because they don't fully understand. But there's something in them that's lovely and hopeful, because they're eager to help the cause of Christ.

In all Christian congregations, we have clusters of people like this, and in some Christian churches most of the members aren't much better. They haven't received enough instruction to know their right hand from their left in spiritual matters. This lack of doctrinal teaching leaves them in the dark. Because they are refused sound doctrine, they remain in semi-blindness, unable to enjoy the blessings, which encourage the eye of the enlightened believer.

Our Lord's Method of Cure

Every part of the miracle holds importance. The first thing we see is a friendly intervention. The blind man's friends brought him to Jesus. Many people don't understand the basic doctrine of the gospel of Christ and need the help of believers. They can generally appreciate religion, but they don't know what they must do to be saved.

The great truth of Jesus' substitutionary death, which is the main point in the gospel, is what they haven't grasped. They barely understand what it means to come to Jesus and rest in him, because he paid the price for their sins. They have a sort of faith, but they have such narrow understanding of the truth that their faith brings them little or no benefit.

Such people might be blessed if more mature Christians brought them under their wing and discipled them to bring them to a clearer knowledge of the Savior. Why can't more mature believers instruct these spiritually blind ones in the sound doctrine they understand? Why can't they explain the Word of God in such a way that might open the eyes of the blind? Why can't they at least share from the Scripture the passage of God's Word, which opened their eyes?

What a mighty work it would be to look for those who aren't hostile to the gospel but simply ignorant of it, who have a zeal for God but lack knowledge, and who would possess the one thing they truly need if they could be given sight. If we are willing to look for the lost souls who are depraved, fill our court systems, and live on the streets, we should be equally ready to seek out these hopeful ones who sit under the noise of preaching that is not sound teaching or who hear the true Word but don't understand it.

Brothers and sisters, you should pray for these people that you might be used by God to answer their questions and enlighten their understanding. If you cared about these children of mist and darkness, it might be the first step to their receiving spiritual eyesight through the work of the Holy Spirit.

Contact with Jesus

When the blind man was brought to the Savior, he first experienced contact with Jesus. Jesus took him by the hand. It's a happy day when a soul comes in personal contact with the Lord Jesus. When we're in a state of unbelief, we sit in the church, and Christ seems to be distant. We hear about him, but he seems to have departed to the ivory palaces and is no longer among us. Even if he passed by, we don't feel his presence. So, we sit and sigh and long to feel his shadow upon us or touch the hem of his garment. But when the soul comes in contact with Jesus, he becomes the object of full attention. Then we feel that there's something to be grasped and realized; he's not distant, but he is real and has influence over us. He will take us by the hand.

Some of you have felt this. It has frequently happened that when we've gathered, you thought you had to pray. You felt the sermon was made just for you, as though someone had told the preacher about you. The truth came so close to home that the details of the preacher's speech fit the condition of your mind. That was our blessed Lord taking you by the hand.

To you the service wasn't comprised of man's words, but a mysterious hand touched you. Your feelings were affected, and your heart became aware of new emotions originating from the presence of the Savior. Of course, Jesus doesn't come into any physical contact with us. He touches our mental and spiritual components. The mind of the Lord Jesus lays its hand upon the minds of sinners, and the Holy Spirit influences the soul for holiness and truth.

A Solitary Position

Note the second step of this healing, because it's a little odd. The Savior led the man to a solitary position. He took him out of the town. I've noticed that when people are converted who have been spiritually blind rather than willfully wicked and haven't been as hostile as they've been ignorant, one of the first signs of their becoming Christians is that they withdraw from their former way of life and recognize their individual responsibility.

> Tens of thousands . . . consider themselves to be part of a nation of Christians, born into a church, but never consider themselves personally responsible to God.

I always have hope for the man who considers his way of life as he stands alone before God. Tens of thousands in England consider themselves to be part of a nation of Christians, born into a church, but never consider themselves personally responsible to God. They recite the confession of sin but always with the whole congregation. They chant the congregational hymns, but they do not connect in a personal way.

But when a man is led to feel as if he is alone, and he grasps the idea that true relationship with God must begin within him, the confession of sin is more fitting from his lips, and a work of grace has begun. There is hope for the blindest understanding when the mind meditates on its own condition and examines its own options. A sure sign that the Lord is dealing with you is if he's taken you out of the town, and you're forgetting about everyone else and thinking about yourself. Don't call it selfishness. This type of selfishness is what God requires. Every man must think of himself when he is drowning; if it's justifiable selfishness to preserve one's own life, it's much more acceptable when we pursue escape from eternal ruin.

When your own salvation is accomplished, you won't have any more need to think of self, but you will care for the souls of others. The wisest thing to do is to think of yourself in your position before God and look to the Savior, so you may have eternal life. *So, taking the blind man by the hand, he led him out of the town.*

Ordained by Despicable Means

Jesus' next act was strange. He healed the blind man under ordained but despicable means. He spit on his eyes. The Savior often used saliva from his mouth to heal. Some say it was recommended by ancient physicians, but I doubt their opinion would have carried much weight with our wonder-working Lord. It seems to me that the use of saliva connected the opening of the eye with the Savior's mouth. That is to say, it connected the illuminating of the understanding with the truth which Christ spoke.

Spiritual eyesight comes from spiritual truth, and the eye of the understanding is opened by the doctrine which Christ speaks. However, we typically associate saliva with disgust, and this was intentionally used by the Savior for that very response. It was nothing but saliva, though it was saliva from the Savior's mouth.

God can bless you by the very truth you once despised, and he may even bless you through the very man you bitterly spoke against. God seems to be pleased to reward those who minister in his name with a gracious kind of vengeance. Many times, those who were the most furious against God's servants received the best blessings from the hands of those same men whom they despised most.

You call it "spit." Nothing but that spit will open your eyes. You say, "The gospel is a simplistic thing." But through that simplicity you will have life. You mocked and declared that a man like him spoke the truth in a coarse and ordinary style. One day, you will bless that ordinary way of communicating and be thrilled to receive the truth even in the coarse way it was presented to you.

Many of us had to come to the realization that the Lord chastised our pride by saying, "Those people whom you thought so poorly of will be made a blessing to you, and the one you held the most prejudice against will be the man to bring you into perfect peace."

When the Savior spit on his eyes, he used no powders from the merchant, no myrrh and frankincense, no costly drugs but just common spit from his lips. If you want to see the deep things of God, it won't be by the philosophers or the profound thinkers of the day, but by the one who says to you, "Trust Christ and live." This man teaches you better philosophy than the philosophers, and he who tells you that in the Lord Jesus dwells all the treasures of wisdom and knowledge tells you in that simple statement more than you could ever learn from Socrates and Plato. Jesus Christ will open your eyes, and it will be by the common spit from his mouth.

Note also that after he had spit on the blind man's eyes, he put his hands on him. Did he do that in the form of heavenly blessing? Did he lay hands on him, bless him, and cause something of his nature to flow into the blind man? I think so.

So, it's not the saliva, and it's not the leading of the man out of the crowd that effects the miracle. It's not the ministry or the preaching of the Word. It's not the hearer's thoughtfulness that will earn spiritual blessings. The blessing from Christ, the one who died for sinners, provides everything. Jesus is exalted on high to provide repentance and remission of sin. He who was despised and rejected by men provides the priceless blessings, such as sight to the blind, which are given to the sons of men.

We must withdraw from the crowd, because solitary reflection is a great blessing. But after we've reflected, we must look up to the Lord, the giver of every good gift, or the spit will do no good. And the outcome of being alone but not looking to Christ would be that the blind man would lose his way and wander deeper into the darkness with less sympathy and help.

From their childhood, many people have attended places of worship without the slightest perception of spiritual life. They would have continued to do so if the Lord hadn't used Christian friends who said, "I think I can tell you something that you might not know."

Through prayer and teaching, these friends brought you into contact with Jesus. The Holy Spirit touched you, influenced your mind, and made you thoughtful. He made you see that there was more to religion than the external, and going to church or chapel wasn't everything. Actually, it wasn't anything at all, unless you learned the secret, the real secret of everlasting life.

Through all this, you realized there is power in the gospel you once despised. And what you made fun of is now the gospel of your salvation. Let's thank God for this, because he opens eyes in this way.

A Hopeful Stage

The Savior gave the man's eyeballs the power to see, but he hadn't completely removed the film that kept out the light. Jesus *asked him if he saw anything.* He looked up, and his first joyful words were *I see!* What a blessing.

Some of you can say, *that having been blind, now I see* (John 9:25). Though I don't have total darkness now, I don't see as much as I should or as much as I hope, but I do see. I knew nothing about many things that now I know something about. The devil himself can't make me doubt that I see. I know I do.

At one time I was quite satisfied with the outward rituals. If I got through the hymns and prayers, I felt satisfied. But now I don't see as well as I want to see, so some darkness must be present. If I can't see salvation, I can see my own ruin, my own wants and necessities. If I don't see anything else, I see these.

If a man can see anything, he certainly has sight. Whether it's something beautiful or something ugly, it doesn't matter. The seeing of anything is proof positive that there's sight in his eyes. So, spiritual perception of anything is proof that you have spiritual life, whether that perception makes you mourn or makes you rejoice. If you see it, you must have the power of sight. But look at what the man said again. He said, *I see men.* That's even better. Obviously, the blind man had once been able to see, or he wouldn't have known the shape of a man. He said, *I see men.*

Some have enough sight to be able to distinguish between one thing and another, enough to know this from that. Even though you were as blind as bats once, nobody can make you believe that baptismal regeneration is the same thing as the regeneration by the Word of God. You can see the difference between these two things now. You might think anybody would know the difference, but many don't.

You can see the difference between formal, external worship and spiritual worship. You know that there's a Savior, that you need a Savior, and that the way of salvation is by faith in Christ. And you understand that the salvation Jesus gives helps us stand in the face of temptation and brings us safe to eternal glory. So, clearly, you can see something and know what that something is.

However, listen to the blind man, because here comes a point in the Word that creates doubt to a certain extent, *I see men; I see that they walk as trees.* He couldn't tell whether they were men or trees; he only saw that they were walking, and he knew trees didn't walk. Therefore, they couldn't be trees. Objects were a confused jumble to his eyes. He knew from how they moved that they must be men, but he couldn't tell exactly by eyesight whether they were men or trees.

Many precious souls wait at this hopeful but uncomfortable stage. They can see. Bless God for that! They will never be completely blind again. If they can see the Man Jesus and the tree on which he died, they can make a single object of them if they want, because Christ and his cross are one. Eyes which can't clearly see Jesus might see him dimly, and even a dim sight will save the soul.

The man in Mark 8 had indistinct sight; a man or a tree, he couldn't tell. Likewise, the first sight that's given to many spiritually blind people is indistinct. They can't distinguish between doctrines. The work of the Spirit and the work of the Savior often confuse them. They possess justification and they possess sanctification, but they probably couldn't tell you which was which. They've received imparted righteousness of heart, and they've also received the imputed righteousness of Christ, but they can't explain the difference. They have them both, but they don't know which is which – at least not well enough to explain it to someone else.

They can see, but not as well as they should. They see men as trees walking. In addition to being indistinct, their sight is very exaggerated. A man isn't as big as a tree, but they compare a human to towering timber. In the same way, half-enlightened people exaggerate doctrines. If they receive the doctrine of election, they stay focused on that one truth, and fail to see how other scripture reconciles with the doctrine of election.

If they grasp the precept of baptism or any other doctrine, they exaggerate its proportions and distort the truth of the doctrine. Some get one odd quirk and some get another, because they don't see clearly and mistake a man for a tree. It's a great mercy that they see doctrine at all and precept at all, but it would be a greater mercy if they could see it as it is, and not as it now appears to them.

This exaggeration generally leads to alarm. If I see a man walking up to me who is as tall as a tree, I'm naturally afraid that he might fall on me, and I get out of the way. Many people are afraid of God's doctrines, because they see them as high as trees. They aren't too high. God made them exactly the right height, but man's blindness exaggerates them and makes them more terrifying than they should be. Men are afraid to read books about certain truths, and they become withdrawn around men who preach and teach about them, because they can't see those doctrines in the right light and are alarmed by their own confused vision.

In addition to this exaggeration and fear, these people also experience an utter loss of the enjoyment which comes from being able to perceive beauty and loveliness. The most excellent part of a man is, after all, his countenance. We like to grasp the non-verbal communication of our friends – that gentle eye, tender expression, winning look, radiant smile, and the expressive glow of compassion. We like to see it all, but this poor man couldn't see any of these. He could barely tell the difference between a man and a tree. There's no way he could see those softer lines of the great master artist which make true beauty. He could only say, "It is a man," but what that man looked like, he didn't know and couldn't describe.

It's the same way with people who have obtained some spiritual sight. They can't see the details of the doctrines, but the beauty lies in the details. If I trust Jesus as my Savior, I will be saved, but the enjoyment of faith in Christ comes from knowing him in his person, in his work, in his past, present, and future. We experience his true beauty by studying him, observing him, and watching him.

We experience his true beauty by studying him, observing him, and watching him.

Our interaction with doctrine works the same way. The whole of doctrine is blessed, but it's when we take a closer look at the working pieces that we gain the purest enjoyment.

"Yes," says the man without understanding, as he looks at a fine painting such as Paul Potter's famous *Bull at The Hague*. "It's a rare picture certainly," and then he walks away. The artist sits down and studies its details. To him beauty exists in every touch and shade, which he understands and appreciates. Many believers have enough light to know the bare essentials of faith, but they haven't learned to walk in the fullness of Christ. The details of that Christ-filled life are where the sweetest comfort will always be found by the spiritually educated child of God. They can see, but they "see men as trees, walking."

Although many have travelled far beyond this stage, a countless number of God's people still linger there. This is to be expected when Satan gets the upper· hand. Sects, parties, and theories arise. If a group of people with good eyes meet together and look at an object, their descriptions will all be similar to each other. However, an equal number of men with weak eyes will cause confusion and quarrel.

"It is a man, because he walks," cries one.

"It is a tree; it's too tall to be a man," shouts the second.

When half-blind men grow arrogant, despise their teachers, and refuse to learn as the Holy Spirit teaches, they make their ignorance out to be knowledge and often lead other half-enlightened ones into the ditch with them. Even when this mischievous result is prevented, spiritual half-sight should still be cause for sadness, because it leaves men in sorrow when they could rejoice and lets them mourn over truth, which could fill their mouths with praise. Many are troubled about the doctrine of election. Now, if there's any doctrine in this book which should make believers sing all day and all night, it's the doctrine of electing love and distinguishing grace. Some people are frightened over this and some over that. But if they understood the truth, instead of fleeing from it like it's an enemy, they would run into its arms.

Ultimate Completeness of the Cure

Be grateful for any light, for without the grace of God, we couldn't have a single ray. One ray of light is more than we deserve. If we were shut up in blackness forever, how could we complain? Don't we deserve to be doomed to perpetual darkness, since we shut our eyes against God?

Be thankful for the littlest gleam of light, but don't value that little bit so much that you fail to wish for more.

A man is still pitifully blind if he doesn't care whether he sees more or not. A horrible sign of unhealthiness is when we have no desire to grow. When we're satisfied that we know all truth and can't be taught any more, we need to start at the beginning. One of the first lessons in the school of wisdom is to understand how much we don't know. The man who is growing conscious of his own deficiency and ignorance is growing in wisdom. But when the Lord Jesus Christ brings a man to see a little and sees his desire to see more, our Lord doesn't leave him until he has led him into all truth.

We read that the Savior touched his patient again to complete the cure. Just as your first touch from Jesus brought a certain amount of understanding, contact with him must be renewed to bring about full sight or understanding. To obtain a close, intimate relationship with Jesus Christ and to understand what it means to be fully dependent on him, we must study his character, desire to commune with him, and seek him with our eyes of faith and not through the eyes of others. This will be what brings about clearer sight. Direct interaction with Christ does it all.

> To obtain a close, intimate relationship with Jesus Christ . . . we must study his character, desire to commune with him, and seek him with our eyes of faith and not through the eyes of others.

When the man's eyes were fully opened, the first person he saw was Jesus, since he had been taken away from the crowd and could only see other men at a distance. What a blessed vision – to drink in the sight of his face and look upon the Lover of our souls. Oh, the joy! Someone might be content in their blindness if there was never a hope to see Christ, but what a heavenly delight to be rescued from the blindness that concealed him from our eyes.

Above all things, pray that you may know him and understand him. With everything else you strive for, make sure you strive for an understanding of him. Consider doctrine precious, but don't make it a ritualistic list of rules. Think of it in the respect that it illustrates the life of Christ. Even if your own experience doesn't point to Christ, it is nothing.

You only grow when you grow in him. *But grow in grace,* says the apostle, *and in the knowledge of our Lord and Saviour, Jesus Christ* (2 Peter 3:18). Paul says, *Grow up into him in all things, who is the head, the Christ* (Ephesians 4:15). Ask to see, but ask to see Jesus. Pray for sight, that *Thine eyes shall see the king in his beauty: they shall behold the land that is very far off* (Isaiah 33:17). Your vision is almost clear when you can see Jesus, but you will come into the brightness of day when you see the Savior instead of trees. Then you can let the men and the trees take care of themselves.

Our Lord instructed the blind man to look up. If we desire to see, we must not look at the ground. The earth produces no light. Likewise, if we desire to see, we must not look within ourselves, which is a dark, black cavern, full of everything that is evil. We must look up.

Every good gift and every perfect gift is from above and comes down from the Father of lights, so we must look up for it (James 1:17). As we meditate and rest on Jesus, we must look up to our God. Our soul must dwell on her Lord's perfection and not dream of her own. She must ponder his greatness and not her own. We must look up, not on other believers or the externals of worship but to God himself. We must intentionally look, and as we do, we will find the light.

At the end of this miracle, Scripture says that *he was whole and saw everyone, far away and clearly.* When the great Physician sends the man home, he is fully cured. He saw every man clearly. I pray this end for the half-enlightened ones. Don't be satisfied with being saved. Desire to know how you are saved and why you are saved – the method by which you are saved. The answer is the rock on which you stand, but think upon the questions: how you were put on that rock, whose love put you there, and why that love was given to you. I pray that all believers aren't only in Christ Jesus but understand him and through that understanding know the assurance they have attained. *Be ready always to respond to every man that asks you a reason of the hope that is in you with meekness and reverence* (1 Peter 3:15).

Many specific teachings in Scripture will save you a world of trouble if you know and remember them. Try to understand the difference between the old nature and the new. Never expect the old nature to improve into the new, because it never will. The old nature can never do anything but sin, and the new nature can never sin. They are two distinct principles, so never confuse them. Don't see men as trees walking. Don't confuse sanctification and justification; fully comprehend that the moment you trust in Christ you are justified as completely as you will be in heaven, but sanctification is a gradual work, which is carried on from day to day by the Holy Spirit.

Distinguish between the great truth that salvation is accomplished completely by God and the great lie that men aren't to be blamed if they're lost. Be fully assured that salvation is of the Lord, but don't lay damnation at God's door. Understand that you are saved by grace, but don't embrace grace as a license to sin.

> Understand that you are saved by grace, but don't embrace grace as a license to sin.

On the other hand, while you hold some responsibility, don't error in believing that man ever turns to God of his own free will. There is a narrow line between the two, so ask for grace to see it. Ask for grace, so you don't fall into the whirlpool or be dashed against the rock. Don't be a slave of this system or that.

Never say of one text of Scripture, "Be silent, I can't endure you," or of another, "I believe you, and you alone." Seek to love the whole Word of God and get an insight into every truth that is revealed. As you receive God's Word as a whole, seek to grasp the truth in Jesus in all its precision and unity.

If you have sight that enables you to see at all, fall on your knees and cry out to the great Sight-giver, "O Master, press on. Take away every bit of film, remove every cataract, and even if it's painful to have my prejudices cut away or burnt out of my eyes, do it, Lord, until I can see in the clear light of the Holy Spirit. Prepare me to enter into the gates of the holy city, where my eyes will see you face to face."

Chapter 4

Jesus Rejected

And all those in the synagogue, when they heard these things, were filled with wrath and rose up and thrust him out of the city and led him unto the brow of the hill upon which their city was built that they might cast him down headlong. But he, passing through the midst of them, went away. (Luke 4:28-30)

Jesus had spent several years in the house of his father at Nazareth. He must have been well known. The excellence of his character and conduct must have attracted notice. At God's appointed time, he left Nazareth, was baptized by John in the Jordan, and began his work of preaching and working wonders. The inhabitants of Nazareth likely said to one another, "Surely, he will come to see his parents. When he comes, we'll all go hear what the carpenter's son has to say." There's always an interest in hearing one of the boys who grew up in the village when he becomes a preacher, and the hope of seeing wonders like he performed in Capernaum heightened this interest.

Curiosity was aroused, and everybody hoped and trusted that he would make Nazareth famous among the cities of the tribes. Perhaps he would settle down and attract a crowd of customers to their shops by becoming the great Physician of Nazareth, the great Wonder-worker of the district. And after some time, the famous Prophet finally visited his own city.

When the Sabbath drew near, interest in him grew intense. As men asked the question, "What do you think? Will he be at the synagogue tomorrow? If he's there, we'll need to get him to say something." The ruler of the synagogue shared the common opinion, and at the proper point of the service, he took up the scroll of the prophet Isaiah and passed it to Jesus, so he could read a passage and share his thoughts.

All eyes were on him. He took the scroll, and opened it, like he was very familiar with it, to a passage which applied to himself. To pay respect to the Word, he stood and read it. Then, he rolled up the scroll and took his seat, not because he had nothing to say, but because it was the custom in those days for the preacher to sit down and the hearers to stand.

The passage that Jesus read to them was suitable and applicable to himself, but the most remarkable point in it wasn't what he read as what he didn't read. He paused almost in the middle of a sentence. He said, *to proclaim the year of the LORD's favour,* and there he stopped. The passage isn't complete unless you read the next words: *and the day of vengeance of our God* (Isaiah 61:2).

Our Lord stopped reading at those words. Maybe he wished the first sermon he delivered would be gentle, without a single threatening word. Maybe he only wanted to read the portion that he was fulfilling at that time, for he said, *Today this scripture is fulfilled in your ears* (Luke 4:21). His heart's desire and prayer for them was that they might be saved, and instead of a day of vengeance, it might be to them the acceptable year of the Lord.

He rolled up the scroll, sat down, and explained the Scripture to them. He taught them who the blind were, who the captives were, who the sick and wounded and bruised were, and he taught them about the grace of God that provided liberty, healing, and salvation. They were all amazed. They had never heard any one speak so fluently and with so much authority, so simply, and yet so nobly.

He had their attention. Soon a buzz went around the synagogue, and they said to each other, *From where does this man have this wisdom and these mighty works? Is not this the carpenter's son? is not his mother called Mary? and his brothers, James and Joseph and Simon and Judas? And his sisters, are they not all with us? From where then does this man have all these things?* (Matthew 13:54-56). They were astonished and envious.

Then Jesus felt it wasn't the point of his ministry to astonish people. His desire was to impress their hearts, so he changed his subject. Knowing their hearts, Jesus appealed to their consciences. If men only give a minister their fascination, they've given him nothing. We desire for you to be convinced and converted. Anything short of this, we fail.

Jesus turned from this subject that seemed fruitful with every blessing. He saw that to them it was no more than pearls to swine, so he spoke to them personally, pointedly, somewhat cuttingly, or so they thought. *Ye will surely say unto me this proverb, Physician, heal thyself; whatever we have heard done in Capernaum, do also here in thy country* (Luke 4:23). Then he told them that he didn't recognize their claims. Even though he might have grown up in that district and lived with them, he was under no obligation to display his power to suit their pleasure.

To emphasize his point, he said:

> But I tell you of a truth, many widows were in Israel in the days of Elijah, when the heaven was shut up three years and six months, when great famine was throughout all the land, but unto none of them was Elijah sent, except unto Sarepta, a city of Sidon, unto a widow woman. And many lepers were in Israel in the time of Elisha the prophet, and none of them was cleansed, except Naaman the Syrian. (Luke 4:25-27)

In this way, the Savior presented the doctrine of sovereign grace.

This, along with other circumstances connected with his teaching, so provoked the anger of the entire congregation that those eyes, which had looked upon him with fascination, now glared at him with eyes like beasts. And their tongues, which earlier were ready to applaud him, howled with rage. United, they rose up to slay Jesus. The curiosity of yesterday had transformed into rage today. A few hours earlier, they may have welcomed the prophet to his own country; now there was refusal.

They dragged him out of the synagogue, broke up their own worship, and with complete disregard for the day to which they paid such high regard, they *rose up and thrust him out of the city and led him unto the brow of the hill upon which their city was built that they might cast him down headlong. But he, passing through the midst of them, went away* (Luke 4:29-30). What an unimaginable end to such a beginning.

You and I would have said, "What a fruitful field we have here – The best of preachers and an audience where everyone is attentive, every ear is open, and the people are fascinated with what he has to say." We would expect countless conversions and for Nazareth to become the stronghold of Christianity, the very metropolis of the new faith. But no such thing happened.

Today some attend church faithfully who are not Christians.

Such is the perversity of human nature. Where we expect much, we get little. The field which should have brought forth wheat a hundredfold, yields nothing but thorns and thistles.

As the Holy Spirit helps and directs me, my plan is to apply this narrative to the hearts and consciences of those who are treating the Savior the same way as these men of Nazareth did in the days of his flesh.

Who were these rejecters of Christ? I ask the question, because I'm convinced that there are certain types and representatives sprinkled throughout Christianity today.

Those Most Closely Related

These people were those who most closely related to the Savior. They were the people of his own town. Ordinarily, you might expect fellow townsmen to show a man the most kindness, but *He came unto his own, and his own received him not* (John 1:11). It's amazing that they would reject him.

Today some attend church faithfully who are not Christians. They are not with Christ, and because of this, they are against him. Still, they are the most closely related to Christ of any unconverted people in the world, because from their childhood they attended religious worship and joined in the songs, prayers, and services in the Lord's house. In addition to these religious practices, they are convinced of the authenticity and divine nature of the Word of God, and they have no doubt that the Savior was sent from God, that he can save, and he is the appointed Savior.

They're not troubled with doubts, and skeptical thoughts don't perplex them. They are, in fact, Agrippas, almost persuaded to be Christians. *Then Agrippa said unto Paul, Almost thou persuadest me to be a Christian* (Acts 26:28). They are not Christians, but they are most closely related to Christians of any people on the face of the earth. You would naturally expect that they would be the best people to proclaim the gospel to, but that has proven not to be the case. These are less likely to be brought to a decision than those who are far off. Some of you might think, "When you say that, you're rebuking us too."

Those Who Knew the Most

These people of Nazareth were those who knew the most about Christ. They were well acquainted with his mother and the rest of his relatives. They knew his whole pedigree. They could tell at once that Joseph and Mary were of the tribe of Judah and might have known why they came from Bethlehem and what caused them to stay in Egypt for a while. They might have known the whole story of the wondrous child.

Surely these knowledgeable people didn't need to be taught the basics. They couldn't possibly need to be instructed in the very elements of the faith. They must have been a very receptive group of people for Jesus to preach to, right? That's not what happened.

Many religious people are like them. You may even be like him. You know the whole story of the Savior and have known it ever since childhood. Even better, you have an intellectual grasp on the doctrines of the gospel. You can discuss gospel truths and delight in them, because you take a deep interest in them. When you read the Scripture, it's not a dark, mysterious book you can't comprehend. You're even able to teach others about the basic principles of the truth.

Yet, how strangely sad it is that you practice so little. I am afraid that some know the gospel so well that it has lost much of its power. It's as well-known as a story told three times. If you heard it for the first time, its freshness would strike you, but you can't experience that sense of newness and wonder at this point. One reason given for the great success of George Whitefield's preaching was that he preached the gospel to people who had never heard it before.

The gospel was a new thing to the masses of England in Whitefield's day. The gospel had been either eradicated from the Church of England and from the pulpits of those who refused to conform, or it only remained with a few within the church and was unknown to the masses outside. The simple gospel of believe and live was so unique that when Whitefield stood in the fields to preach to tens of thousands, they heard the gospel as if it was a new revelation fresh from the skies.

Some of you have become gospel-hardened.

But some of you have become gospel-hardened. It would be impossible to put it into a new shape for your ears. The angles, the corners of truth, have become old to you. Sunday follows Sunday, and you attend church. You take your seats and go through the service. It has become as much of a routine with you as getting up and dressing yourselves in the morning.

The Lord knows I dread the influence of routine on myself. I must always stay alert, so it never becomes a routine for me to deal with the souls of men. I pray to God that he would deliver you and me from the deadly effect of religious routine. It would be better for some to change their place of worship than to sleep in the old one. Go and hear somebody else if you've attended a church for a long time and received no blessing. It's better to go elsewhere than to sit in the pew and slowly die under the Word, lulled to sleep by the gospel, which is meant to stimulate you. Let some other voice speak to your ear, and let some other preacher see what God may do through him, if only the Spirit of God saves you. It will bring me equal joy if it's under the words I speak or those spoken by someone else. Here's the reality: it's sad indeed that men so closely related to Christianity, who know so much about Christ, should still reject the Redeemer.

Those Who Supposed They Had a Claim on Christ

Here we have people who supposed they had a claim on Christ. They didn't think it would be a great kindness on the part of the Lord Jesus to heal their sick. They no doubt argued, "He's a Nazareth man, and of course he's duty bound to help Nazareth." In a way they considered themselves to be his owners, who could command his powers at their own discretion. Our Savior rejected that idea and wouldn't wear their yoke.

Sometimes I fear that some who are children of godly parents or seat-holders or subscribers to various religious organizations imagine in your hearts that if anyone is to be saved, surely it must be you. Yet, your claim has no foundation in truth. I desire that each of you would be completely and altogether saved.

Perhaps the very fact that you think you have a claim on grace may be the stone which lies in your path. You think, surely Jesus Christ will look on us with favor, even if others perish. I tell you, he will do as he wills, and politicians and prostitutes will enter into the kingdom of heaven before some of you if you think you have a right to mercy. The mercy of God is God's sovereign gift. He has said it with a voice of thunder, *I will have mercy on whom I will have mercy, and I will have compassion on whom I will have compassion* (Romans 9:15). If you kick against his sovereignty, you will stumble on a stone and be broken. *Whosoever shall fall upon that stone shall be broken, but on whomsoever it shall fall, it will grind him to powder* (Luke 20:18).

But if you feel you have no claim upon God, if you can put yourself into the position of the publican who, *standing afar off, would not lift up so much as his eyes unto heaven, but smote upon his breast, saying, God, reconcile me, a sinner,* you are in a position in which God can bless you with the dignity of his own sovereignty (Luke 18:13).

Take the position which grace accepts. You must be beggars and not choosers. He who asks for grace must not set himself in a position to dictate to his God. He who desires to be saved, even though he's unworthy, must come to God as a beggar and humbly plead that the Lord would be merciful and grant his gift of love.

A bit of this kind of spirit may be in the minds of some of you. If so, you are the people who have rejected Christ. *Hear, O heavens, and give ear, O earth!* (Isaiah 1:2). We call the skies and the earth to witness; here are those who are near to being Christians, who know the gospel by the letter, who think they have a claim on the Savior, yet they remain disobedient to the divine command, "Believe and live." They turn their backs and reject the Savior. They will not come to him, so they can have life. Hear it, O heavens, and be astonished, O earth!

Why They Reject the Messiah

Let's consider our unconverted friends who give us so much concern because of their enmity to Jesus. Why did they reject Christ? I think to say that one cause is responsible would be too general of a statement. Usually, a complex set of circumstances is unique to each individual. Or to say it another way, the fires of their anger fed upon several kinds of fuel.

The Gospel Is for Someone Else

Many feel that they themselves aren't the people to whom the Savior claimed to have a commission. Observe in the eighteenth verse that he was *anointed to preach the gospel to the poor* (Luke 4:18). The poorest ones in the synagogue may have rejoiced at the Word, but it was almost a belief among the Jewish rich that few besides the rich could enter heaven. The very proclamation of a gospel for the poor must have sounded to them democratic and extreme, and it must have laid in their minds the foundation of prejudice.

Jesus meant, of course, the *poor in spirit*, whether they are poor in pocket or not. Those are the poor whom Jesus comes to bless. *Blessed are the poor in spirit, for theirs is the kingdom of the heavens* (Matthew 5:3). But this concept was so contrary to all they had been accustomed to, it made them bite their lips. They said within themselves, "We're not poor in spirit. We've kept the law." Some of them said, "We've worn our phylacteries and made broad the borders of our garments. We haven't eaten with unwashed hands. We've strained out all gnats from our wine, kept the fasts and the feasts, and made long prayers. Why should we feel any poverty of spirit?"

Because of this, they thought Christ's mission had nothing for them. Next, when he mentioned the brokenhearted, they weren't aware of any need for a broken heart. They felt wholehearted, self-satisfied, and perfectly content. Who can preach to the brokenhearted when all his hearers think that they have no reason to rip open their hearts with repentance?

When he spoke of captives, they claimed to have been born free and not to have been in bondage to any man. They rejected with scorn the very idea that they needed anyone to free them, because they were as free as free could be. *They answered him, We are Abraham's seed, and we have never served anyone; how sayest thou, Ye shall be set free?* (John 8:33).

Then Jesus spoke of the blind. "Blind!" they said, "does he insult us? We are far-seeing men! Let him go and preach to some of the outcasts who are truly blind, but as for us, we can see into the very depths of all mysteries. We need no instruction about opening of eyes from him."

Finally, he spoke of those who had been bruised, as though they had been scourged for their sins. They said, "We have no sins for which we should be bruised. We have been honorable, upright people and have never been chastened with the scourge of the law. We don't want liberty for those who deserve to be bruised. What difference does the acceptable year of the Lord make to us if it's only for bruised captive ones? We aren't those people."

> Here you see the reason so many of your respectable attendees at our places of worship reject salvation by grace. It's because they don't feel that they need a Savior.

At a glance, you understand the reason Jesus Christ is still rejected by so many church-going and chapel-going people. Here you see the reason so many of your respectable attendees at our places of worship reject salvation by grace. It's because they don't feel that they need a Savior. *Because thou sayest, I am rich and increased with goods and have need of nothing and knowest not that thou art wretched and miserable and poor and blind and naked* (Revelation 3:17).

They claim to be intelligent, thoughtful, and enlightened, but they don't know that until a man sees Christ, he walks in darkness, is stone blind, and sees no light. They say they are not bruised. Perhaps God has left them, because it was of no use to bruise them. What would the point be? They only rebel more and more. They feel no pain of conscience and have no reverence for God's law. Therefore, Jesus Christ was unable to produce fruit in them; they were like a root out of a dry ground. They despised him in the same way as the healthy man laughs at the physician and as the man who is rich doesn't care about the needs of the poor.

If you don't feel your need for a Savior, the need still exists, even though you don't recognize it.

Let me remind you, if you don't feel your need for a Savior, the need still exists, even though you don't recognize it. You were born in sin and formed in iniquity, and no baptismal waters can wash away your defilement. Beside this, you have sinned from the time you were a child in heart and word and thought. You are condemned already, because you have not believed in the Son of God.

You may not have been openly wicked, yet there's a text I must remind you of. *The wicked shall be put into Sheol, all the Gentiles that forget God* (Psalm 9:17). That last list includes you who forget, postpone, play around, and wait for a more convenient season. You live with the gospel in front of you and don't comply with its commands. You say to your sins, "I love you too well to repent of you," and to your self-righteousness, "I am too fond of this foundation to leave it to build on the foundation which God has laid in the person of his dear Son."

Conceit makes the empty bag think itself full and makes the hungry man dream he has feasted and is satisfied. Self-righteousness damns the souls of thousands. There is nothing so ruinous as self-confidence. I pray that the Lord will make you feel undone, ruined, lost, and cast away. Then there's no fear of your rejecting Christ, because he who is perfectly bankrupt is willing to accept a Savior. He who has nothing of his own falls flat before the cross and gladly receives all things which are stored up in the Lord Jesus. Self-confidence is the first and perhaps the greatest reason why men reject the Savior.

High Claims

I entertain little doubt that the men of Nazareth were angry with Christ because of his exceedingly high claims. He said, *The Spirit of the Lord is upon me because he has anointed me to preach the gospel to the poor; he has sent me to heal the brokenhearted, to proclaim liberty to the captives and recovery of sight to the blind, to set at liberty those that are broken, to proclaim the acceptable year of the Lord* (Luke 4:18-19). They balked at that. They might have been willing to admit he was a prophet. If he meant it in that sense, they would be patient. But when he said, *he has anointed me to preach*, claiming to be none other than the promised Messiah, they shook their heads and murmured, "He claims too much."

When Jesus placed himself side by side with Elijah and Elisha, claimed to have the same rights and spirit as those famous ones, and by inference compared his hearers to the worshippers of Baal in Elijah's day, they believed he set himself up too high and put them down too low. I see another master reason here that so many good people reject our Lord and Master. He sets himself too high. He asks too much of you. He puts you down too low. He tells you that you must be nothing, and he must be everything. He tells you that you must give up that idol god of yours, the world, and the pleasures that go with it, and that he must be your Master and not your own passions and desires.

He tells you that you must pluck out the right eye of pleasure if it comes in the way of holiness and tear off the right arm of profit rather than commit sin. He tells you that you must take up your cross and follow him outside the camp. You must leave the world's religion and the world's irreligion, no longer conformed to the world but becoming a nonconformist to its self-love, customs, and sins. He tells you that he must be the Prince Imperial in your souls, and you must be his willing servants and his loving disciples.

These claims are too high for human nature to produce. Yet, remember that if you don't yield to them, a much worse thing awaits you. *Kiss the Son lest he be angry, and ye perish from the way when his wrath is kindled in a little while. Blessed are all those that put their trust in him* (Psalm 2:12). Those who don't kiss the scepter of silver will be broken with the rod of iron. *Thou shalt break them with a rod of iron; thou shalt dash them in pieces like a potter's vessel* (Psalm 2:9).

Those who refuse to have Christ reign over them in love will have him rule over them in terror in the day when he puts on the garments of vengeance and dyes his vesture in the blood of his foes. I pray that you acknowledge him as he is covered with his own blood, so you don't have to acknowledge him when he is covered with yours. Accept him while you can, because you won't be able to escape him when his eyes, which are like eyes of fire, flash devouring flame upon his adversaries. This is a common source of failure for the sons of men. They can't give King Jesus his due but would willingly throw the Lord of glory into a corner. O, corrupt hearts, how can you kick against so dear, so great, so good a king?

They Craved Miracles

Another reason they rejected the Messiah might be the fact that they wouldn't receive Christ until he had exhibited some great wonder. They craved miracles. Their minds were in a sickly state. They wouldn't receive the gospel they needed or the miracles they demanded. Many today also demand signs and wonders, or they won't believe.

Some young women set their hearts on feeling the same horror of conscience and the same gloom of soul as John Bunyan, or they refuse to believe in Jesus. What if you never feel it, because you probably won't? Will you go to hell out of spite for God, because he won't do what he did for someone else?

A young man I know said, "If I had a dream like So-and-so or a special spiritual experience, then I would believe." You demand that my Lord and Master is to be dictated to by you.

You are beggars at his gate, asking for mercy, and you think you must draw up your list of demands as to how he will give that mercy. Do you think he will ever submit to this? My Master possesses a generous spirit, but he has a righteous and royal heart. He rejects all demands and maintains his sovereignty of action. Why do you crave signs and wonders in the first place? Isn't it enough of a miracle that Jesus invites you to trust him and promises that you will be saved? Isn't it enough of a sign that God has extended so wise a gospel as *Believe and live*? Isn't the gospel its own sign, its own wonder, and its own proof, because he who believes has everlasting life? Isn't it a miracle of miracles, that *God so loved the world that he gave his only begotten Son, that whosoever believes in him should not perish but have eternal life*? (John 3:16).

Surely the precious word, *whosoever will, let him take of the water of life freely,* and the solemn promise, *he that comes to me I will in no wise cast out,* are better than signs and wonders (Revelation 22:17; John 6:37). A truthful Savior ought to be believed. He never lied.

Why would you ask for proof of the truth from the one who cannot lie? The demons themselves declared him to be the Son of God. Will you stand against him? Sovereign, mighty, irresistible grace, come and conquer this wickedness in the hearts of men and make them willing to trust Jesus, whether they see signs and wonders or not.

Election

Perhaps this time, I'll hit the nail on the head. In some cases, part of the irritation which exists in the minds of men like those of Nazareth is caused by the peculiar doctrine on the subject of election. I wonder if that wasn't the real issue all along. Jesus declared that God had a right to give his favors in whatever ways he pleased. In doing so, he often selected the most unlikely people. For instance, he supplied the needs of a widow in idolatrous Sidon, while the widows of Israel were left to go hungry (1 Kings 17:8-16). At the time of Elisha, God healed a leper from the idolatrous land of Assyria and left the Israelite lepers to die (2 Kings 5:9-15).

The men from Nazareth didn't like this, and I suppose even among those I teach, some are uneasy when the doctrine is presented as a moot point, because it's so offensive to human nature. Though most are accustomed to strong statements dealing with the sovereignty of God, and we aren't ashamed to preach predestination and election as clearly as we preach any doctrine, some continue to find it offensive.

The church of Rome hates Calvinism because it can't stand the doctrine of grace where God can save whomever he desires or the doctrine of salvation separate from the hands of priests and our own worthiness.

God holds the keys to grace and distributes it as he pleases. This doctrine makes men so angry that they don't know what to say about it. But I trust this isn't the reason you refuse to believe in Jesus, because if it is, it's a most foolish reason. Scripture tells us, *whosoever believes in him should not perish.* While it's true that the Lord will have mercy on whomever he will have mercy, it's equally true that he desires to have mercy and has already had mercy on every soul that repents of its sin and puts its trust in Jesus.

What's the sense of quibbling about a truth just because you can't understand it? Why do you kick against the truth to your own detriment, when it won't be changed by all your kicking? The Lord of Hosts has ordained the doctrine of grace to stain the pride of all earthly glory and cause all worldly excellence to become distasteful. *So then it is not of him that wills, nor of him that runs, but of God that has mercy* (Romans 9:16).

I the LORD have brought down the high tree, have exalted the low tree, have dried up the green tree, and have made the dry tree to flourish, so no flesh can glory in his presence, but the Lord may be exalted (Ezekiel 17:24). Bow to sovereign grace! Shouldn't he be King? Who else should rule but God? And if he's a King, doesn't he have the right to forgive a felon condemned to die and not provide you with a reason?

> **If you refuse Christ until you understand all mysteries, you will perish in your sins.**

Leave that question, and all others, behind and come to Jesus, who welcomes you with open arms. He says, *Come unto me, all ye that labour and are heavy laden, and I will give you rest* (Matthew 11:28). If you wait until you've solved all your doctrinal difficulties, you'll never come at all. If you refuse Christ until you understand all mysteries, you will perish in your sins. Come while the gate is opened. He said, *he that comes to me I will in no wise cast out* (John 6:37).

Plain Talk

I see another reason for the quarrel of the Nazarenes with our Lord. It was probably because they didn't love such plain, personal speaking as the Savior gave them. Some people are easily offended. You must not call a spade a spade; it's an agricultural implement and should only be spoken of in grander terms.

Our Lord was a plain-speaking man, and he spoke to men plainly. He knew that men would go to hell, so he wanted to be as plain and direct as possible; in this way his audience wouldn't have the excuse that they couldn't understand the preacher. He put the truth so clearly that not only could they understand it, but they couldn't misunderstand it if they tried. His preaching was most personal. He didn't speak about Capernaum but all about Nazareth, but this also made them angry.

Blessing for the Gentiles

Jesus also hinted that he intended to bless the Gentiles. Elijah had fed and Elisha had healed a Gentile, and this didn't sit well with the Jews. They feared that their monopoly of blessing was coming to an end, and grace would be given to others besides the sons of Israel. A Gentile dog would be expected to be admitted into the family, to be permitted not only to eat the crumbs that fell from the table but to be changed into a co-heir. The Jews just couldn't bear it.

This monopolizing spirit still exists among self-righteous people. I've heard people say, "Oh, they're having meetings to get those girls off the street. It's no use, you can try, but it's really no use trying to reform them. There are other people looking after these undesirables and going into those nasty slums. If people get there, that's where they belong. We shouldn't stoop to their level to look after such good-for-nothing people. The church is there to take care of such people, and if they choose not to go, that's their decision."

> I don't know which God looks at with more disgust: the open sinner or the openly, good-living person whose inward pride stands against the gospel.

Some people turn their noses up at the idea of reaching out to those who need it most. This is just the same horrible old Jewish monopolizing of the gospel. Often, these people are treated as if they aren't as good as you because of their sins and poverty. But, while their sins may be clearly visible, they aren't one bit more detestable than the pride of some people who boast of a self-righteousness which doesn't exist.

I don't know which God looks at with more disgust: the open sinner or the openly, good-living person whose inward pride stands against the gospel. The physician doesn't care whether he sees the eruption outside the skin or knows it's inside. He might even think it's harder to get at the second than the first. Our Lord Jesus Christ makes it clear that however good you are, you must come to him the same way as the vilest of the vile. You must come as guilty; you cannot come as righteous. You must come to Jesus to be washed, and you must come to him to be clothed. You think you don't need washing? You believe you're clothed, covered, and beautiful to look at?

The garb of outward respectability and outward morality is often nothing more than a thin film to hide hideous leprosy until God's grace changes the heart. God *dost desire truth in the inward parts, and in the secret things thou hast made me to know wisdom* (Psalm 51:6). But this superficial country of ours is satisfied with external politeness, and you can be as rotten as you want within your heart, but the living God will have no part of pretense. You must be born again, which is another doctrine which people can't endure. They'll say all sorts of terrible things about the preacher, but if he proclaims that you must be born again, they reject Christ. In doing so, they reject their own mercy and seal their own destruction.

I wish that the Lord would thrust you into the furnace and make you like melted iron. Then the hammer of the gospel and the law together could beat you into something resembling an evangelical shape, and you might be saved. God's arm is strong enough, and his fire fierce enough to melt even the iron of self-righteousness.

What Came of It?

This is what came of it. First, they thrust the Saviour out of the synagogue, and then they tried to hurl him over the edge of a steep hill. These were his friends and good, respectable people. Who would have believed it of them? You saw that large group of people in the synagogue who sang so sweetly and listened so attentively. Would you have guessed that there was a murderer inside every one of their hearts? They worked together to throw Jesus down the hill. We don't know how much wickedness exists inside any one of us. If we aren't renewed and changed by grace, we are heirs of destruction along with all the others.

The description given in Romans 2 is a truthful picture of every child of Adam. He may look respectable, but he's a deadly snake. While the snake sleeps, you may play with it. But if it wakes up, you'll see that it's a deadly thing. Sin can lie dormant in the soul, but there may come a time when it wakes up. And there may come a time in this country, when those good people who hang on the skirts of Christ and attend our places of worship may actually develop into persecutors. It has already happened in the past in England when they burned the servants of the Lord at the stake.

Your opposition to Christ may not take that active form, but unless you are converted, you are an enemy of Jesus. You deny it? Then I ask why you don't believe in him? Why don't you trust him? If you aren't opposed to him, why don't you yield to him? As long as you don't trust him, I can only add you to his list of enemies. The most obvious proof is that you refuse to be saved by him.

> Unless you are converted, you are an enemy of Jesus.

If a man was drowning, and another put out his hand to save him, but the drowning man said, "No, I won't be saved by you, I would sooner be drowned," wouldn't that prove they were enemies? That's your case; you refuse to be saved by Christ's grace. Oh, what an enemy of Christ from the bottom of your heart you must be!

But what came of the situation in Nazareth? Though they thrust him out of the city, they could not hurt the Savior. The hurt was all their own. Christ didn't fall from the hill; he escaped by his miraculous power. And the gospel won't be hurt even though you reject it and set yourself in opposition to it.

Jesus Christ glides through the midst of his enemies uninjured. Through the persecutions of Nero and Diocletian, the true Christ of God went on his way. Through all the burnings of Mary, the hangings of Elizabeth, and right on through the persecuting times of Claverhouse and his soldiers, the gospel remained unconquered by its adversaries. It's alive and well to this very day. It escapes from all the anger of its most deadly foes.

But what became of the Nazarenes? They rejected Christ, and he left them. He left them unhealed because of their unbelief. Now it's ancient history, and in a few more years when the great trumpet sounds, all those men who tried to throw him over the edge of the hill will have to look at him and see him seated where they can't grab him, abuse him, or cast him down. What a sight it will be for them! Will they say to one another, "Isn't this Joseph's son?" When they see him sitting on the throne of his glory with his holy angels, will they say, *Is not this the carpenter's son? is not his mother called Mary? and his brothers, James and Joseph and Simon and Judas? And his sisters, are they not all with us?* (Matthew 13:55-56). Will they then say to him, *Physician, heal thyself?*

Oh, what a change will come over those arrogant faces. For every sneer, there will be a blush, and for each word of anger, there will be weeping, wailing, and gnashing of teeth. The same thing will happen to you if you reject the Savior. Within a few more years, you and I will have mixed our bones with the earth. After that will come a general resurrection. We will live and stand in the end times upon the earth, and Christ will come in the clouds of heaven.

> If you heard the gospel and despised him, what will you say?

If you heard the gospel and despised him, what will you say? Have your apology ready, because you'll be called on to say why judgment shouldn't be pronounced upon you. You can't say you didn't know the gospel, or you weren't warned about what would happen if you rejected it. You knew, but your heart wouldn't receive what you knew.

When the Lord says *unto those who shall be on the left hand, Depart from me, ye cursed, into eternal fire, prepared for the devil and his angels* (Matthew 25:41). What claim will you have in your defense? It will be futile to say, *We have eaten and drunk in thy presence, and thou hast taught in our streets* (Luke 13:26). That would only be an aggravation that the kingdom of heaven came so close to you, and you didn't receive it.

When the thunderbolts are launched, he who was once the Lamb so full of mercy will take his position as the Lion of the tribe of Judah, full of majesty. That thunderbolt will punctuate the fact that you rejected Christ. You heard him but turned a deaf ear to him. You neglected perfect salvation and refused God's gift of grace.

Because I can't even hope to find words that can express the force of God's own language, I will leave you with these few words, which I beg you to allow to penetrate your heart.

> *Because I have called and ye refused; I have stretched out my hand, and no one responded; for because ye have disregarded all my counsel and rejected my reproof: I also will laugh at your calamity; I will mock when your fear comes upon you; when what you have feared comes as destruction, and your calamity comes as a whirlwind; when tribulation and anguish come upon you. Then they shall call upon me, but I will not answer; they shall seek me early, but they shall not find me: Because they hated knowledge and did not choose the fear of the LORD: They rejected my counsel: they despised all my reproof. Therefore they shall eat of the fruit of their own way, and be filled with their own counsel.*
> (Proverbs 1:24-31)

I pray that God will save you from that curse.

Chapter 5

Young Man, Is This for You?

And it came to pass the day after that he went into a city called Nain, and many of his disciples went with him, and many people. Now when he came near to the gate of the city, behold, there was a dead man carried out, the only son of his mother, and she was a widow; and many people from the city were with her. And when the Lord saw her, he had compassion on her and said unto her, Weep not. And he came and touched the bier, and those that bore him stood still. And he said, Young man, I say unto thee, Arise. And he that was dead sat up and began to speak. And he delivered him to his mother. And there came a fear on all, and they glorified God, saying, That a great prophet is risen up among us, and, That God has visited his people. And this word of him went forth throughout all Judaea and throughout all the region round about. (Luke 7:11-17)

We observe in this passage the overflowing power of our Lord Jesus Christ. He had just performed a great miracle upon the centurion's servant, and the very next day, he raised the dead man. *And it came to pass the day after that he went into a city called Nain.* Each day testified of his deeds of goodness. Did he save your friend yesterday? His fullness is the same. If you seek him, his love and grace will flow to you today. He blesses today, and he blesses tomorrow. Our divine Lord is never compelled to stop until he has accomplished his purpose. His excellence proceeds from him forever. These thousands of years that have passed since he walked the earth as a man have not diminished the strength and ability of his power to bless.

We must also take into consideration how our Savior was quick and willing to share his life-giving power. As he journeyed, he worked miracles along the way, and *He went into a city called Nain*. Outside the city gates, he met a funeral procession. At once he restored life to this dead young man. Our blessed Lord doesn't seem to have come to Nain at anyone's request for the display of his love. He was simply passing through the gate into the city for some reason which isn't recorded.

The Lord Jesus is always ready to save.

The Lord Jesus is always ready to save. He healed the woman who touched him in the crowd when he was on the road to another person's house. The bits of grace spilled out onto those he came into contact with by chance are marvelous. Here he gave life to the dead when he was en route. He scattered his mercy along the roadside. No time or place found Jesus unwilling or unable. When Baal was on a journey or sleeping, his deluded worshippers had no hope for his help. But when Jesus journeyed or slept, we always found him ready to conquer death or calm the storm.

The meeting of these two processions at the gates of Nain would be a thing to behold, which could give someone with a vivid imagination an opportunity to develop his poetical genius. We start with a procession, which descended from the city. Our spiritual eyes see death upon the pale horse coming from the city gate in victory. He had taken another captive. The procession carried the spoils of the dreaded conqueror on their shoulders. Mourners confessed the victory of death with their tears. Like a general riding in triumph to the Roman capital, death carried his spoils to the tomb. What could hinder him?

Suddenly, the procession came face to face with another. A company of disciples and a large crowd ascended the hill. We don't need to look at the crowd. Our eyes rest upon the one who stood in the center, a man who carried himself in lowliness, but somehow majesty was also present. It was the living Lord, and in him death had met his destroyer.

The battle was short and decisive. No blows were struck, because death had already done all he could do. With a word, the spoil was taken from death, and the captive was delivered. Death fled, defeated, from the gates of the city while the mountains of Tabor and Hermon, which looked down upon the scene, rejoiced in the name of the Lord. This was a small-scale rehearsal of what will happen in the future, when those who are in their graves hear the voice of the Son of God and live. Then the last enemy will be destroyed. When death comes into contact with him who is our life, it is compelled to relax its hold on whatever spoil it has captured. Soon, our Lord will come in his glory. Then, in front of the gates of the New Jerusalem, we will witness the miracle at the gates of Nain, multiplied a myriad of times.

Our subject leads us to the doctrine of the resurrection of the dead, which is one of the foundation stones of our faith. I will declare this grand truth to you again and again. But right now, the text I've selected is for a very practical purpose. It concerns the souls of some for whom I'm greatly worried.

The narrative we see records a fact, a literal fact, but it may also be used for spiritual instruction. All our Lord's miracles were intended to be parables. They were intended to instruct as well as influence. They are examples for us to see, just as his spoken words were meant to be heard. We see here how Jesus can deal with spiritual death and how he can freely give spiritual life at his pleasure.

The Spiritually Dead Cause Great Grief

If an ungodly man is blessed to have Christian family, he causes them much grief. This dead young man, who was being carried to his burial, caused his mother's heart to burst with grief. Her tears showed that her heart overflowed with sorrow. The Savior said to her, *Weep not*, because he saw how deeply she was troubled.

Many of my dear young friends should be thankful they have friends who grieve over them. It's a sad thing that your conduct grieves them, but it's a hopeful situation for you when those around you grieve in this way. If everyone approved of your evil ways, you would continue in them and rush to your destruction. Cautionary voices are a blessing when they hinder you. Our Lord might listen to the silent words of your mother's tears and bless you for her sake. Look at how Luke put it: *When the Lord saw her, he had compassion on her and said unto her, Weep not.* Then he said to the young man, *Arise.*

Many young people who are good-natured and hopeful but spiritually dead cause great sorrow to those who love them the most. A son probably doesn't intend to inflict all this sorrow. He actually thinks it's quite unnecessary, but he's a daily burden to those he loves. When his mother ponders his behavior in the dead of night or in her prayer closet, she can't help but weep. Her son went with her to church when he was a boy, but now he finds his pleasure elsewhere. Beyond all control, the young man doesn't choose to go with his mother.

She doesn't want to deprive him of his freedom, but her heart breaks that he exercises that freedom so unwisely. She mourns that he doesn't have a desire to hear the Word of the Lord and become a servant of his mother's God. She hoped he would follow in his father's footsteps and unite with the people of God, but he chooses a much different course.

She has noticed a lot about his behavior that caused her anxiety to grow. He has developed friendships and other connections which are harmful to him. He has a distaste for the peaceful environment of home and has exhibited a spirit which wounds her. Maybe what he has said and done isn't meant to be unkind, but it grieves the heart that tenderly watches over him. She sees a growing indifference to everything good and a blatant intention to pursue the darker side of life.

She knows a little and imagines more about his present condition, and she dreads that he'll go from one sin to another until he ruins himself for this life and the next. An unconverted child brings a huge amount of grief to a gracious heart. That grief is multiplied if the child is a mother's only boy, and she's a widow whose husband has been snatched away.

To see a dear son pursue spiritual death causes a mother to mourn in secret and pour her soul out before God. Many mothers have grieved over a son and cried, "It would be better if he had never been born!" Thousands upon thousands of cases are like this.

If you fit this description, take my words home with you and reflect on them. The cause of grief is this: we mourn because they are in such a situation. In the account we're looking at, the mother wept because her son was dead. We are filled with sorrow because our young friends and family are spiritually dead. There is a life more important than the life which brings about the end of our material bodies.

Those who are not renewed don't know anything about this true life. To us, it's a dreadful thing for someone to be dead to God, dead to Christ, and dead to the Holy Spirit. Some are dead to the divine truths that are the delight and strength of our souls, dead to holy motives that restrain us and spur us on to virtue, and dead to the sacred joys that bring us near the gates of heaven. We can't look at any dead man and feel joy in him. A corpse, however well-dressed he is, is a sad sight.

> **We are filled with sorrow because our young friends and family are spiritually dead.**

We can't look at poor dead souls without crying out, "O God, will it always be this way? Will these dry bones never live? Won't you bring them to life?" The apostle Paul speaks of one who lived in pleasure, and he said of her, *She that lives in pleasure is dead while she lives* (1 Timothy 5:6). Many people are dead when it comes to everything that is true, noble, and of God. Yet, in other respects, they are full of life and activity. Oh, to think that they can be dead to God and still full of amusement and energy! Don't be amazed that we grieve for them.

We Lose Help and Comfort

This widowed mother mourned for her boy, not only because he was dead, but because in him she lost her earthly way of life. She must have considered him as the one she could depend on and the comfort in her loneliness. *She was a widow.* I wonder if anybody besides a widow understands the full sorrow of that word. Through sympathy, we can attempt to put ourselves into the position of one who has lost the partner of her life, but the tenderest sympathy can't fully realize the fullness and desolation of love's loss.

She was a widow. If the sun of her life was gone, there remained a star shining. She had a boy, a dear boy, who promised her great comfort. He would supply her necessities and cheer her in her loneliness. In him, her husband would live again, and his name would remain among the living in Israel. She could lean on him as she went to the synagogue. She would have him to welcome home from his work in the evening and to keep the little home together. Then that star was swallowed up in the darkness.

He died, and this was the day he was carried to the cemetery. Spiritually, it's the same for us in regard to our unconverted friends – those who are dead in sin. We miss the aid and comfort, which we should receive from them in our side-by-side service of the living God. We want fresh laborers in our Sunday school work, our mission among the masses, and in all manner of service for the Lord we love.

> Some of you have dear ones you love, and they love you, but they can't have any spiritual fellowship with you, nor you with them.

Ours is a gigantic burden, and we long for our sons to put their shoulders to it. You are our sons. We looked forward to seeing you grow up in the fear of God and stand side by side with us in warfare against evil and in holy labor for the Lord Jesus. But you can't help us, because you're on the wrong side. You even hinder us by causing the world to say, "See how those young men are acting!" We have to spend thought, prayer, and effort on you, which could have benefited others. Our burden for the dark world that lies all around us is very heavy, but you don't share it with us. Men are perishing from a lack of knowledge, and you don't lift a finger to help us enlighten them.

No Fellowship

The mother at Nain couldn't have fellowship with her dear son because he was dead, and the dead can't know anything. He can never speak to her, nor she to him, because he's on the funeral platform, *a dead man carried out.*

Some of you have dear ones you love, and they love you, but they can't have any spiritual fellowship with you, nor you with them. You never pray together or share common matters of spiritual concern.

Young man, when your mother's heart leaps for joy because of the love of Christ poured out on her soul, you can't understand her joy. Her feelings are a mystery to you. If you are a dutiful son, you don't say anything disrespectful about her religion, but neither can you share in its sorrows or its joys. Regarding the best things in life, a gulf as wide as if you were actually dead in a casket exists, and she stood weeping over your corpse.

I remember my overwhelming anguish when I feared that my beloved wife was about to be taken from me, but I was comforted by the loving prayers of my two dear sons. We had fellowship and shared commonality, not only in our grief but in our confidence in the living God. We knelt together and poured out our hearts to God, and we were comforted. I praised God that I had such sweet support in my children.

Suppose they had been ungodly young men. I would have looked in vain for holy fellowship and for aid at the throne of grace. In many households, the mother can't have fellowship with her own son or daughter in the things that are most vital and enduring, because they are spiritually dead, and she has been brought into newness of life by the Holy Spirit.

Obvious Causes for Sorrow

Moreover, spiritual death soon produces obvious causes for sorrow. In Luke 7, the time had come for her son's body to be buried. She wouldn't want to have his dead body in the home with her any longer. This reminds us of the terrible power of death, that it conquers love when it comes to the body. Abraham loved his Sarah, but after a while he said to the sons of Heth, *Give me a possession of a burying place with you, that I may bury my dead out of my sight* (Genesis 23:4).

It happens in some unfortunate cases that a person's reputation becomes so bad that nothing in life can be enjoyed while the erring one is in the home. We've known parents who felt they couldn't have their son at home, because he had become completely immersed in a lifestyle of drunkenness and debauchery. Sometimes they tried to send the young man away to a distant relative in the hope that when he was removed from the bad influences, he might do better. Very seldom does such an experiment succeed. I've known mothers who couldn't think of their sons without feeling pain far worse than they endured at their birth. Woe to him who causes such heartbreak.

What an awful thing when love's hope gradually disintegrates into despair and turns from prayers of hope into tears of regret. Words of admonition bring about such anger and blasphemy that their loving caution silences them. Then we end up with the dead young man carried out to his grave.

A sorrowful voice sobs, "He worships idols, leave him alone." Am I talking to one whose life preys upon the tender heart of his own mother? Do I speak to one whose outward conduct has become so wicked that he's a daily death to those who gave him life? Young man, can you bear to think of this? Have you turned to stone? I can't believe that you ponder your parents' heartbreak without feelings of regret. God forbid that you should.

The Future of Men Dead in Sin

This mother, whose son had already died and was to be buried out of sight, also had the knowledge that something worse would happen to him in the tomb to which he was being carried. It was impossible for her to think calmly about the decomposition that follows at the heels of death. When we think of what will become of you who refuse the Lord Christ, we are appalled. *And as it is appointed unto men to die once, and after this the judgment* (Hebrews 9:27).

We could more easily describe details about putrefying corpses than we could analyze the state of a soul lost forever. We don't dare to linger at the mouth of hell, but we're forced to remind you of a place *where their worm does not die, and the fire is never quenched* (Mark 9:44). Those who are driven from the presence of the Lord and from the glory of his power must dwell in this place.

The thought that anyone will be cast into the lake of fire, which is the second death, is unbearable. *But the fearful and unbelieving and the abominable and murderers and fornicators and sorcerers and idolaters and all liars shall have their part in the lake which burns with fire and brimstone, which is the second death* (Revelation 21:8). I'm not surprised that those who aren't completely honest are afraid to tell you about this end and that you do your best to doubt it. But with the Bible in your hand and a conscience in your being, you can't help but fear the worst if you remain separated from Jesus and the life he freely gives. If you continue in your sin and unbelief to the end of life, you must be condemned in the day of judgment. The most solemn declarations of the Word of God assure you that those who believe will not be damned. *He that believes and is baptized shall be saved, but he that believes not shall be condemned* (Mark 16:16).

> **If you continue in your sin and unbelief to the end of life, you must be condemned in the day of judgment.**

To think that this should be the case with any one of you is heartbreaking. You played at your mother's feet and kissed her cheek in devoted love. Why will you choose to be separated from her forever? Your father hoped you would take his place in the church of God. How did it happen that you don't even care if you follow him to heaven? The day will come when *one shall be taken, and the other left* (Luke 17:36).

Do you reject all hope of being with your wife, your sister, or your mother at the right hand of God? You can't wish for them to go down to hell with you, and still you have no desire to go to heaven with them? To those who imitated their gracious Savior, he will say, *Come, ye blessed of my Father, inherit the kingdom prepared for you from the foundation of the world* (Matthew 25:34). To those who refuse to be made like the Lord, he will say, *Depart from me, ye cursed, into eternal fire, prepared for the devil and his angels* (Matthew 25:41). Will you choose to receive your penalty with the accursed ones?

With great difficulty, I express my heart's feelings. I wish I possessed the forceful words of an Isaiah or the passionate cries of a Jeremiah to rouse your affections and your fears. Still, the Holy Spirit can use even me, and I beg him to do so. It's enough. One thing I am sure of – the spiritually dead cause great grief to their family members who are spiritually alive.

There is a Helper

For this type of grief there is only one Helper, but there is a Helper. This young man is being carried out to be buried, but our Lord Jesus Christ met the funeral procession. Notice the "coincidences," as skeptics call them, but we call them "providences" of God. This is a fine subject for another time, but consider this one case.

How did it happen that the young man died at that time? How was that exact hour selected for his burial? Perhaps because it was evening, but that wouldn't have fixed the precise moment. Why did the Savior arrange on that particular day to travel twenty-five miles to arrive at Nain in the evening? How did it happen that he travelled from an area, which led him to enter that particular gate where the dead would be carried out?

He ascended the hill to the little city at the exact moment when the head of the funeral procession was coming out of the gate. He met the dead man before the procession reached the tomb. A little later and he would have been buried. A little earlier and he would have been at home, lying in the darkened room, and maybe no one would have called the Lord's attention to him. The Lord knows how to arrange all things. His forecasts are precise to the tick of the clock.

I hope some great purpose is fulfilled by the writing of these words. I don't know why you happen to be reading this book, as I'm led to share on this particular subject. But here you are. And Jesus is here too. He came here on purpose to reveal himself to you and usher you into newness of life. There's no chance about it. Eternal plans have arranged it all, and we'll take part in observing the blessing. You who are spiritually dead are meant to come into contact with him in whom eternal life is found.

The blessed Savior saw the whole situation with a glance. He identified the chief mourner out of that procession and knew her inmost heart. He was always tender to mothers. He fixed his eyes on that widow, because he knew her without anyone telling him. The dead man was her only son. Our Lord perceived all the details and nothing was hidden from his infinite mind.

Young man, Jesus knows all about you. Your mother's heart and yours are both open to him. Jesus has seen the tears of those who have wept for you. He sees how some of them despair for you and in their grief act like mourners at your funeral.

Jesus Enters Your Grief

Jesus saw it all and entered into it all. How we should love our Lord, because he pays attention to our griefs, particularly our spiritual griefs about the souls of others. You, dear teacher, want your class saved. Jesus sympathizes with you. You, dear friend, have been passionate to win souls. Be comforted that in all this you are workers together with God. Jesus knows all about our soul's struggle, and he is with us in the midst of it.

> Jesus knows all about our soul's struggle, and he is with us in the midst of it.

Our struggle is his own struggle worked out in us according to our measure of humility. When Jesus enters into our work, it cannot fail. Enter, O Lord, into my work right now, I pray, and bless these feeble words to my hearers.

Our Lord entered the funeral scene by saying to the widow, *Weep not*. Now, he says to you who are praying and agonizing for souls, "Don't despair! Don't mourn like those who are without hope! I intend to bless you. You will once again rejoice over life given to the dead." Let's follow this advice and dismiss all unbelieving fear.

Our Lord then went to the funeral platform that the mourners carried and laid his hand upon it, and *those that bore him stood still*. Our Lord has a way of making those who carry death stand still without a word. Perhaps a young man is being carried further into sin by his natural passions, his unfaithfulness, his bad company, and his drunkenness. It may be that pleasure, pride, willfulness, and wickedness are carrying the four corners of the casket, but our Lord can make the bearers stand still. Evil influences become powerless, and the man doesn't know how.

Then those who carried the dead man stood still. We might imagine there was a hush. The disciples stood around the Lord, the mourners surrounded the widow, and the two crowds faced each other. Jesus and the dead man were in the middle of it all. The widow may have pushed away her veil, gazed through her tears, and wondered what was coming. The Jews from the city halted, just as the bearers had done. What will he do?

In that short time, the Lord may have heard the unspoken prayers of that widow. I don't doubt that her soul could have whispered, half in hope and half in fear, "Oh, if only he would raise my son!" Jesus heard the flutter of the wings of desire, even if it wasn't fully faith. Surely her eyes spoke as she gazed at Jesus, who had so suddenly appeared. Let us be as quiet as the scene before us. Let us be hushed for a minute and pray for God to raise dead souls at this time.

Jesus is Able to Work the Miracle of Giving Life

Quickly the Great Life-Giver began his gracious work. Jesus Christ has life in himself, and he gives life to whomever he desires. *For as the Father raises up the dead and gives them life; even so the Son gives life unto whom he will* (John 5:21). There is so much life in him that he says, *he that believes in me, though he is dead, yet shall he live* (John 11:25). Our blessed Lord immediately approached the dead man. What lay in front of him? It was a corpse. He could receive no help from that lifeless form. Those in the funeral procession were sure he was dead, because they carried him out to bury him. No deception was possible. His own mother believed he was dead, and you can be sure that if there had been a spark of life in him, she wouldn't have given him up to the jaws of the grave. So, there was no hope from the dead man, no hope from anyone in the crowd of bearers, and no hope from the disciples. They were all powerless. In the same way, you can't save yourself, and neither can any of us.

There's no help for you, dead sinner, in yourself or in those who love you the most. But the Lord has provided help in the one who is mighty to save. If Jesus wants even the smallest bit of help, you can't provide it, because you are dead in your sins. There you lie, dead on the funeral platform, and nothing but the sovereign power of divine omnipotence can put heavenly life into you. Your help must come from above.

While the men who carried the dead man stood still, Jesus spoke to the dead young man. He spoke to him personally, *Young man, I say unto thee, Arise.* Master, personally speak to those we know. Speak to the young, speak to the old, but speak the word which brings life to them. What we desire is your personal call. Speak, Lord, we beg you!

He said, *Young man, I say unto thee, Arise.* He spoke as if the man was alive. This is the gospel way. He didn't wait until he saw signs of life before he commanded him to rise, but to the dead man he said, *Arise.* This is the model of gospel preaching. In the name of the Lord Jesus, his chosen servants speak to the dead as if they were alive. Some of my brothers fuss about this and say that it's inconsistent and foolish, but all through the New Testament this is the model.

We read, *Awake thou that sleepest and arise from the dead, and the Christ shall shine upon thee* (Ephesians 5:14). I don't attempt to justify it. It's more than enough for me that I read it in the Word of God. We are to command men to believe on the Lord Jesus Christ, even though we know they're dead in sin, and that faith is the work of the Spirit of God. Our faith enables us in God's name to command dead men to live, and they live. We command unbelieving men to believe in Jesus. Power accompanies the Word, and God's elect believe.

> The voice of Jesus can do what your mother can't. How often has her sweet voice pleaded with you to come to Jesus?

It's by this word of faith, which we preach, that the voice of Jesus reaches dead men. The young man who couldn't rise, because he was dead, rose when Jesus commanded him. Likewise, when the Lord speaks through his servants and the gospel command, *Believe and live,* is obeyed, men live.

But the Savior spoke with his own authority, *Young man, I say unto thee, Arise.* Neither Elijah nor Elisha could have spoken in this way. But he who spoke was God come in the flesh. Though he was concealed as a man and clothed in humility, he was the same God who said, *Let there be light, and there was light* (Genesis 1:3). If any of us are able by faith to say, "Young man, Arise," we can only say it in his name. We have no authority except what we receive from him.

Young man, the voice of Jesus can do what your mother can't. How often has her sweet voice pleaded with you to come to Jesus but pleaded in vain. We pray that the Lord Jesus would inwardly speak to you, and he would say, *Young man, Arise.* I trust that while you read these words, the Lord is speaking in your hearts by his Holy Spirit. If that's the case, within you a gentle prodding of the Spirit is encouraging you to repent and yield your heart to Jesus. This will be a blessed day to the spiritually dead young man if he accepts his Savior and submits himself to be renewed by grace. No, they won't bury you! I know you've been very bad, and those who love you may feel tempted to give up, but as long as Jesus lives we can't give up on you.

> **In an instant, the Lord can save a sinner.**

The miracle was accomplished, immediately. To the astonishment of everyone around him, he sat up. His was an extreme case, but death was conquered, because he sat up. He had been called back from the innermost dungeon of death, even from the mouth of the grave, but he sat up when Jesus called him.

It didn't take a month, a week, or an hour. It didn't even take five minutes. Jesus said, *Young man, Arise,* and he who was dead sat up and began to speak. In an instant, the Lord can save a sinner. It's possible that the words you've read did more than enter your ear, and the divine flash of power which gives you eternal life may have penetrated your heart. You've become a new creature in Jesus Christ, already beginning to live in newness of life. There's no reason to ever feel spiritually dead or to return to your old corruption. New life, new feeling, new love, new hope, and new fellowship are yours, because you've passed from death into life.

This Will Produce Evidence

To give life to the dead is no small matter. The evidence will be clear. First, let's look at the young man. Would you like to see him as he was? Let me pull the sheet back from his face. Observe what death has done. He was a fine young man, and to his mother's eye he was the mirror of manhood.

But his face has taken on an ashen color, and his eyes have sunk into their sockets. You feel sad, and you can't bear the sight. Come, look into his grave, where corruption has progressed in its work. Cover him up! We can't even bear to look at the decomposing body.

But when Jesus Christ says, *Arise*, what a change takes place! Now look at him. His eyes have the light of heaven in them. His lips are pink with life. His face and expression is handsome and full of thought. Look at his healthy complexion, what a fresh look there is about him – like the dew of the morning!

He's been dead, but now he lives, and no trace of death remains. While you're looking at him, he begins to speak. What music to his mother's ear! What did he say? That, I can't tell you. Speak, yourself, as a newly living one. Then I'll hear what you say. I know what I said. I think the first word I said when I was made alive was, "Hallelujah." Afterward, I went home to my mother and told her that the Lord had met with me.

No words are given here, and it doesn't matter what those words were, because any words proved he was alive. If you know the Lord, I believe you'll speak of heavenly things. I don't believe our Lord Jesus has a mute child in his house. They all speak to him, and most of them speak about him. The new birth reveals itself in confession of Christ and praise of Christ.

When this mother heard her son speak, I doubt she criticized what he said. She didn't say, "That sentence is grammatically incorrect." She was just glad to hear him speak. Newly saved souls often talk in a way, which they wouldn't after years of experience. When people reflect back on revival meetings, they often say that there was a lot of excitement, and certain young converts talked in ways that showed their immaturity. That's very likely. But if genuine grace was evident in their souls, and they testify about their new life in the Lord Jesus, no one should judge too harshly. Be glad if you can see any proof that they're born again. To the young man himself, a new life from among the dead had begun.

A new life also began for his mother. What a life-changing experience for her to receive her son back from the dead. From that point forward, he would be doubly precious to her. Jesus helped him down from the funeral platform and returned him to his mother. We don't know what words were used, but we're sure he made the presentation most gracefully. He gave the son back to the mother as one presents a choice gift. He looked at that happy woman with majestic delight, as he *delivered him to his mother*. She would never forget the thrill of her heart.

It's important to note that our Lord, when he puts the new life into young men, doesn't want to take them away with him from the home where their first duty lies. Occasionally, one is called to leave his home to be an apostle or a missionary. Usually, however, he wants them to return home to their friends and family and make them happy and holy. He doesn't present the young man to the priest, but to his mother.

Don't say, "I'm converted, so I can't go to work anymore or try to support my mother by the work of my hands." That would prove that you weren't converted at all. You could possibly serve as a missionary in a year or two if it's what you're supposed to do, but don't rush into something you're not prepared for. For now, go home to your mother and make your home happy. Win your father's heart and be a blessing to your brothers and sisters. Give them a reason to rejoice because he *was dead and is alive again; he was lost and is found* (Luke 15:24).

What was the next thing that happened? All the neighbors feared and glorified God. A young man could be at the music hall last night and come home drunk at another time, but when he is born again, everyone around him will be amazed at the change. If a young man who got himself out of a situation by gambling or some other wrong doing is saved, we'll all feel God's real presence. If a young man who's known to associate with women with bad reputations is transformed to be pure minded and gracious, people around him will be awestruck.

The young man may have led many others astray, so if the Lord leads him back, it will make a great uproar, and people will ask about the reason for the change. They will see that God has the power to change lives. Conversions are miracles. These extraordinary examples of power in the moral world are just as remarkable as extraordinary examples in the material world. We want conversions so matter-of-fact, so real, so supernatural that those who doubt won't be able to doubt, because they clearly see the hand of God.

Finally, this miracle not only surprised the neighbors and affected them, but rumor of what took place spread everywhere. If a convert is made this morning, the result of that conversion may be felt for thousands of years, if the world stands that long. A conversion will be felt when a thousand years have passed and even throughout eternity.

Trembling, I have dropped a smooth stone into the lake. It fell from a feeble hand and a hopeful heart, but I can see the first circle on the water's surface. Other wider circles will follow as these words are spoken of and read. When you share what God has done for your soul, it will create a wider ring. No one can tell how wide the circle will become. Ring upon ring, the word will spread itself until the shoreless ocean of eternity feels the influence of this word.

No, I'm not dreaming. According to our faith, so shall it be. Grace today, granted by the Lord on one single soul could affect the whole mass of humanity. Pray for God to grant his blessing of life forever. My dear friends, I beg you, for the sake of Jesus Christ, pray for me. Amen.

Chapter 6

Lifting Up the Bowed Down

And he was teaching in one of the synagogues on the sabbath. And, behold, there was a woman who had a spirit of infirmity eighteen years and was bowed together and could in no wise lift herself up. And when Jesus saw her, he called her and said unto her, Woman, thou art loosed from thine infirmity. And he laid his hands on her, and immediately she was made straight and glorified God. (Luke 13:10-13)

I believe that this woman's sickness wasn't only physical but spiritual. Her outward appearance reflected her deep and chronic depression of mind. Her body was doubled over, and she was bowed down by her sadness of mind. A close relation exists between body and soul, but it's not always as visible as it is in this woman's case. Imagine for a moment the effect on our congregation if our inner condition showed on our outward forms. If someone had eyes like our Savior, gazed upon us, and saw the inward man reflected in our outward appearance, what would we look like? Horrific sights would be evident to all, because there would be dead people sitting in many of the pews, gazing out of the glassy eyes of death. Those would be seen for what they are. Now they appear alive on the outside but are actually spiritually dead.

You would shudder if you found yourself next to a corpse. However, the corpse wouldn't shudder but would remain as indifferent as ungodly people usually are. Even though the precious truth of the gospel rings in their ears, it produces no life. A large number of souls will be found in all congregations who remain *dead in trespasses and sins* (Ephesians 2:1). They sit with God's people and can't be visibly discerned from the living. Even in those cases where there is spiritual life, it wouldn't be attractive to look at. We would see a man blind, another mangled, and a third disfigured. Spiritual deformity takes many forms, and each form is painful to look upon.

> A large number of souls will be found in all congregations who remain dead in trespasses and sins.

A paralyzed man with a trembling faith, made visible by a trembling body, would be an uncomfortable neighbor. A person prone to fits of rage or despair would be equally undesirable if his body took on those characteristics. How sad it would be to have people around us who suffered with a fever or burned almost to fanaticism at one moment and then iced over with complete indifference.

I won't try to fill in further detail regarding the lame, blind, and helpless people we all come in contact with. If the flesh were formed according to the spirit, our churches would be turned into hospitals, and each man would flee from his brother and wish to run from himself. If any one of us were transformed so our inward ailments were made visible externally, we wouldn't linger long at the mirror or even think about the hideous sight which our eyes would see.

Let's end the imaginary scene with this comforting thought: Jesus is in our midst even though we are sick. Even though he doesn't see anything of beauty according to the law, his mercy takes pleasure in relieving human misery in the midst of countless ailing souls.

In that synagogue on the Sabbath, the poor woman described in the text must have been one of the least visible. Her particular disease would cause her to be very short in stature. She had been ailing for eighteen years, and like other very short people, she would be almost lost in a standing crowd. A person so bent over might have come in and gone out without being noticed by anyone standing in the meeting place. Jesus always took a position from which he could spot those who were bowed down. His quick eye didn't miss its mark. She was likely the least visible of all the people in the company, but our Lord's gracious eyes passed over all the rest and settled on her. His gaze remained on her until he worked his deed of love.

Someone reading this may be the least observed of anybody, but is noticed by the Savior. He doesn't see like man sees. He sees those whom man passes over as not worth their time. Nobody knows you or cares for you. Your peculiar trouble remains unknown, and you wouldn't reveal it to the world. You feel completely alone. No loneliness is like the kind experienced in a large gathering of people, and that's where you're at now. But don't give up, because you still have a friend. We receive great joy in the fact that as our Master observed this woman on that Sabbath in the synagogue, we can trust him to do the same today. His gaze will come to rest on you, even you. He won't pass you by but will pour out a special blessing on your weary heart. Though you count yourself among the last, you will be placed first by the Lord's working of a notable miracle of love upon you. Since we hope that this will be the case, we will proceed with the help of the Holy Spirit to look into the gracious deed, which Jesus performed for this poor woman.

The Bowing Down of the Afflicted

We read that *there was a woman who had a spirit of infirmity eighteen years and was bowed together and could in no wise lift herself up*. I can imagine that when she was a girl, she was sure-footed, her face was dimpled from smiling, and her eyes sparkled with childish glee. She possessed her share of the brightness and beauty of youth and walked upright like everyone else. She looked up at the sun by day and the sparkling stars at night, rejoicing in everything around her.

But an infirmity crept over her, which dragged her down, probably a weakness of the spine. Either the muscles and ligaments tightened, so she was drawn more and more towards the earth, or the muscles relaxed, so she couldn't retain her upright position, and her body dropped forward more and more. I suppose either of these might cause her to be bowed together, so she *could in no wise lift herself up*.

For eighteen years, she hadn't gazed at the sun. For eighteen years, no stars in the night sky brought her joy. Her face was drawn downward toward the dirt of the ground, and all the light of her life was dim. She walked around like she was searching for a grave. And I suspect she often felt that it would have brought her gladness to find one. She was as shackled as though she was bound in iron and as much in prison as though she were surrounded by stone walls. Unfortunately, we know children of God who are in much the same condition. They're perpetually bowed down, and though they remember happier days, the memory only deepens their gloom. They might sing:

> Where is the blessedness I knew when first I saw the Lord?
> Where is the soul-refreshing view of Jesus and his word?
> What peaceful hours I then enjoyed!
> How sweet their memory still! But they have left an aching void
> The world can never fill.
>
> (William Cowper)

Those who are spiritually bowed down seldom enter into fellowship with God and seldom or never gaze lovingly at the face of the Well-beloved. They try to hold on by believing, and they succeed, but they have little peace, little comfort, and little joy. They've lost the crown and choicest part of spiritual life, though that life still remains. I'm fairly certain that I am addressing more than two or three who are in such a situation, and I pray for the Comforter to bless my words to them.

This poor woman was bowed towards the things which were depressing. She seemed to grow downwards. Her life was stooping. She bent lower and lower as the weight of years pressed upon her. She constantly looked earthward. Nothing heavenly, nothing bright could pass before her eyes. Her line of sight was narrowed to the dust, and to the grave.

Likewise, the thoughts of some of God's people sink like lead, and their feelings run in a deep groove, constantly cutting a deeper channel. You can't give them delight, but you can easily cause them alarm. Oddly, they can squeeze the juice of sorrow from a cluster of grapes. Where others would leap for joy, they stoop for grief. They constantly embrace the negative and believe that joyous things aren't meant for people like them.

They refuse to accept medicine, expressly prepared for mourners, and the more comforting they are, the more they're afraid to receive them. If there's a dark passage in the Word of God, they're sure to read it and say, "That applies to me." If there's a thundering portion in a sermon, they remember every syllable of it. Although they wonder how the preacher knows them so well, they're sure he aimed every word at them. If anything happens, either good or bad, instead of accepting it as good, they manage to translate it into a sign of evil. They say, "All these things are against me." They can see nothing but the earth and can't imagine anything but fear and distress.

She Couldn't Lift Herself Up

We've known certain wise but somewhat unfeeling people who blame afflicted people and criticize them for being discouraged. That brings us to our next observation: that she *could in no wise lift herself up*. Blaming her would not be helpful. At a previous time her older sisters may have said, "Sister, you should stand up straight. If you keep slumping over, you could become deformed." Advice given to depressed people is usually unwise and causes pain and aggravation of spirit.

Maybe if those who are quick to give advice had suffered themselves, they would have the wisdom to hold their tongues. What benefit is there to advise a blind person to see or the deformed person to walk upright and not look at the ground so much? Such words are not constructive, and unsolicited advice just serves to increase the person's misery.

Some people who pretend to be comforters might be better classified as tormentors. A spiritual infirmity is as real as a physical one. When Satan binds a soul, it's as truly bound as when a man binds an ox or a donkey. It can't get free, because it's in bondage.

Some people have bravely attempted to rally their own spirits. They've tried a change of scenery and entered into godly company. They've asked Christian people to comfort them, attended church, and read consoling books, but without a doubt they are still bound. You never know what type of reaction to expect when joy is forced upon broken spirits. Some distressed souls are so sick that they despise all matters of spiritual significance and draw near death instead. If anyone finds himself in this predicament, however, he doesn't have to despair, because Jesus can lift the most dejected and disabled.

Perhaps the worst point about the poor woman's case was that *she had lived with her affliction for eighteen years.* Her disease was chronic and her illness confirmed. Eighteen years! That's a long, long time. Eighteen years of happiness fly by, and then they're gone. Eighteen years of happy life passes quickly. But eighteen years of pain, eighteen years of being bowed down to the earth, would be eighteen long years, each one with twelve dreary months dragging like a chain behind it.

> The devil may take eighteen years to forge a chain, but it doesn't take our blessed Lord even eighteen minutes to break it. He can set the captive free.

Can a child of God exist for eighteen years in despair? I'm forced to answer, "Yes." Mr. Timothy Rogers wrote a wonderful book on religious melancholy, *A Discourse Concerning Trouble of Mind and the Disease of Melancholy.* He spent twenty-eight years in despair.

Similar accounts are well known to those familiar with religious biographies. Individuals have been locked up for many years in the gloomy den of despair, and in the end they've risen to joy and comfort. Eighteen years in this condition must be a frightful affliction, but there's an escape. The devil may take eighteen years to forge a chain, but it doesn't take our blessed Lord even eighteen minutes to break it. He can set the captive free. Build your dungeons, O Fiend of Hell, and lay the foundations deep. Place the foundation of granite so close together that nothing can shift. But when he comes, the sovereign Master will destroy all your works, for all he must do is speak, and all your work will vanish into thin air. Eighteen years of affliction don't prove that Jesus can't set the captive free, but they give him an opportunity to display his gracious power.

Even though this poor woman was bowed down in mind and body, she frequented the house of prayer. Our Lord was in the synagogue, and there she was. She could have easily said, "It's very painful for me to go into a public place. I should be excused." But no, there she was. The devil might have suggested to you that it's pointless for you to go to hear the Word. Go anyway. He knows you're likely to escape from his hands if you hear the Word, so if he can keep you away, he'll do so. This woman found her liberty while in the house of prayer, and you might find it there also. Continue to gather with the church no matter what afflicts you.

The whole time, she was *a daughter of Abraham*. The devil had tied her up like a beast of burden, but he couldn't take her position. She was still a daughter of Abraham, a believing soul trusting in God by humble faith. When the Savior healed her, he didn't say, "Your sins are forgiven." There was no particular sin in her case. He didn't address her as he did those whose infirmity had been caused by sin. With the exception of being bent over, all she needed was comfort not rebuke. Her heart was right with God, which is evident because the moment she was healed, she glorified God. That praise was waiting in her spirit for the glad opportunity. She received some measure of comfort in going up to the house of God, even though for eighteen years she was afflicted. Where else should she have gone? What good could she have gained by staying at home? A sick child is best in its father's house, and she was best where prayer was likely to be made. May the Holy Spirit encourage your hearts with this description.

The Hand of Satan in this Bondage

We would never have known that it was Satan who bound this poor woman for eighteen years unless Jesus had told us. He must have cleverly bound her to make the knot hold all that time, because he doesn't appear to have possessed her. You'll notice that our Lord never laid his hand on a person possessed with a demon. Satan had not possessed her, but he bound her eighteen years earlier, and she had not been able to break free in all that time.

In a moment the devil can tie a knot, which you and I can't untie for eighteen years. He had securely bound this victim that no power she or others possessed could free her. When he's permitted, he can tie up any one of God's people in a very short time and by almost any means. Perhaps one word from a preacher, which was never meant to cause sadness, makes a heart sorrowful. A single sentence out of a good book or one misunderstood passage of Scripture might be enough in Satan's cunning hand to bind a child of God for a long time.

Satan bound the woman to herself and to the earth. There's a cruel way of tying a beast, which is somewhat similar – the animal's head is fastened to its knee or foot. Satan bound the woman in a similar fashion. Some of God's children, whose thoughts are all about themselves, turned their eyes, so they look only at themselves and the transactions of their little world.

They complain about their own weakness, mourn about their own impurity, and allow their own emotions to govern their decisions. The one and only subject of their thoughts is their own condition. If they ever change to another subject, it's only to gaze at the earth beneath them and groan about this poor world with its sorrows, miseries, sins, and disappointments. In this way, they are tied to themselves and to the earth. They can't look up to Christ like they should or let the sunlight of his love shine full upon them. They plod through life in mourning without the sun and pressed down with cares and burdens. Our Lord uses the figure of an ox or donkey, as he explains that even on the Sabbath, its owner would release it for watering.

This poor woman was restrained from what her soul needed. She was like a work animal, which can't get to the trough to drink. She knew the promises, because she heard them read every Sabbath day. She went to the synagogue and heard of him who would come to set the captives free, but she couldn't rejoice in the promise or enter into freedom. Multitudes of God's dear people are fastened to themselves and can't get to watering, can't drink from the river of life, and can't find comfort in the Scriptures. They know how precious the gospel is and how its blessings provide comfort, but they cannot enjoy the comfort or the blessings. They sigh and cry but remain bound.

There is still hope. Satan had done a good deal to the poor woman, but he had done all he could do. You can be assured that whenever Satan afflicts a child of God, he doesn't hold back. He knows nothing of mercy, and nothing else restrains him. When the Lord delivered Job into Satan's hand for a time, Satan unleashed destruction and havoc in

Job's life. He didn't spare a child, a sheep, a goat, a camel, or an ox. He caused ruin to Job's whole estate.

When he touched Job in his bone and in his flesh, nothing would satisfy the devil but covering him from the sole of his foot to the crown of his head with boils.

> *But put forth thy hand now and touch his bone and his flesh,*
> *and thou shalt see if he does not blaspheme thee to thy face.*
> *And the LORD said unto Satan, Behold, he is in thy hand,*
> *but preserve his life. So Satan went forth from the presence of*
> *the LORD and smote Job with sore boils from the sole of his*
> *foot unto the crown of his head.* (Job 2:5-7)

Satan might have inflicted pain quite sufficiently by torturing one part of his body, but that wasn't good enough. He indulged himself with vengeance upon Job's entire body.

The devil would do all he could, so he covered him with running sores. Yet, in Job's case there was a limit. It was the same here. Satan bound this woman, but he didn't kill her. He might bend her toward the grave, but he couldn't bend her into it. He might make her droop over until she was bent double, but he couldn't take away her poor feeble life. With all his wicked expertise, he couldn't make her die before her time.

At the same time, she was still a woman, and he couldn't make a beast of her. The devil can afflict you, but he can't kill you. He worries those whom he can't destroy and derives wicked pleasure from that. He knows there's no hope of your destruction, because you're beyond the shot of his gun if you belong to God.

But if he can't wound you with the shot, he'll attempt to frighten you with the powder. If he can't slay you, he will bind you in such a way that it appears he's preparing you for the slaughter. He knows how to make a desperate soul feel a thousand deaths by fearing one. But even in all this, Satan was unable to touch this woman's true position. She was a daughter of Abraham when the devil first attacked her, and she was a daughter of Abraham eighteen years later when the fiend had done his worst.

If you are ever in the position where you feel the Lord's love for you has been removed for eighteen years, you are still his beloved. If he never once gives you any token of his love, which brings you pleasure, or if you remain confused and distracted such that your eyes only see your own misery, you still belong to Jesus, and no one can pluck you out of his hands. The devil may bind you tightly, but Christ has bound you with immovable cords of everlasting love which must and will hold you to the end.

That poor woman was being prepared by the work of the devil to glorify God. Nobody else in the synagogue could glorify God like she could when she was finally set free. Every one of the eighteen years made her thanksgiving all the sweeter. What a joy it would have been to hear her tell the story of the liberating power of the Christ of God.

The devil must have thought that all his work was for nothing. He must have regretted that he hadn't left her alone those eighteen years, since his torment only qualified her to tell the story of Jesus' wondrous power.

The Liberator at Work

We've looked at the woman bound by the devil, but then the Liberator came, and the first thing we read of him is that *he saw her*. His eyes looked around and read every heart, as he glanced from one to another. At last he saw the woman. Yes, she was the one he was looking for. We shouldn't think that he saw her in the same common way we see each other.

He saw every line of her character and history, every thought of her heart, and every desire of her soul. Nobody told him that she had been bound for eighteen years, but he knew all about it. He knew how the affliction happened, what she suffered during the time, how she prayed for healing, and how the infirmity still pressed upon her. In a single moment he had read her history and understood her case. He saw her.

Our Lord had wonderful eyes. All the painters in the world will never be able to produce a satisfactory picture of Christ, because they can't duplicate his eyes. Heaven was calmly displayed in his eyes. They weren't only bright and penetrating, but they were full of power, an irresistible tenderness, and a strength that secured confidence. As he looked at the poor woman, I suspect that tears formed in our Lord's eyes. But they weren't tears of sorrow, because he knew he could heal her, and he anticipated the joy of doing so.

When his gaze came to rest on her, he called her to himself. Did he know her name? He knows all our names, so his calling is personal and unmistakable. *I have named thee; Thou art mine* (Isaiah 43:1). See the poor creature coming up the aisle? The pitiful mass of sorrow, even though she's bent over, she is moving. Is it a woman at all? You can hardly see she has a face, but she's moving toward him who called her. She couldn't stand upright, but she could come bent as she was.

> I rejoice in my Master's way of healing people, because he comes to them where they are.

I rejoice in my Master's way of healing people, because he comes to them where they are. He doesn't present them with a plan that requires them to accomplish something before he will finish the job. He begins and ends. He commands them to approach him as they are and doesn't ask them to improve or prepare. I pray that my blessed Master looks at some of you until you say, "The preacher's Master is looking at me." Then may a voice ring out from within your ears saying, "Come to Jesus just as you are."

May you have grace to reply, "Just as I am – poor, wretched, and blind – I come."

When the woman came, the great Liberator said to her, *Woman, thou art loosed from thine infirmity.* How could that be true? She was still as bent as she was before. He meant that the influence of Satan was removed from her, and the power which disabled her was broken. She believed this in her inmost soul, even as Jesus said it, even though her physical state remained unchanged.

My desire is that some of you who are God's dear people would have the power to believe that the end of your despair has come and your time of doubt and depression is ended. I pray that God would give you grace to know that freedom has been extended to you. I bring good news from the Lord. Step forward, prisoners. Jump for joy, those of you held captive. Jesus has come to set you free today.

The woman was set free, but she couldn't actually enjoy the freedom, and I'll tell you why. After he pronounced her freed, our Lord *laid his hands on her.* She suffered from a lack of strength. By putting his hands on her, I believe the Lord poured his life into her. The warm stream of his own infinite power and life came into contact with the lethargic stream of her painful existence. This infusion invigorated her so that she lifted herself up. The deed of love was done, and Jesus had done it.

If we could get those of you who struggle in bondage away from thinking about yourselves to thinking about our Lord Jesus and from looking at your own cares to thinking of him, what a change would take place. If his hands could be laid upon you – those dear pierced hands that bought you, those mighty hands that rule heaven and earth on your behalf, those blessed hands that are outstretched to plead for sinners, those dear hands that will hold you in his loving arms forever – then you would recover your joy and renew the resilience of your spirit. The bowing down of your soul would pass away like a bad dream and be forgotten forever. O, Spirit of the Lord, make it so.

The Bound Set Free

We read that *she was made straight* at once. Notice that she must have lifted herself up; this was her own act and deed. No pressure or out-side force was placed on her; she lifted herself up. Yet, she was *made straight.* She was passive in the fact that a miracle was performed on her, but she was active too. Being enabled, she lifted herself up. What a wonderful meeting there is here of the active and the passive in the salvation of men.

The Arminian says to the sinner, "Now, sinner, you are a responsible being. You must do this and that."

The Calvinist says, "Truly sinner, you are responsible enough, but you are also unable to do anything of yourself. God must work in you first to activate your will and so you can do."

What will we do with these two teachers? They started fighting a hundred years ago. We won't let them fight now, but what should we do with them? We'll let them both speak and believe what is true in both their testimonies. Is it true when the Arminian says that there must be effort on the sinner's part or he'll never be saved? It is true without question. As soon as the Lord gives spiritual life, there's spiritual activity.

Nobody is ever lugged into heaven by his ears or carried there asleep on a feather bed. God deals with us as responsible, intelligent beings. That is true, so what's the use of denying it?

Now, what does the Calvinist have to say? He says that the sinner is bound by the disease of sin and can't lift himself up. When he does so, it's God who does it all, and the Lord must have all the glory. Isn't that true too?

The Arminian says, "I never denied that the Lord is to have the glory. I will sing a hymn with you to celebrate his divine honor, and I'll pray the same prayer with you for God's divine power." All Christians are thorough Calvinists when it comes to singing and praying, but it's a pity to doubt what we profess on our knees and in our songs. It is most true that Jesus alone saves the sinner and equally true that the sinner believes to receive salvation.

> There has never been a grain of true faith or true repentance in this world unless it was initiated by the Holy Spirit.

The Holy Spirit never believed for anybody. A man must believe for himself and repent for himself or be lost. But there has never been a grain of true faith or true repentance in this world unless it was initiated by the Holy Spirit. I'm not going to explain these difficulties, because they're not difficulties except in theory. They're plain facts of practical everyday life. The poor woman knew where to put the crown. She didn't say, "I straightened myself." No, she glorified God and credited all the work to his gracious power.

The most remarkable fact is that *she was made straight immediately,* because there was more than her infirmity to overcome. Suppose someone suffered from a diseased spine or a disorder of the nerves and muscles for eighteen years. Even if the disease that caused the deformity could be entirely removed, what would the effect be? The effects of the disease would remain, because the body would have become accustomed to one posture.

In India a man might hold his hand up for years to fulfill a vow, but when the years of his penance are over, he can't bring his hand back down. It has become fixed and immovable. In the case of this woman, the bond, which held her poor bent body, was taken away, and at the same time the stiffness from lack of use was removed. In a moment, she stood up straight. This was a double display of miraculous power. If the Lord visits you this morning, he won't only take away the cause of your sadness, but he will even remove your tendency for depression. The long grooves, which you've worn into the floor, will be smoothed; the ruts in the road of sorrow, which you've worn by sadness, will be filled up, and you'll *be strong in the Lord and in the power of his might* (Ephesians 6:10).

The perfect cure caused the woman to rise up and glorify God. I wish I could have seen that hypocritical ruler of the synagogue when he made his angry speech. I wish I could have heard the Master silence him so completely. But most of all, I would have rejoiced to see this poor woman stand upright and to hear her praise the Lord.

What did she say? It's not recorded, but we can maybe imagine something like this: "I've been in and out among you for eighteen years. You've seen me and know what a poor, miserable, wretched body I possessed. But God lifted me up. Blessed be his name, I've been made straight."

What she spoke with her mouth wasn't even half of what she expressed. No reporter could have taken it down. She spoke with her eyes, her hands, and every limb of her body. She probably moved around just to see if she was really straight and to make sure it wasn't all a delusion. She must have been a living mass of joy. With every movement, she praised God from the soles of her feet to the crown of her head. She was like one newly born, delivered from a long death, joyous with all the novelty of a fresh life. It is expected that she would glorify God.

She didn't mistake how the cure came about. She traced it to a supernatural power, and she gave glory to that divine power. Are you able to glorify Christ, because he has set you free? Even though you've been bound, you don't need to be bound any longer. Christ is able to deliver you. Trust him, believe him, be made straight, and then go and tell everyone you know, "You know how depressed I was, because you tried to cheer me up. Now I have to tell you what the Lord has done for my soul."

Expect the Lord Jesus to Do the Same Thing Today

What was Jesus' reason for setting this woman free? According to his own statement it was, first of all, human kindness. He says, *does not each one of you on the sabbath loose his ox or his ass from the stall and lead it away to drink?* (Luke 13:15). This is good reasoning and leads us to believe that Jesus will help the sorrowful. Wouldn't you untie an ox or an ass if you saw it suffering? "Yes," you say.

Don't you think the Lord will release you? Do you have more mercy than the Christ of God? Let's not think so little of our Master. If your heart would cause you to pity a beast of burden, don't you think his heart will cause him to pity you? He hasn't forgotten you. His tender humanity motivates him to set you free.

More than that, there was a special relationship. He told the master of the synagogue that a man would loose his own ox or his own ass. He might not think it's his business to go and unhitch an animal that belonged to another man, but if it was his own ass and his own ox, he would free it. And don't you think that the Lord Jesus will release you? He bought you with his own blood; his Father gave you to him, and he has loved you with an everlasting love. Don't you think he'll release you? You are his property. Don't you know that he sweeps his house to find a lost coin and runs over hills and valleys to find his lost sheep? And won't he come and untie his poor tied-up ox or ass? Won't he free his captive daughter? Certainly, he will. Won't he set you free if you are a daughter of Abraham, a child of faith? Depend on it. He will.

> Jesus Christ came into the world to destroy the works of the devil.

Next, there was a point of antagonism which prompted the Savior to act. He said, *This daughter of Abraham, who, behold, Satan had bound eighteen years* (Luke 13:16). If I knew the devil had tied anyone up, I'm sure I would try to free him, wouldn't you? We can be sure some mischief is going on when the devil is working, so it must be a good deed to undo his work. But Jesus Christ came into the world to destroy the works of the devil. So when he saw the woman tied up like an ox, he said, "I will free her if for no other reason than I will undo what the devil has done." However much your sorrow can be traced to satanic influence, Jesus Christ will be more than a match for the devil, and he will set you free.

Think of her pitiful condition. An ox or an ass tied up without water would soon be in a very sad situation. Pity the poor thing. Imagine the lowing of the ox hour after hour as it cries out in thirst. Wouldn't you pity it? Don't you think the Lord pities his poor, tested, tempted, and afflicted children? Do those tears fall for nothing? Will those sleepless nights be ignored? Will that broken heart, which is willing but struggles to believe the promise, be denied attention? Has the Lord forgotten to extend grace? Has he shut off his mercy in anger? No, he will remember your sorrowful condition and hear your groaning. He even puts your tears into his bottle. *Thou tellest my wanderings; put my tears into thy bottle; are they not in thy book?* (Psalm 56:8).

The last reason, which moved the heart of Christ, was that she had been in that state for eighteen years. The master of the synagogue might have said, "She's been bound for eighteen years. She can wait until tomorrow. It's only one more day."

"No," said Christ, "if she's been bound for eighteen years, she won't wait another minute. She's already waited too long. She will be set free right now."

Don't argue that because of the length of your affliction, it won't come to an end. Instead, argue that because of the length of it, your release is near. The night has been so long, it must be so much closer to morning. You've been scourged for so long, it must be much nearer the last stroke, because the Lord doesn't allow the affliction or the grieving of the children of men forever and without purpose.

Be strong and courageous. Pray that our divine Master will come and do what I wish I could do, but can't. Pray that he make every child of God leap for joy.

I know what being bound by Satan means. The devil hasn't tied me up for eighteen years at a stretch, and I don't think he ever will, but he has brought me into bondage many times. Every time, my Master comes and sets me free again. He leads me out to water, and what a drink I get at those times! I feel like I could drink up the Jordan in one huge gulp when he pours out his promises, and I drink my fill of his sweet love.

By this, I know that he will lead other poor souls to the water. And when he does, I pray you will drink like an ox. You may be tied up again, so drink as much as you can of his grace and rejoice while you have the opportunity. *Hearken diligently unto me, and eat ye that which is good, and let your soul delight itself in fatness* (Isaiah 55:2). Be glad in the Lord and shout for joy all you who are upright in heart, because the Lord frees the prisoners. May he free many now. Amen.

Chapter 7

Only Trust Him

And as he entered into a certain village, ten men that
were lepers met him, who stood afar off and lifted up their
voices and said, Jesus Master, have mercy on us. When he
saw them, he said unto them, Go show yourselves unto the
priests. And it came to pass that as they went, they were
cleansed. (Luke 17:12-14)

S everal interesting topics are found in these verses. We see the fruit
of sin in the form of ten lepers and the abundance of divine power
to overcome it, because they were all cleansed. We also see how Christ
must come first and ceremonies second. First comes the work of grace
and then the outward showing of it. The Lord's tenderness towards outcasts, his attention to prayers from a distance, and his consideration for
the ceremonial law could provide important lessons. However, I want
to stress the importance of only one. If I could, I would engrave this
lesson on the hearts and minds of all who desire to find eternal salvation. I pray that the Holy Spirit would imprint it on every living soul.

These ten lepers had to perform an act of faith in Christ before
they had the slightest outward evidence that he had performed a life-
changing miracle upon them. Before they felt their foul blood cleansed
and before the horrible dryness of leprosy had yielded to healthy per-
spiration, Jesus commanded them to go to the house of the priest to be

examined and pronounced clean. They were to display faith in Jesus' power to heal them by going to show themselves, even though they were not yet healed.

They started their journey to the place where they would be examined by the priest, believing Jesus had healed them or would heal them, even though they had no evidence that their flesh would become like that of a little child. Here's the point I wish to stress: the Lord Jesus Christ asks sinners to believe in him and trust their souls to him, even though they may not yet discern any work of his grace in themselves. Just as these men were lepers and nothing but lepers, you may be sinners and nothing but sinners, but you are commanded to display faith in Jesus Christ while you are just what you are.

You, with all your sinfulness still present and your sense of condemnation heavy on your soul, are to believe in Jesus Christ just as you are.

These men were commanded to go to the priest with all their leprosy still clearly upon them, as if they were already healed. In the same way, you, with all your sinfulness still present and your sense of condemnation heavy on your soul, are to believe in Jesus Christ just as you are, and you will find everlasting life on the spot. This is my point, and it's of critical importance. Sinners, as sinners, are to believe in Jesus for everlasting life. The words to each one of them is, *Awake thou that sleepest and arise from the dead, and the Christ shall shine upon thee* (Ephesians 5:14).

Signs Commonly Looked For

I shall note what signs are commonly looked for by unconverted men as reasons for believing in Christ, which are actually not reasons. Then I shall show what the real reason for faith in Christ is, and last I will show how the issue of a faith in Christ is similar to that of the lepers.

First, we are to believe in and trust Jesus Christ to heal us from the disease of sin, even though we may not yet have a sign that he has done this great work in us. We are not to look for signs and evidences within ourselves before we trust our souls to Jesus.

Often unbelievers think they need a consciousness of great sin and a horrible dread of God's wrath, leading to despair. We often encounter people who say, "I could believe in Jesus Christ if I felt more burdened by a sense of sin. I could trust him if I was consumed with despair, but I'm not depressed enough. I'm not brokenhearted enough, so I can't trust Christ."

It's a strange concept, that somehow if the night was darker, we could see the better. Or if we were closer to death, we would have a better hope of life. These concepts are in direct disobedience to Christ. He wants you to trust him, not on the ground of you feeling much or little, or even of you feeling anything at all, but simply because you're sick and he came to heal you; he is able and willing to cure you.

If you say, "Lord, I can't trust you unless I feel this or that," then you're in effect saying, "I can trust my own feelings, but I can't trust God's appointed Savior." What does this accomplish other than make a god out of your feelings and a savior out of your own inner griefs? Is your own heart going to save you by its dark resistance against divine love? Is unbelief somehow going to bring you salvation, because you refuse to believe God? And should you trust despair instead of the Savior whom God sent into the world to save sinners? Is there a new gospel and does it proclaim, "He who denies the power of Jesus and despairs about his love will be saved"?

You know that Jesus justifies the ungodly and cleanses the wicked from their sin through his precious blood. And though you know this is true, you say, "I can't trust the Crucified One. I can't rely on his full payment for my sins unless I feel that my guilt is unpardonable." I pray that you never feel how you foolishly think you should feel, because feelings of despair dishonor the Lord and offend his Spirit and certainly can't be good for you.

It comes to this – you are making a god out of your despair and a christ out of your horrors. You're setting up an antichrist in the place where Christ alone should be. Although you haven't been terrified, alarmed, and heartbroken to the same extent as some, will you trust Christ with your soul? I pray that you trust Jesus once and for all.

Cast thy guilty soul on him,
　　Find him mighty to redeem;
At his feet thy burden lay;
　　Look thy doubts and cares away;
Now by faith the Son embrace;
　　Plead his promise, trust his grace.

(Augustus Toplady)

That's the point. Can you trust Jesus? That's what he's asking you to do. It seems so strange that anyone would even raise a question about trusting him. How insane and insulting to be willing to trust our feelings and not trust the Savior. These ten lepers felt no change at the point where Jesus commanded them to go and be examined by the priest, but they went. And as they went, they were made whole. Trust Jesus Christ just as you are without those feelings, which you have believed to be necessary as a sort of preparation. Trust him right now and follow him. He will make you whole before you've taken very many steps along the path of faith and obedience. O, Lord God, lead all my readers to trust your Son at once.

Many people also think they must experience a blaze of joy before they can trust Christ. One said, "I heard a Christian say that when he found the Savior, he was so happy he didn't know how to contain himself, and he sang like a whole band of music in one, 'Happy day, happy day, when Jesus washed my sins away.' If only I could be as full of joy as these 'happy day' people!"

Are you going to find evil even in our delights? Will you feed your unbelief on the joy of the Lord? What a strange thought process. You say, "Shouldn't I be happy before I can believe in Christ?" What? Why would you have the joy before you exercise the faith? That's unreasonable. If we tell you that a certain seed produces a sweet fruit, will you say that you must have the fruit before you will accept the seed? Surely that's bad reasoning.

We who have experienced this joy came to Christ in order to obtain it and didn't wait until we found it, or we would have waited forever. We came to Jesus just as we were. Some of us were vile, but we came just as we were. We trusted Christ, and we were made whole. Then came the joy and peace. If we had waited until we felt joy and peace before we came, we would have been standing in opposition to the gospel plan, which says men are to trust the Savior before they feel the slightest benefit from him.

Isn't that common sense? Aren't we required to take the medicine before we're cured by it? Don't we have to eat the bread before it removes our hunger or open our eyes before we see? Before you have any awareness of the Lord's comfort or healing, you must come and do just what he asks you to do and trust in him to save you. Neither the gloom of horror or the blaze of delight should be sought before faith. Faith comes before everything else, and that faith is a simple, humble reliance on Christ.

> Before you have any awareness of the Lord's comfort or healing, you must come and do just what he asks you to do and trust in him to save you.

Some expect to have a text impressed upon their minds. A superstition has arisen that a special Scripture must somehow impact your mind and continue there, so that you can't get rid of it. Then you can believe you're saved. In long-established families, a superstition says white birds come to a window before a death. I hold the same distrust for the superstition that if a text continues on your mind day after day, you can safely conclude it's an assurance of your salvation.

I certainly hope you never draw any such a conclusion from anything I've said. I would never want to assist you in a confidence which has such a questionable foundation. The Spirit of God does often apply Scripture with power to the soul, but this is never presented as the rock for us to build on. Do you find anything in the Bible to support the assumption that the impression of a certain text is a seal of conversion? It's not uncommon for some Word of God to greatly comfort the soul, but we don't have any right to demand this.

Do you have any right to say, "I won't believe God's Word unless I read it and then he impresses it on me in some special way"? Is it a lie if the scripture reading isn't accompanied by a special revelation? "No, it's true," you say. Remember, if it's not true, an impression on your mind won't make it true. If it is true, why don't you believe it? If it's true, accept it. If there's any power in a promise, pray for God to make you feel its power, and you should feel its power. If you don't, sin waits at your door. But as a reader of the Scriptures, you must not fall into the habit of thinking that you are to wait until some Scripture burns its way into your soul. You must read with a willing heart and believe what the Lord God says to you.

You must read with a willing heart and believe what the Lord God says to you.

Remember, it's not reading the Scripture that saves you; it's believing in Christ. What did Christ himself say? He said to the Bible readers of his day, *Search the scriptures, for in them ye think ye have eternal life; and they are those who testify of me. And ye will not come to me, that ye might have life* (John 5:39-40).

As good as searching the Scriptures is, it's nothing without coming to Christ. You will only read about your own condemnation in the Bible if you remain out of Christ. Even the Bible itself can be made into a stumbling block if you substitute Bible reading for closing the deal with Christ and putting your trust in him. Your immediate business is to trust Jesus, and no amount of reading will compensate for neglect of faith.

What if no special text of Scripture was ever laid on your heart at all, yet here it stands, *Believe on the Lord Jesus Christ, and thou shalt be saved* (Acts 16:31). That's your job if you're going to get peace. Who among you will put his trust in Jesus? If you do so, you'll surely find eternal salvation the moment you believe in his dear name.

There's another way some men try to get out of believing in Christ; they expect an actual conversion to be obvious in them before they will trust the Savior. You must understand that Christ has never brought about salvation in a man who is unconverted. There must be a perfect turning around of us – a repentance and complete conversion from sin to holiness. That is salvation and not a preparation for salvation. Conversion is the proof of Christ's healing power. But you won't have this before you trust him. You're supposed to trust him for this very thing.

When a man with a disease goes to a prominent physician, does he say, "Doctor, I'll trust you with my case when I have reached a certain stage"?

"No," says the physician, "if you've reached that state, you'll be feeling better, and you won't want me."

Your wisest plan is to go to your physician just as you are. If you're sure that he's a competent doctor, just put yourself in his hands as if you knew nothing, and he knew everything. Go to him as if you wouldn't have a choice or say in your treatment but would leave yourself entirely in his capable hands.

That's what you need to do with the Lord Jesus, the perfect Physician of the souls of men. You say, "I am not a saint. I can't be saved." Who said you were a saint? It's Christ's job to make you into a saint. "Oh, but I don't repent like I should." It's Christ's work to make you repent like you should, and you must come to him for repentance. "Oh, but my heart won't break." It is Christ who will break your heart. You don't break it and then come to him with it already broken.

Come to Jesus just as you are with your hard, stony, senseless heart and trust that and everything else to his saving power. "I don't even seem to have a strong desire," you might say. Christ himself gives every spiritual desire through his Holy Spirit. He's a Savior who begins the alphabet of mercy at A. He doesn't ask you to get as far as B, C, or D, and then promise to meet you. He begins at the beginning.

When the Good Samaritan found the man beaten by the thieves, he came where he was. That's what Jesus does. He doesn't say, "Now, then, you wounded man, get up and come to me, and I'll pour the oil and wine into you." No. He goes to where the wounded one lies in utter helplessness, stoops over him, cleanses his wounds, pours in the oil and wine, lifts him up, and carries him to the house of mercy. Poor soul! Our Master isn't a half Savior but a whole one. If you're lying at the gates of death right next to the doors of hell, he's as able to save you as if you were sitting on the doorstep of heaven. Just where you are and as you are, trust Christ to save you, and you will be saved. Don't look for conversion first, but expect it as the result of faith.

We've known some who hold to a very curious idea which I can hardly put into words. They believe that if they were to be saved, they would experience some very unique-to-them sensation. They could believe in Christ if they felt a mysterious physical sensation. It's rather difficult to understand people, but when I've talked to some, it seems they thought that they should experience some sort of physical sensation within their bodies. One said to me, "I was quite sure I was saved, because I felt so light." Poor fool; what does it matter whether you felt light or heavy? Perhaps you were lightheaded or half out of your mind with absurd excitement. Beware of such nonsense. To feel light could be interpreted as being weighed in the balances and found wanting, a sensation which could frighten as much as comfort. Another might say, "But I felt so special." Yes, and many who are now in hospitals could say the same. What does it matter what you felt? It is not a feeling that will save you.

Believing in Jesus will bring you the blessings of grace. However, strange feelings might be produced by what you've eaten, the weather, hysteria, or a hundred other things. Don't you know that when politics or some other controversial topic is discussed, an effective speaker will often provoke men with excitement to the point of agitation? Excitement doesn't save anybody. Many are melted to tears by a novel or a play, but what's the benefit? You may be moved with religious excitement, and half the emotion may be purely physical, but there may be nothing of the grace of God in it. The wiser way is to calmly sit down and say, "Here's God's way of salvation through his crucified Son, Jesus Christ. And he's promised that if I trust his Son, he'll save me from sinning, make a new man of me, and heal me of my spiritual diseases. I'll trust him, because I'm sure that the Word of God is true."

By that simple and deliberate act of faith you are saved. The power and ability to believe God is the evidence that the cure has begun and begun well. If you've trusted him, Jesus has set your case in motion, and he will save you.

The very fact that you can and do believe contains within it the necessary power by which you will be delivered from the battle of your mind. God is no longer an enemy to him who believes. Those whom we trust, we soon learn to love. This demands no unique or special sensation or excitement. It's plain and clear enough.

Someone might say, "But don't we have to be born again?" Yes, and he who believes in Christ is born again. Although he doesn't know it yet, the first mark of life is within the soul, because the first token of spiritual life is trusting Jesus Christ alone. The best evidence doesn't come from trusting marks, signs, evidences, inward feelings, impressions, and so on. It comes from trusting Jesus. That's the bottom line of the saving change; it's getting from self to the Lord God in Christ Jesus.

Imagine a mariner with a fine anchor, one of the best constructed anchors ever used in the navy. He has it on board his ship, but it's not worth a penny to him. While he has it on board his ship, it doesn't serve the purpose of an anchor. His vessel drifts with the anchor on board. He drags it out on deck and looks at it. What an anchor! Wouldn't that hold in the midst of a storm? He admires his anchor as if it was made of gold. The winds howl and the waves roar, but he feels safe with his anchor on board.

> The best evidence doesn't come from trusting marks, signs, evidences, inward feelings, impressions, and so on. It comes from trusting Jesus.

What a fool! An anchor is of no use to you while you can see it. A ship's anchorage can't be in the ship itself. "Suppose I hang the anchor from the side of the ship." It's of no use there. What do you need to do with it? Fling it overboard. Let it down into the deep, even to the bottom of the sea. It's gone. You can't see where it is. Good! That will do.

Now, soul, fling your anchor of trust overboard. Don't let it hang on your feelings or your impressions or anything that is in you. Let it go overboard, deep into the waters of infinite love, and let it get a grip on Jesus. Your hope must be outside of you. Because as long as your confidence is within you or has any dependence upon you, it's like an anchor on board; it can only increase the weight of the ship but certainly can't help in the midst of a storm. There's the truth. I pray that God grants you grace to accept it.

Reason for Believing in Jesus Christ

What assurance do I have as a sinner for trusting myself with Jesus Christ? We don't need to look for any assurance within ourselves. Our assurance for believing Christ is found in God's witness concerning his Son Jesus Christ. God, the Everlasting Father, has declared Christ *as the reconciliation for our sins, and not for ours only, but also for the sins of the whole world* (1 John 2:2). God the Father says to men, "I am able to forgive you and serve justice through the death and righteousness of my Son. Trust me, and I will save you." What more do you want than that? *He that believes in the Son of God has the witness of God in himself; he that does not believe God has made God a liar; because he does not believe the witness that God has testified of his Son* (1 John 5:10). Surely, if God declares something, you don't need further evidence. *For God is true, and every man a liar* (Romans 3:4).

What can be firmer than the voice of God who can't lie? I shouldn't need to bring any other evidence before you. I feel like I'm insulting the Lord by trying to defend him, as if his perfect truth needs my testimony to support it. Angels never doubt God. Those bright and glorious beings are never suspicious of their Maker. How can you doubt the God who made you? Oh, let it not be so. When his testimony is that he is a God ready to pardon the guilty and forgive all those who trust his Son, why should we doubt such a gracious declaration? My soul, I command you to trust your Savior and raise no more questions, but let the matter be settled within you.

The next assurance for our belief is Jesus Christ himself. He provides evidence on earth as well as the Father, and his witness is true. Consider who this Christ is – the one we are commanded to trust. Look at his person. He is God. Can we doubt him? He is perfect man and has taken perfect manhood upon himself for our sakes. Can we doubt him? He lived a perfect life. When did he ever lie? Who can accuse him of falsehood?

He died, *the just for the unjust, that he might bring us to God,* and God accepted the sacrifice of his dear Son (1 Peter 3:18). What clearer proof of his truthfulness can he give us than his death for us? Why would you refuse to put your confidence in one so worthy of it? Can you doubt Calvary? Will you despise the cross? Will you say, "I want some other assurance or proof for trusting Christ besides his own person and his finished work"? I feel almost ashamed to be pleading for something like this.

Tell me in what way my Lord was ever false. Tell me about a single time when he refused to receive a sinner who came to him. You know that he is risen from the dead and gone into heaven where he sits at the right hand of God and will return shortly. Do you dare treat him as a mere pretender? Can you dare distrust him? Do you want signs and wonders over and above those, which he displayed in himself? If one rose from the dead, you wouldn't believe if you don't believe Jesus. Because you have more than Moses and the prophets when you have Christ himself risen from the dead. *And he said unto him, If they do not hear Moses and the prophets, neither will they be persuaded, even though one rose from the dead* (Luke 16:31). Won't you trust him?

> Cast your soul on him right now and believe him just as you are, and he will save you.

I would like to grab you by the hand and put it to you personally, "Do you mean it – that you are suspicious of my Savior and can't trust your soul with him? Do you mean it?" I beg you with tears, don't treat him so badly. Cast your soul on him right now and believe him just as you are, and he will save you. He won't back out on his word, but he'll wash away your guilt in his own blood if you'll consent to be cleansed.

Let's look at this from another perspective. Do you want to know why you should believe? Your reason for believing lies in the fact that God commands you to believe. The Scriptures say, *He that believes and is baptized shall be saved, but he that believes not shall be condemned* (Mark 16:16). Then, *Believe on the Lord Jesus Christ, and thou shalt be saved* (Acts 16:31). And we've received this commandment from our Master – to preach this gospel to every creature under heaven. We preach it in his name, commanding you in the name of Jesus Christ, the Son of God, that you believe in him. This divine command is reason enough for you. If God commands you to do it, you don't need to ask, "May I do it?" The command includes permission. When the law of the gospel comes from God himself, what is there to do but to obey it and believe at once? The door is open; enter. The feast is spread; eat. The fountain is filled; wash.

Then there's the promise made to you and every creature, *Believe on the Lord Jesus Christ, and thou shalt be saved* and *he that believes not shall be condemned*. Do you hear that? *He that believes in the Son has eternal life* (John 3:36). He has eternal life; he has it now. These promises are rich and free for you. What more do you want? I don't know what more I can say. When Jesus commands you and when Jesus invites you, how can you stand back? I pray that the Holy Spirit would make this plain to men and lead them to believe.

I'll only add this one last thing. I'll be bold and say that these poor lepers believed in Jesus because they had heard of other lepers whom he had cleansed. Here I stand before you, a representative of many more in this world, who would stand up and say the same. I came to Jesus full of sin, guilty, and lost, with a hard heart and a heavy spirit. I looked to him and trusted him alone to save me, and he saved me. He has changed my nature; he has blotted out my sin, and he has made me love him. He has caused me to love all that is good and true and generous for his sake. I am not the only one who will tell you this, but countless many others who have experienced the same miracle of divine mercy. Trust the Lord Jesus, and you will experience the same miracle worked in you. If I have money to give away, I don't have to persuade anybody to take it. Jingle a few coins, and what ears men have! They'll rush to where the coin produces its golden notes. Give bread away in a cold winter or a little soup, and the poor will crowd to get it. But when we say, "Trust Jesus, and your sin will be forgiven, and your nature will be changed, and you'll be saved from sinning, and you'll be made pure and holy," men not only require an invitation, they need to be prodded to come.

> Dear Savior, draw reluctant hearts.
> To thee let sinners fly,
> And take the bliss thy love imparts,
> And drink, and never die.

> (Anne Steele)

The Result of This Kind of Faith

What does the doctrine of "only trust Jesus" lead to? What is the result and outcome of trusting in Jesus without marks, signs, evidences, or tokens?

The very existence of that type of faith in the soul is evidence that there is already a saving change. You say, "I don't see that. How can it prove that I'm a new man, because I trust myself to Christ?" Consider that it will be evidence of a saving change already performed, because it will show that you have come to be obedient to Jesus on a matter which your proud will has struggled against for a long time.

Every man in his sinful nature kicks against simply trusting in Christ. When he finally yields to the divine method of mercy, it's a direct surrender of his own will, the end of rebellion, and the establishment of peace. Faith is obedience. Faith is the evidence that the warfare has been ended by uncondi-tional surrender. They said to Jesus, *What shall we do that we might work the works of God? Jesus answered and said unto them, This is the work of God, that ye believe in him whom he has sent* (John 6:28-29).

> You want to be saved by something in yourself, but God says that he will save you if you trust in Christ.

In one sense, faith isn't a work at all. In another sense, it's the grand-est of all works. Here's where God and you are at odds. The central point of the quarrel is that you want to be saved by something in yourself, but God says that he will save you if you trust in Christ. If you do trust Christ just as you are, your trust will be evidence that you've been obedient to God, so obedient that a complete, deep-seated, radical renewal of your nature has taken place.

This trust will be evidence that you are humble. It's pride that makes men want to do something or be something for their own salvation or to be saved in some wonderful way, so they can tell other people how wonderfully they were saved. When you're willing to just be saved like the poor, good-for-nothing sinner that you are, you're already saved from pride. I won't compliment you. You're a good-for-nothing wretch of a sinner. If you'll trust Jesus, it will prove that you're humble and provide solid evidence that a change has taken place.

Faith in Jesus will be the best evidence that you are reconciled to God, but the worst evidence of your hatred of God is that you don't like God's way of salvation. You dislike God so much that you won't receive heaven on his terms. As a sinner, you are so much at war with God that you will go to hell rather than be saved in God's way. That's what it comes to.

When you give that up and say, "Lord, as long as I can be made whole and can be made to love you, I'm willing to be saved however you say," there will be evidence of a radical change in you. When you cry, "Lord, I will be saved in your own way, and I will trust Christ as you have commanded me," then God and you are reconciled on a point of primary importance. There's no battle between you now, because you're of one mind about trusting Christ.

God has trusted his honor in Christ's hands, and you trust your soul in his hands, so God and you are now in agreement to honor Jesus. The moment you have trusted Christ, that simple act of trust becomes indisputable proof that a great change has taken place in your relationship to God and in your feelings toward him.

Before long, you will become delightfully conscious of the fact that you are saved. Many people are saved, and for a time they question the truth of God's work of grace. In time, the blessing is made clear to them. When a man trusts Jesus in the way these ten lepers did and acts upon his trust, good always comes of it. Picture the ten men. They're going toward the priests even though they haven't felt that they're healed yet. They're acting on Christ's authority, and he won't make fools of them. *For the scripture says, Whosoever believes on him shall not be ashamed* (Romans 10:11).

Those lepers had to start on their walk before they could feel the healing, but as they were going they felt it. In the same way, when you trust Christ without any sense of any good thing, it won't be long before you feel his blessed power at work on your heart. For example, while I was coming to Christ, I didn't know I was coming. And when I trusted in Christ, I didn't know if I did it right. But when I finally felt that Jesus had healed me, I knew what I had done.

God has given me many blessings, which I didn't realize until sometime after I received them. I've read about the feelings of some good men, and I've said, "I wish I felt like them." Then sometime later, when I looked back, I realized I was actually following their same path and experiencing the same things. When a man wishes he was humble, he is humble, because he doesn't think of himself as humble. A person might sigh, "I wish I had a tender heart." But I'm sure his heart is tender, because he mourns its hardness. He desires to be deeply sensitive before the Lord, and it's clear that he possesses a tenderness which he doesn't recognize. His goal of tenderness is very high and therefore he dreads falling short of it.

If you trust Jesus in the dark, you will one day enter into the light. Even if you never enjoy comfort, you would still be safe. If you have trusted Christ, you will be saved, because he can't allow faith in him to be exercised in vain. If you trust Jesus, you will know his love. Trust him as you sink, and you will swim. Trust him as you feel yourself dying, and you will live. If you trust him before you feel any work of grace upon you, you will soon discover that there was a work upon you, even though you didn't realize it at the time. If you trust the Lord, you are under the authority of a divine power, because nothing short of all-powerful grace could have led you to believe and live.

The act of faith is simplicity itself. But to bring us into that simplicity, God must create a new us. To summarize, if you're ready to come to Christ and trust him without any miracles, signs, or evidences but simply trust him alone, you have within you a power that will carry you through life and preserve you in holiness to the end.

When the Amalekites burned Ziklag and took all their wives, David's men talked of stoning him (1 Samuel 30:1-6). David fell back on God alone. This account has a parallel to the beginning of faith in the sinner. Your beginning is impressive when you begin by trusting Christ alone saying, "Without anything good in me and without anything I can grab hold of, I will cast myself, sink or swim, upon Christ Jesus the Savior of sinners. And if I perish, I perish." This is a glorious beginning.

This type of faith in the Lord alone has been the final achievement, but you can exercise this same faith while you're still a babe in Christ. You will often need to trust like this in your future life, so you might as well get started right from the beginning. Circumstances in business, family, and various trials of life will require you to exercise this type of faith on a regular basis. So, I would prefer that you learn the lesson while you're young.

You will have to say, "Even though I'm weak and poor and don't see how I might be provided for, I see that the ravens and the sparrows are fed, so I will be too. I give my need of clothing to God and my hunger for food to God. I give my very life to him, so he can preserve it for me from the jaws of death."

This is glorious faith, and it's the place you must begin, because if you don't, you haven't started to build on the rock. Your foundation must be

This is a glorious faith to die with, as well as to live with.

on solid rock, or everything else will be unstable. To begin well is half the battle. Make sure that you get a foundation, which can never be moved. Life has many trials, and suffering comes to the man whose foundation fails him.

This is a glorious faith to die with, as well as to live with. When your hearing and eyesight start to fail, your soul is about to launch into the unseen world. What will you do now? Simply faint into the arms of your Father and your God. If you have learned to trust from the first because of what Jesus is and not because of what you are, then you will know how to die.

When that time comes, fears, doubts, and terror will come if you are looking within or looking back on your past life and trying to find comfort there. But if you can say, "My Savior, into your hands I commit my spirit. I place my naked and exposed soul into your pierced hands again;" then you can take your last breath in peace. *I am not ashamed, for I know whom I have believed and am persuaded that he is able to keep that which I have committed unto him against that day* (2 Timothy 1:12).

When John Hyatt, an English clergyman in the early nineteenth century, lay dying, one of his friends said, "Mr. Hyatt, can you trust your soul with Jesus even now?"

"Man," he said, "trust him with one soul? That's nothing. I could trust him with a million souls if I had them. I know that he is able to save all who trust him."

I want you to begin as these poor lepers did. Just take Christ at his word and move forward in the strength of that word before you feel any hopeful change inside you. When your time to die comes, you can watch for glory and expect it, even though the brilliance of eternal live has not yet changed you. You can watch for the eternal crown, the face of the Well-Beloved, and bliss unspeakable. You can expect these things even though the clouds gather around you. Before you pass the gates of pearl or cross the chilly sea, you can enjoy the sight of this beautiful vision through your unchanging faith.

Hope that is seen is not hope. The faith that sees him who is invisible and grasps the substance of the things to come is glorious. By this faith I even now anticipate the joys of heaven. I encourage you to try to do the same. To know of heaven will be lovely, even though you haven't seen it or felt it, because you knew and trusted the Lord of heaven. You know the promise is true. Now trust the Lord for your eternal glory in the same way you trusted him for grace, and you'll find that his richest promises are true and trustworthy.

God save every one of you, beloved. And I pray that he does so at this very hour for his dear Son's sake. Amen.

Chapter 8

Where Are the Nine?

Then one of them, when he saw that he was healed, turned back and with a loud voice glorified God and fell down on his face at his feet, giving him thanks; and he was a Samaritan. And Jesus answering said, Were there not ten cleansed? but where are the nine? Were there not found any returning to give glory to God, except this stranger? And he said unto him, Arise, go; thy faith has saved thee. (Luke 17:15-19)

Leprosy is as a very horrible disease. I think it's one of the worst. We should be more grateful than we are that this disease is scarcely known in our country. You've also seen what an accurate example it is in human flesh of what sin is in the human soul – how it pollutes and destroys. I don't need to go into that sad subject.

But here was a pitiful sight for the Savior – ten men who were lepers. What sights our Lord still sees every day in this sin-defiled world. Not ten men or even ten million are in this dreadful condition today, but on this earth there are billions of men diseased within their soul. It is a miracle of mercy that the Son of God would even set foot in such a place as this.

Observe the grace of our Lord Jesus to the ten men who were lepers. It would make a man a fortune or crown him with lifelong fame to heal one leper, but our Lord healed ten lepers at once. He is such a fountain of grace. He so freely gave his grace that the ten men were commanded to go and show themselves to the priests, because they were healed. On the way to the priests they found it to be true.

None of us can imagine the joy they felt when they realized they were healed. It must have been a sort of new birth to them to find their flesh as perfect as that of a little child. It would have been wonderful if all ten hurried back, fell at Jesus' feet, and lifted up their voices in praise. The sad thing is that nine of them, even though they were healed, went on their way to the priests. We never hear of their return. They drop out of the story completely. They've obtained a blessing and go their way.

Only one of them, a Samaritan, returned to express his thanks. Misery has strange company, as we can see by the nine lepers of the seed of Israel associated with an outcast Samaritan, and he was the only one who made his way back to Jesus, fell down at his feet, and glorified God. If you search the whole world, you will barely find gratitude. It should be as common as the dew drops that hang on the plants in the morning, but the world is dry of thankfulness to God. Gratitude to Christ was scarce enough in his own day. It was nine to one that nobody would praise him. One day in seven is for the Lord's worship, but only one man in nine is devoted to his praise. Our subject is thankfulness to the Lord Jesus Christ.

The Singularity of Thankfulness

More people receive benefits than ever give praise for them. Nine people healed, and one person glorified God. Nine people healed of leprosy, and only one person knelt down at Jesus' feet and thanked him for it. If men only thank the Lord in the proportion of one to nine for a gift this generous, what should I say about what we call God's common mercies? They're only common because he's so extravagant with them, but each is priceless beyond measure. Life, health, eyesight, hearing, domestic love, the faithfulness of friends . . . I can't even attempt to list all the benefits we receive every day. But is there one man in nine who praises God for these? A cold "Thank God!" is all that is sometimes given. Others of us do praise him for these benefits, but what poor praises! Dr. Isaac Watts's hymn is sadly true: "Hosannas languish on our tongues, and our devotion dies."

We don't praise the Lord properly, proportionately, or intensely. We receive a continent of mercies but only return an island of praise. He gives us blessings new every morning and fresh every evening, great is his faithfulness. *It is of the LORD's mercies that we are not consumed because his mercies never diminish. They are new every morning; great is thy faith* (Lamentations 3:22-23). We let the years roll by and seldom observe a day of praise. How sad to see all God's goodness and all of man's ingratitude. The number of those who receive blessings may say, "My name is Legion," but the names of those who praise God are so few that a child could write them down.

Something else is more remarkable than this: the number of those who pray is greater than the number of those who praise. These ten lepers all prayed. Their voices had become poor and feeble through disease, but they lifted them up in prayer and cried together, "Jesus, Master, have mercy on us!" They all joined together, "Lord, have mercy

> **The number of those who pray is greater than the number of those who praise.**

on us! Christ, have mercy on us!" But when they came to singing a song of thanksgiving, magnifying and praising God, only one of them sang the song. One would think that all who prayed would praise, but it's not so. In some cases a whole ship's crew prayed during a storm, but none of that crew praised God when the storm became calm. Multitudes of our fellow citizens pray when they're sick and near dying, but when they get well, their praises die on their lips. The angel of mercy, listening at their door, heard no melody of love and no song of thankfulness. Sadly, it's more pray than praise!

I'll put it another way to you who are God's people – most of us pray more than we praise. You pray, but nowhere near what you should. But praise, where's that? At our family altars we pray but seldom praise. In our closets we constantly pray, but do we praise nearly as often? Prayer isn't as heavenly an exercise as praise. Prayer is for a time, but praise is for eternity, so praise deserves the first and top priority. Does it not?

Let's get started on the job we will occupy for all eternity. Prayer is for a beggar, but a man is a poor beggar if he doesn't also give praise when he receives a gift. Praise should follow naturally on the heels of prayer, even when it doesn't go before it. If you are afflicted, if you lose money, if you fall into poverty, if your child is ill, if correction visits you in any form, you pray, and I don't blame you for it. But should it be all praying and no praising? Should our lives have so much salt and so little sweet in them? Should we so often get a drink from the rock of blessing and so seldom pour out a drink offering to the Lord Most High? Come, let's scold and correct ourselves as we acknowledge that we offer so much more prayer than praise.

In the same way, let me say that more believers obey ritual than ever praise Christ. When Jesus said, *Go show yourselves unto the priests*, off they went, all ten of them. Not one stayed behind, but one came back to recognize a personal Savior and praise his name. Today you'll go to church, you'll go to chapel, you'll read a book, and you'll perform outward religious actions, but how little praising God, how little lying at his feet and feeling that we could sing our souls away for gratitude to him who has done such great things for us. External religious exercises are easy and common enough, but the internal matter, the exposing of the heart in thankful love, is scarce. Nine obey ritual and only one praises the Lord.

Let's make this more personal: there are more who believe than there are who praise. These ten men believed, but only one praised the Lord Jesus. Their faith was about the leprosy, and in agreement with their faith, so the healing was given to them. Even though it only had to do with their leprosy, this faith was still a wonderful faith. Remarkably, they believed the Lord Jesus when he didn't even say, "Be healed." He didn't speak a single word to them to that effect. He simply said, *Go show yourselves unto the priests*. With parched skin and death burning its way into their hearts, they marched off in confidence that Jesus intended to bless them. It was admirable faith, but none of the nine who believed ever came back to praise Christ for the mercy they received.

I'm afraid that there's much about faith which concerns spiritual things that still hasn't flowered into practical gratitude. Perhaps it blooms late in the year like the chrysanthemum. It certainly hasn't flowered in springtime like the primrose and the daffodil. It's a faith which produces few blossoms of praise.

I scold myself sometimes that I have wrestled with God in prayer like Elijah on Mt. Carmel, but I haven't glorified the name of the Lord, like Mary of Nazareth. We don't praise our Lord in proportion to the benefits we receive. God's treasury would overflow if the amount of thanks due was more honestly paid. There would be no need to plead for missions or stir up God's people to self-denial if praise was proportionate to our faith.

We believe for heaven and eternity but don't praise the Lord like we should for earth and time. It's real faith, but it's faulty in execution. Faith was only real in these lepers as far as their leprosy was concerned. They didn't believe that our Lord was the Son of God or believe for eternal life. Even today, men get benefits from Christ and even hope they're saved, but they don't praise him. They spend their lives examining their own skin to see if their leprosy is gone. Their religious lives reveal a constant searching of themselves to see if they are really healed. What a poor way to spend one's energies.

> You can sin in company and go to hell in company, but when you obtain salvation, you come to Jesus all alone.

That tenth leper knew he was healed; he had full assurance on that point. The next impulse of his spirit was to hurry back to where the one stood who had been his glorious Physician, fall at his feet, and praise him with a loud voice, glorifying God. I pray that we would all do the same.

The Characteristics of True Thankfulness

This man's simple act may show the character of praise, and it doesn't take the same shape in everybody. Love to Christ, like living flowers, takes many forms; only artificial flowers are all alike. Living praise is marked by individuality. This man was one of ten when he was a leper, but he was all alone when he returned to praise God. You can sin in company and go to hell in company, but when you obtain salvation, you come to Jesus all alone. When you are saved, you will delight to praise God with others if they join with you, but if they don't, you will happily sing a solo of gratitude.

This man left the company of the other nine and came to Jesus. If Christ has saved you and your heart is right, you will say, "I must praise him. I must love him." You won't be held back by the lack of enthusiasm of your old companions or by the worldliness of your family or by the lukewarm church. Your personal love for Jesus will make you speak even if heaven and earth are silent.

Your heart burns with adoring love, and you feel like it's the only heart under heaven that loves Christ. So, you must feed the heavenly flame, and you must indulge its desires and express its longings. The fire is in your bones and must have a vent. Since there's an individuality about true praise, come and let's praise God, each one in his own way.

> Oh, may the sweet, the blissful theme,
> Fill every heart and tongue,
> Till strangers love thy charming name,
> And join the sacred song!
>
> (Anne Steele)

The next characteristic of this man's thankfulness was promptness. He returned to Christ almost immediately. I can't imagine that the Savior lingered at the village gate for hours that day. He was too busy to be in one spot for very long. The Master travelled around doing good. The man who was healed returned quickly. When you're saved, the quicker you can express your gratitude the better.

Some say that second thoughts are best, but this isn't the case when your heart is full of love for Christ. Carry out your first thoughts and don't stop for the second unless your heart is so on fire with heavenly devotion that the second one consumes the first. Go at once and praise the Savior.

What spectacular plans some of you have made regarding your future service for God, and what small results have followed. It's better to lay one brick today than to plan to build a palace next year. Magnify your Lord in the present for present salvation. Why should his mercies be set aside for future use? Why should praise be kept waiting at the door for a night? He praises often who praises at once; but he who does not praise at once praises never.

The next quality of this man's praise was spirituality. We observe this in the fact that he paused on his way to the priests. It was his duty to go to the priests, and he had received a command to do so, but all things have priorities, and some responsibilities are more important than others. He thought to himself, *I was ordered to go to the priests, but I'm healed. This new circumstance changes my priorities. The first thing I should do is to go back, tell the people, glorify God in the midst of them all, and fall down at Christ's feet.* It's a good thing to have holy priorities.

Worldly minds place ritualistic duty first. That which is external comes before that which is spiritual in their lives. But love allows us to see that substance is more precious than things passing away. And to bow at the feet of the great High Priest is a greater duty than to go before lesser priests, so the healed leper went to Jesus first. The spiritual overrode the ceremonial, and he felt that his main duty was to adore the divine person who had delivered him from his horrible disease.

Let's go to Jesus first and bow before Him in spirit. Go to church and join in regular worship, but if you love the Lord, you will want more than this. You will long from the depth of your being to get to Jesus himself and tell him how you love him. You will desire to show the gratitude of your heart to the Christ of God.

True thankfulness also manifests itself in intensity. Intensity is seen in this case, as the leper turned back and with a loud voice glorified God. He could have praised in a quieter way, but when you're cured of leprosy, and your voice is restored to you, you can't whisper out your praises. You know it would be impossible to be restrained and proper when you're newly saved. This man glorified God with a loud voice. You would also feel the need to cry out:

> Fain would I sound it out so loud
> That earth and heaven should hear.
>
> (Philip Doddridge)

Some of our converts are wild at times, and they become what some might consider excessive. Don't blame them. Why not indulge them? It won't hurt you. We are so proper and orderly that we can afford to have an extravagant one among us now and then. I pray that God would send more of that sort to wake the church up, so we might all begin to praise God with heart and voice, with soul and substance, with our entire being. Hallelujah! My own heart feels the glow.

In true thankfulness, there is also humility. This man fell down at

There is no place as honorable as at the feet of Jesus.

Jesus' feet. He didn't feel like he was in the right position until he was lying there. "I am nobody, Lord," he said with his actions, so he fell on his face. The perfect place for his demonstration of humility was at Jesus' feet.

I would rather be nobody at Christ's feet than everybody anywhere else. There is no place as honorable as at the feet of Jesus. What joy to lie there, love him wholly, and let self die out. Oh how wonderful to have Christ standing over you as the one overshadowing your life from that point forward and forever. True thankfulness lies humbly before the Lord.

Added to this, there was worship. He fell down at Jesus' feet, glorified God, and gave thanks to him. Let's worship our Savior, and let others think what they want about Jesus, but we'll put our finger into the print of the nails and say, "My Lord and my God!" We will never cease to adore him who has proved his divine authority by delivering us from the leprosy of sin. May all worship be to his supreme majesty!

One last thing about this man's thankfulness is his silence when it comes to censuring others. When the Savior said, *Where are the nine?* I notice that this man didn't reply. The Master said, *Where are the nine? Were there not found any returning to give glory to God, except this stranger?* But the adoring stranger didn't say, "O Lord, they've all gone off to the priests. I'm shocked that they didn't return to praise you!" We have enough to do to worry about our own business when we feel the grace of God in our own hearts. If I can get through my service of praise, I won't even think about accusing those who are ungrateful. The Master said, *Where are the nine?* But the poor healed man at his feet has no word to say against those cruel nine; he's too occupied with his personal adoration.

The Blessing in Thankfulness

This man was more blessed than the other nine. They were healed, but they weren't blessed as he was. There is a great blessing in thankfulness.

First, because it is right. Shouldn't Christ be praised? This man did what he could. There's always a sense of peace when you feel that you're doing all you can in a worthy cause, even though you may fall short of your own desire. At this moment, magnify the Lord.

> Meet and right it is to sing,
> In every time and place,
> Glory to our heavenly King,
> The God of truth and grace.
> Join we then with sweet accord,
> All in one thanksgiving join,
> Holy, holy, holy Lord,
> Eternal praise be thine!

> (Charles Wesley)

Next, there's the blessing that thankfulness is a manifestation of personal love. I love the doctrines of grace. I love the church of God. I love the Sabbath. I love the ordinances. But I love Jesus most. My heart never rests until I can glorify God personally and give thanks to Christ personally. That we are able to indulge in the personal love of Christ is one of the sweetest things we receive as believers. And the best way you can indulge that personal love is by personal thankfulness expressed through your heart, mouth, and actions.

There's another blessing in thankfulness: it has clear views. The thankful eye sees with clarity. The man healed of leprosy gave thanks to Jesus before he continued to glorify God. If he had thanked Jesus and stopped there, I would have said that his eyes weren't entirely open, but when he saw God in Christ and glorified God for what Christ had done, he showed a deep insight into spiritual truth. He had already begun to discover the mysteries of the divine and human person of the blessed Lord.

We learn a lot through prayer. Didn't Luther say, "To have prayed well is to have studied well"? I would like to add to what Luther said so well: To have praised well is to have studied better. Praise is a great instructor. Prayer and praise are the oars by which a man may row his boat into the deep waters of the knowledge of Christ.

The next blessing about praise is that it is acceptable to Christ. The Lord Jesus was evidently pleased. He was grieved to think the other nine didn't come back, but he was delighted with this one man who did return. The question *Where are the nine?* carries within it a commendation of the one. Whatever pleases Christ should be carefully cultivated by us. If praise is pleasant to him, let's continually magnify his name. Prayer is the straw of the wheat, but praise is the ear. Even more than Jesus loves to see the blade grow up, he loves to pluck the golden ears when the harvest of praise is ripe.

Notice too that thankfulness receives the largest blessing. The Savior said to this man what he had not said to the others, *thy faith has saved thee.* If you desire to live victorious in Christ Jesus, live a life of praise. Some of you are depressed and downtrodden like this man. He was a Samaritan. But through his praise to God, he became a singer of praise rather than a stranger. I've often noticed how the worst sinner becomes the greatest praiser. Those who were furthest from Christ, hope, and purity when they were saved, feel that they owe the most, so they love the best. Even if we weren't originally among the vilest of the vile, may it be our life's ambition to feel that we owe Jesus most. Therefore, we will praise him most and receive the richest blessings from his hands.

> Personal praise to a personal Savior must be our life's object.

Let's learn from all this to put praise in a high place. Let's hold praise meetings and consider it a great sin to neglect praise or restrain prayer.

Then let us offer our praise to Christ himself. Whether we go to the priests or not, let's go to Christ. Let's praise him personally and intensely. Personal praise to a personal Savior must be our life's object.

And last, if we work for Jesus and see converts, but they don't turn out as we expected, let's not be disappointed about it. If others don't praise our Lord, let us be sorrowful, but don't let us be disappointed.

The Savior had to say, *Where are the nine?* Ten lepers were healed, but only one praised him. We have many converts who don't join the church. We have many people converted who don't come forward for baptism or to the Lord's Supper. Many get a blessing, but don't feel enough love to own it. Those of us who are soul-winners are robbed of our wages by those who hide their faith. I thank God that lately we have many who profess their conversion, but if the other nine would come, we would need more space. Unfortunately, many have vanished after professing their faith. *Where are the nine?*

You who hold small gatherings and go around with tracts are doing more good than you will ever know. You don't know where the nine are, but even if you only bless one out of ten, you'll have a reason to thank God.

One says, "I've seen so little success. I've only had one soul saved!" That's more than you deserve. If I fished for a week and only caught one fish, I might be disappointed. But if that fish happened to be a sturgeon, a royal fish, I would feel that the quality made up for lack of quantity. When you win a soul, it's a great prize. Can you estimate the value of one soul brought to Christ? If one is saved, you should be grateful to the Lord and persevere. Even though you wish for more conversions, you won't be disappointed as long as at least a few are saved.

Above all, you won't be angry if some of them don't thank you personally or join in church fellowship with you. Ingratitude is common towards soul-winners. Ministers often bring sinners to Christ and feed the flock, but when he grows old or feeble, they want to get rid of him and try a new broom, which will sweep cleaner. They say, "Poor old gentleman, he's quite out of date!" So they get rid of him like gypsies turn an old horse loose to graze or starve; they don't care which.

If anybody expects gratitude, I'll remind them of the benediction, "Blessed are they who expect nothing, for they will not be disappointed." Even our Master didn't receive praise from the nine, so don't be amazed if you bless others, and others don't bless you. If only some poor soul would come to Christ, or some leper would be healed of sin sickness or he finds healing, let him magnify the Lord who has dealt so graciously with him.

Chapter 9

Obeying Christ's Orders

And the third day there was a marriage in Cana of Galilee, and the mother of Jesus was there, and Jesus and his disciples were also called to the marriage. And being short of wine, the mother of Jesus said unto him, They have no wine. Jesus said unto her, Woman, what have I to do with thee? My hour is not yet come. His mother said unto the servants, Whatsoever he saith unto you, do it. (John 2:1-5)

It doesn't take a strong imagination to picture Mary, probably by that time the widowed mother of our Lord. She was full of love and of a naturally kind, sympathetic disposition. She was at a wedding and was very pleased that her Son was there with the first handful of his disciples. Maybe their presence placed a greater demand on the provisions than was expected, and the supply ran short. So Mary, with an anxiety that was natural to such a mother of her years and gentle spirit, decided to speak to her Son. She told him, *They have no wine.*

There wasn't anything wrong in that, but our Lord, who doesn't see as man sees, saw that she was exercising her motherly authority at a time when it was becoming necessary for it to be in the background. History has shown how truly necessary it was. Take for example the apostate church of Rome which actually made Mary a mediator and offers prayers to her. She's even been asked to use her maternal authority with her Son.

It was a good thing for our Savior to put in place anything that might tend to give any credibility to the idolatrous worship of Mary. It was necessary for him to speak to his mother with a bit more of sharpness than, perhaps, her conduct alone might have required. So her noble Son said to her, "*Woman, what have I to do with thee?* I'm not your son as a miracle-worker. I can't work to please you. If I work a miracle as the Son of God, it can't be as your son; it must be in another role. What do I have to do with you in this matter?" Then he gave his reason: *My hour is not yet come.*

This gentle rebuke was absolutely necessary, because he knew of all that would follow. It's easy to picture how Mary took it. She knew Christ's gentleness, his infinite love, and how he had never done anything that had grieved her spirit for thirty years, so, she graciously received the reproof and gently removed herself from the situation. I'm sure she thought much more than she said, because she always laid these things up and pondered them in her heart. We see in her conduct after this point in time that she thought a great deal about what Jesus said to her.

Even with the very best intentions, we sometimes err in our relationship with our Lord. If he rebukes us, corrects us, disappoints our hope, or doesn't permit our ambitious plans to prosper, let's follow Mary's example. Let's just feel that he must be right, and in silence remain in his presence.

Let's pay attention to how Mary quieted herself; she ceased to say a word and quietly drank it all in. Then observe her wise admonition to the servants who were there to wait at the feast. Just like she had run before him, she would have these servants follow after him. She very wisely and kindly said to them, "*Whatsoever he saith unto you, do it.* Don't go to him with any of your remarks. Don't try to hurry him. Don't badger him. He knows better than we do. Stand back and wait until he speaks. Then be quick to obey every single word he utters."

I wish that when we've learned a lesson, we would try to teach it to others. Sometimes our Master rebukes us just for ourselves, and we wouldn't tell anybody else what he said. In our private fellowship with him, he has spoken to our conscience and our heart, and we don't need to go and repeat that, just as Mary didn't.

But once we've learned the lesson well, let us share what we've learned with our friend, saying, "Don't make the same mistake I made. You can avoid the rock I just ran into. I fear that I grieved my Lord. If you can learn from my mistake, you don't have to grieve him." Don't you think we would build up the body if we did that? Instead of focusing on the faults of others, let's share the lessons we've learned from our own errors to help those who are around us.

This holy woman must have spoken with a good deal of authority. Her tone must have been peculiarly forceful, and her manner must have made a great impression upon the servants, because you'll notice that they did exactly what she told them. It's not every servant who will let a guest come into the house and assume the role of mistress, but that was the case when she spoke to those servants with her deep, earnest tones, as a woman who had learned something she couldn't tell, but who had extracted a lesson for others out of that experience. She must have spoken with a wonderful melting force when she said to them, *Whatsoever he saith unto you, do it.* They all looked on with awe after she spoke and drank in her message to them as she had drunk in the message of the Lord.

Now I would like to try to teach that lesson to myself and to you. I think our own experience shows us that wisdom and our best chance of success is found in our cautiously keeping behind Christ. We must be sure to never run before him, never force his hand, never tempt him, or demand for him to do this or that. But, in holy, humble obedience, we must take these words as our life motto, *Whatsoever he saith unto you, do it.*

We Are Asked to Obey

What are we asked to do? In a word, it is to obey. You who belong to Christ and are his disciples pay attention to this word of exhortation, *Whatsoever he saith unto you, do it.*

Notice that these words were spoken, not to the disciples of Christ but to the servants who are called *diakonois* in the Greek. They were the people who were brought in to wait on tables and serve the guests. I don't know if they were paid servants or friends who kindly volunteered their services, but they were the waiters at the feast. They weren't told to leave their master or asked to give up their jobs as waiters. They were servants, and they were to remain servants, but they were also required to acknowledge Christ as their Master without disregarding their obedience to the host of the feast. Mary didn't say to these people, "Put down those pots and stop carrying those dishes." While they continue to do what they were doing, she said to them, *Whatsoever he saith unto you, do it.* I thought that point was worth nothing – that these servants, still doing their job, were to obey Christ.

That obedience would be prepared obedience. Mary came to get their minds ready to do what Christ would command them. No man will obey Christ all of a sudden and keep doing so. We must weigh and consider. There must be a thoughtful, careful knowledge of what his will is and a preparedness of heart to do that will, whatever it is.

At first these servants did nothing. The guests wanted wine, but the servants didn't go to Jesus and say, "Master, wine is needed." No, they waited until he asked them to fill the waterpots with water. Then they filled them to the brim and did nothing more until he commanded them. A large part of obedience lies in not doing. I believe that. In the anxiety found in many trembling hearts, the very best faith will be seen in not doing anything. When you don't know what to do, do nothing. And doing nothing will sometimes be the very hardest work of all.

In the case of a businessman who has come into a difficulty or of a woman with a sick child or husband, you know the impulse is to do something. Maybe we don't feel the need to do the first thing that comes to mind, but we feel that we must do something. And many people have made their situation worse by doing something, when it would have been infinitely better for them if they had bravely done nothing and left it in God's hand. *Whatsoever he saith unto you, do it.*

However, don't do whatever whim or fancy your poor brain urges you to do; don't run before you are sent. Those who run before God's cloud will have to come back again, and they'll be very happy if they find their way back. Where Scripture is silent, you be silent. If there's no command, you better wait until you can find some guidance. Don't press on in anxiety, or you might find yourself in the ditch. *Whatsoever he saith unto you*, do that. But until he speaks, you sit still. My soul, be patient before God, and wait until you know his command.

True obedience isn't always seen in what we do or don't do. Our obedience becomes obvious in our perfect submission to the will of God and our strong resolve that saturates everything that makes us who we are through and through. Whatever he asks us we will do.

> True obedience isn't always seen in what we do or don't do. Our obedience becomes obvious in our perfect submission to the will of God.

Let your obedience be perfect obedience. *Whatsoever he saith unto you, do it.* It is disobedience and not obedience, which causes us to pick and choose from the commands of Christ which ones we will obey. If you say, "I will choose which of Christ's commands I will obey," you have in fact said, "I will not do what Christ commands me, but I'll do what I please." If obedience isn't complete, it isn't obedience.

Imagine a soldier in the army who omits this or that and says that he can't help it or that he even plans to leave certain things undone instead of obeying every command of his commanding officer. Be careful before you carelessly discard any precept of the Lord. Every word he has spoken to you is more precious than a diamond. Prize it. Store it up. Wear it. Let it be your ornament and your beauty. *Whatsoever he saith unto you, do it*, whether it relates to your service to the church of God, your walk among your fellowmen, your relationship within the family, or your own private service for the Lord. *Whatsoever.* See, there are no trimmings here and no cutting off of certain things. *Whatsoever he saith unto you, do it.* Breathe this prayer right now: "Lord, help me to do *whatsoever* you have said. May I have no choice. Never allow me to let my own will come in and interfere. If you have commanded me to do anything, enable me to do it, whatever it may be!"

This obedience that is prepared and perfect is also to be practical obedience. Don't think about it for a very long time and then wait until you feel more led or until there's a more convenient time. *Whatsoever he saith unto you, do it.*

One of the great evils of our time is that of mulling over a plain command of Christ and asking, "What will be the result of it?" What do you have to do with results? "But if I follow Christ in all things, I may lose my job." What do you have to do with that? When a soldier is commanded to go up to the cannon's mouth, he's very likely to lose his job and something else, but he's bound to do it. "Oh, but I might lose my opportunities of usefulness!" What do you mean? That you're going to do evil so good may come? That's really what it comes to. Will you really before God look at that matter honestly? *Whatsoever he saith unto you, do it.* At any expense, at any risk, do it. I've heard some say, "I don't like doing things in a hurry." Alright, but what did David say? *I made haste and did not delay to keep thy commandments* (Psalm 119:60).

> If there's anything in the Bible that disagrees with you, you are wrong.

Remember, we sin every moment that we delay to do something commanded by Christ. Whether every moment of delay is a fresh sin, I can't say, but if we neglect any command of his, we are living in a condition of perpetual sinning against him. That is not a desirable position for any of Christ's disciples to live in. *Whatsoever he saith unto you, do it.* Don't argue against it or try to find some way of getting out of it.

I've known some believers who didn't want certain passages of Scripture read at the family altar, because they troubled their consciences. If there's anything in the Bible that disagrees with you, you are wrong. You need to come to terms with it right away, and the only terms will be obey, obey, obey your Lord's will.

I'm not presenting this to you as a way of salvation. You know I would never think of doing that. I'm speaking to those of you who are saved; you are Christ's servants, his saved ones. Now you're experiencing the holy discipline of his house, and this is the only rule: *Whatsoever he saith unto you, do it.* Do it in practice. Have we been talking too much about what should be done by our friends or observing what others don't do? I pray that the Spirit of God would come upon us, so our own walk can be close with God, our own obedience be precise and exact, and our own love to Christ be proven by our continual following in his steps. Ours should be obedience in our practice.

It must also be personal obedience. You know how much is done by proxy today. Charity is a great example. A is in a great deal of need; B hears of it and is very sorry indeed, so he asks C to come and help A. Then B goes to bed and feels that he's done a good thing. Or, when A has told his story to B, B finds out if there's some charitable organization that will help him. However, B never subscribes to the organization, because he never thinks of doing that. His part is just to pass A on to C, or to the charity, and having done that, he feels satisfied.

In the last great day, do you want the Savior to say, "I was hungry, and you sent me to somebody else," or, "I was thirsty, and you directed me to the church faucet for a drink"? Nothing of the kind. We must personally do something for Christ. This is how it is when we're trying to win souls to Christ. There's nothing like personally speaking to people, looking them in the eye, talking about your own personal experience with them, and pleading with them to fly to Christ for refuge. Personal obedience is necessary.

When the command came from Christ to fill the waterpots, if one of the servants at the wedding had said, "John, you go and do that, or William, you go and do that," he wouldn't have followed out Mary's command, *Whatsoever he saith unto you, do it.* If I'm touching your conscience, from this time forth stop being a servant of God by proxy, unless you were saved by proxy, and to be saved by proxy would mean you are lost. If you trust Christ for yourself, then serve him for yourself. And by his mighty grace, *Whatsoever he saith unto you, do it.*

It must also be prompt obedience. Do it right away. Delay will take the bloom from the obedience. *Whatsoever he saith unto you,* stand ready to obey. As soon as a soldier receives the command to march, he marches. The moment a command comes to your heart, and you see it confirmed in the Word of God, do it. Oh, the murdered resolutions that lie at the feet of most men's lives! What they would have done, what they could have done, if they had only done it. But they have been building castles in the air, imagining lives they would like to live, and not actually doing Christ's commands. We must seek a prompt, personal, practical service to the Lord Jesus Christ.

And our obedience is to be perpetual obedience. Mary said to the waiters, *Whatsoever he saith unto you, do it.* "Keep on doing it, not only the first thing he says, but *whatsoever he saith unto you.* As long as this feast lasts, and he is here, do what my Son commands you." So, as long as we're in this world, until life's final hour, may the Holy Spirit enable us to do just what Jesus commands us to do. You must be able to say:

> Jesus, I my cross have taken
> All to leave and follow Thee.

Is it your wish that until you enter into his rest, you would always bear his yoke and follow his footsteps? Temporary Christians are not Christians. Those who ask for vacation from this divine service have never entered it. We've put on our uniforms to never take them off, just like certain old knights in times of war slept in their armor and had their lance and shield always at hand; so must the Christian be from this time forward and forever.

Temporary Christians are not Christians.

"Ours is not to reason why;" ours is not to delay when the command comes (Alfred Lord Tennyson). But ours, while there is breath in our body and life in our spirit, is to serve him who redeemed us with his precious blood. We are to obey Christ's orders.

Why Do We Obey?

Why would these men do what Jesus asked them? Let that melt into, "Why would you and I do what Jesus commands us?"

First, Christ is worthy of obedience. I count it an honor to serve Christ. He is a perfect Man who rises nobly above us all. He is perfect God and infinitely majestic in his two natures, so we should love to follow his commands and desire to be conformed to his image. Here we find rest for our aspiring spirit and the glory, honor, and immortality for which we so intensely desire. *Whatsoever he saith unto you, do it.*

Besides that, Christ is our only hope. All our prospects for the future depend on him. Glorify his blessed name. There is none like him. If he was removed from us, and we couldn't trust in him, life would be an endless darkness and an abyss of woe. Because of all the glory of his nature, all that we owe to him, and all that we look for from him, I urge you – *Whatsoever he saith unto you, do it.*

More than that, he is all wise, and this makes him fit to lead. Who but Jesus could get these people out of their trouble at the feast when they ran out of wine? He knew the way out of it all, a way that would clearly show his own glory, make his disciples believe in him, and make everybody present happy. But if he didn't show the way, nobody could, so let us obey him, because his commands are wise. He's never made a mistake, and he never will. Let's commit our path to him, and whatsoever he says to us, let us do it.

Besides, Christ has already rewarded our obedience. Did you ever act in all good conscience and after the fact, find it was a mistake? Some of us have had to do very difficult things in our lives that have gone against our natural inclinations. Would we do them again? Yes, we would, even if they cost ten times as much. Looking back, no man has ever regretted that he followed his conscience and the dictates of God's Word, and he never will, even if he went to prison or death for Christ's sake.

You may lose for Christ, but you will never lose by Christ. When all accounts are settled in the end, you will come out with greater gain because of your apparent loss. He has never deceived you or misled you. Obedience to him has always brought you real solid peace. Therefore, *whatsoever he saith unto you, do it.*

Christ is our Master, and we must obey him. I hope that there's no one who would call him Master and not do the things that he says. We don't talk about him as one who was once great but is gone away, and whose influence is fading, because he is not current and relevant. No, he still lives, and we still fellowship with him. He is our Master and Lord. When we were baptized into his death, it wasn't a mere matter of form. We were dead to the world, and we lived to him. When we took his sacred name and called ourselves Christians, it was no sham. We promised that he would be Captain, King, and Master of our spirits.

He is no Baal, a domineering lord. He is our Man, our Husband, and in his husbandly relationship, he is Lord and Master of every thought and everything we do. Jesus, Jesus, your yoke is easy, and your burden is light. It is easy and joyous to bear it. To walk away from it would be misery. That's one reason I say, *Whatsoever he saith unto you, do it.* If you don't, you cast off your devotion to him; what are you going to do then?

To whom will you go if you turn away from him? Every man must have a master. Will you be your own master? You can't have a greater tyrant. Will you let the world be your master? Are you going to be a servant of society? There are no more pitiful slaves than these. Are you going to live for self, for honor, or for what is called pleasure? You might as well go down to Egypt to the iron furnace at once. Jesus, to whom can we go if we go away from you? *Thou hast the words of eternal life* (John 6:68).

Bind the sacrifice with cords, even unto the horns of the altar (Psalm 118:27). Throw another bond of love around me, another cord of sweet constraint, and let me never even think of parting with you. Let me be crucified to the world and the world to me. Do your hearts pray in that way? What joy to be entirely Christ's, forever Christ's! Yes, we will obey the command, *whatsoever he saith unto you, do it.*

The Result of Obedience

Suppose we do whatever Christ commands us, then what? The first thing is that you'll feel free from responsibility. The servant who has done what his master has commanded may think that some dreadful consequences could follow, but he says to himself, "It won't be my fault. I did what I was asked to do." If you want to get rid of the burdens of life, by faith do whatsoever Christ commands you. If the heavens seem like they're about to fall, it won't be your job to shore them up. You don't have to mend God's work and keep it right.

I remember what Mr. John Wesley said to his preachers, "Now, brethren, I do not want you to mend my rules. I want you to obey them." That's pretty strong from John Wesley, but it's appropriate from our Lord Jesus Christ. He doesn't want us to spend our time and resources altering, mending, touching up, and looking at consequences. No, do exactly what he tells you, and you won't need to concern yourself with the consequences. You may have to live with them, but he will give you grace to do that. It will be your joy to bear all negative consequences that come from firm obedience to Christ.

This kind of doctrine didn't suit the year 1889. If you go over to Scotland and see where the graves are of those who opposed government involvement in the Presbyterian Church, anybody who thinks according to the spirit of this age will say that they were fools to be so stubborn and strict about doctrine as to die for it. I wonder whether there's any "modern" doctrine that would be worth a rodent's life. According to the teaching of the government-run school, what's supposed to be true today may not be true tomorrow, so it's not worth dying for.

We might as well put off the dying until the thing is altered. And if we wait a month, it will be changed again, and you might get the old doctrine back again. Lord, send it, and send us a class of men who will obey what he asks them, do what he tells them, and believe what he teaches them. Send men who will lay their own wills down in complete obedience to their Lord and Master, and they will feel free from responsibility.

> You can't walk in disobedience to Christ and still enjoy fellowship with him.

You will feel a sweet flow of love to Christ. The disobedient child won't be kicked out of the house because he won't do what his parents ask. But when he doesn't submit to house rules, he has a hard time of it, and he should. After continued disobedience, that evening kiss isn't as warm as it would have been; that morning greeting has no happiness in it, and the kinder father and mother are, the more unhappy he is.

The sweet love of Christ makes us unhappy in disobedience. You can't walk in disobedience to Christ and still enjoy fellowship with him. The more dear and near he has been to you makes the gap seem so much wider when you're not doing what he asks.

There's no living your faith except by doing as he commands you. Faith that lies only in a list of beliefs or in a little religious book isn't good for much. Faith does what Christ asks it to do, and it's happy to sacrifice itself when Jesus calls for it. Faith can't be satisfied without bearing fruit, and the fruit of faith is obedience to him in whom we believe.

I also think that if we will obey Christ in what he says, we will be learning to be leaders. Wellington used to say that no man is fit to command until he has learned to obey, and I'm sure that's true. We will never see a race of godly, obedient people unless our boys and girls are required to obey their parents in their childhood. The essential priority of manhood is lost when disobedience is tolerated, and in the church of God, the Lord disciplines those he loves. Affliction is our school. Before we can deal with others, God must deal with us. If you won't obey, you will not be placed in a position to command.

And last, I believe that learning to obey prepares us for the enjoyments of heaven. Those in heaven have no will but God's will. Their will is to serve him and delight themselves in him. If you and I don't learn what obedience to God is and practice it, how could we hope to be happy in the midst of obedient spirits? If you never learn to trust and obey Christ, how can you go to heaven? You would be so unhappy that you would ask God to let you run to hell for shelter, because nothing would cause you more horror than to be in the midst of perfectly holy people who find their delight in the service of God. I pray that the Lord would bring us to this complete obedience to Christ. Then this world will be an inclined plane or a ladder as in Jacob's dream, which we will happily travel to the top and find our heaven in perfect obedience to God.

Mary does not speak to you now, but the church of God does. The church is the mother of all who truly love Christ, and she says to you, *Whatsoever he saith unto you, do it.* If you'll do it, he will turn the water into wine for you. He'll make your love happier than it ever would have been without obeying him, and he'll provide for you. Obey him, and he will comfort you. Obey him, and he will perfect you. Devote yourself to being committed to him, and you'll be with him in the home of glory.

The Lord grant this of his infinite grace – that he would allow us to know the will of Christ and then work in us to desire and to practice his perfect will! Amen and Amen.

Chapter 10

The Waterpots at Cana

Jesus said unto them, Fill the waterpots with water. And they filled them up to the brim. (John 2:7)

Y ou know the story. Jesus was at a wedding feast, and when the wine ran short, he bountifully provided for it. I don't think that I would accomplish any good if I enter into the discussion of what sort of wine our Lord Jesus made on this occasion. It was wine, and I'm quite sure it was very good wine, because he would only produce the best.

Some have raised a question regarding the great quantity of wine. I suppose there must have been no less than one hundred and twenty gallons and probably more. Someone might say, "They didn't want all that."

Another says, "Even if it was of the weakest kind of wine, it would be way too much." But you're thinking of an ordinary wedding here, where there are ten or twelve or maybe thirty or forty in someone's living room.

A wedding in Jesus' time was quite another affair. Even if it was only a village like Cana of Galilee, everybody came to eat and drink, and the feast lasted for a week or two. Hundreds of people must be fed as they come and go during this time. Nobody is refused, so a huge quantity of food and drink is required. Besides, they may not have consumed all the wine at once. When the Lord multiplied the loaves and fishes, they ate them immediately, or the bread would have grown moldy, and the fish would rot. But wine could be stored and used for months afterwards. I have no doubt that the wine Jesus Christ made was as good for keeping as it was for using. And why not set the family up with a reserve? They weren't very rich people. They could even sell it if they wanted. At any rate, that's not what I want to discuss. I choose to abstain from alcoholic drink in every form, and I think others would be wise to do the same, but each one must follow his own convictions on this matter.

Jesus Christ set the gospel dispensation in motion, not with a miracle of vengeance like when Moses turned water into blood, but with a miracle of generosity, turning water into wine. He didn't only supply necessities, but he gave luxuries. This is a highly significant aspect of the kingdom of his grace, where he not only gives sinners enough to save them but gives abundantly, grace on top of grace.

The gifts of his promise are not held back or stunted; they aren't small in quantity or quality. He gives men not only the water of life, so they may drink and be refreshed, but the best of wine, so they may greatly rejoice. He gives lavishly like a king without counting the cups and bottles. One hundred and twenty gallons is so small when compared with the rivers of love and mercy which he bestows freely out of his generous heart upon the most needy souls. You can forget all about the wine question and all about wine, bad, good, or indifferent. Let's instead think about our Lord's mercy, and let the wine serve as a type of his grace, and the abundance of it as the type of the abundance of his grace, which he so liberally gives.

Concerning this miracle, notice how simple and practical it was. We might have expected that when the great Lord of heaven and earth came here in human form, he would begin his miraculous career by summoning at least the scribes and Pharisees, if not the kings and princes of the earth, to see the evidence of his work and the authority of his mission. We could easily picture him gathering them together to work some spectacular miracle before them, as Moses and Aaron did before Pharaoh, to convince them of his Messiahship.

He did nothing of the kind. He went to a simple wedding among poor people, and in the simplest and most natural way, he displayed his glory. When he determined his first miracle to be the turning of water into wine, he didn't call for the master of the feast or the bridegroom or any of the guests and say, "You clearly see that your wine is all gone. Now, I'm about to show you a great marvel and turn water into wine."

No, he did it quietly with the servants; he told them to fill the waterpots, and he didn't ask for new vessels but used what was there. He made no fuss or a big scene. He used water, of which they had an abundance, and worked the miracle in the most commonplace and natural style. That's just the style of Jesus Christ. If it had been a Roman-style miracle, it would have been done in a very mysterious, theatrical, sensational way with no end of props. But being a genuine miracle, it followed as closely to the model of nature as the supernatural can go. Jesus didn't have the waterpots emptied and then fill them with wine; he used water to make the wine. In the process, he followed the miraculous patterns of his divine nature, which are at work every day in the world around us.

> Whenever you serve Jesus Christ, don't make a fuss about it, because he never made any fuss in what he did, even when he worked amazing miracles.

When water falls from heaven, it flows into the earth to the roots of the vine. Then the clusters of grapes swell with crimson juice. Through water, wine is produced. There's only a difference of time whether the wine is created in the cluster or in the waterpots. Our Lord didn't call for any strangers to do it; he asked ordinary servants to bring ordinary water. While they were drawing the water or what appeared to them to be water, the servants saw that the water had been turned into wine.

Whenever you serve Jesus Christ, don't make a fuss about it, because he never made any fuss in what he did, even when he worked amazing miracles. If you want to do a good thing, go and do it as naturally as you can. Be simple hearted and simple minded. Be yourself. Don't act like you're going to walk to heaven on stilts. Walk on your own feet and display your love and devotion for Christ in your everyday relationships. If you have an important job to do, do it with genuine simplicity, because everything that is gaudy and showy is petty and inadequate.

Nothing but simple naturalness displays this genuine beauty. That's the type of beauty there is about this miracle Jesus performed.

Principles We See in Our Lord's Procedure

When Christ was about to bestow a blessing, he usually gave a command. This is a fact which your memories will help you to establish in a moment. It's not always the case, but as a general rule, a word of command goes before a word of power or along with it. When he was about to give wine, the process didn't consist of him saying, "Let there be wine." It began with a command addressed to men, *Fill the water-pots with water.*

When Christ was about to give sight to the blind man, he put clay on the man's eyes and said, *Go, wash in the pool of Siloam* (John 9:7). When Christ was going to restore the withered hand of another man, he said, *Stretch forth thine hand!* (Matthew 12:13).

The principle even held true in cases where it wouldn't seem to apply. To the ruler's dead daughter he said, *Maid, arise!* (Luke 8:54). And, in the case of Lazarus, who by this time would be stinking since he'd been buried for four days, he cried, *Lazarus, come forth* (John 11:43). In this way, he provided a benefit through a command. Gospel benefits come with a gospel command.

Are you surprised that this principle, which we see in his miracles, is also observed in the wonders of his divine grace? Let's say a sinner is ready to be saved. What does Christ say to that sinner? *Believe on the Lord Jesus Christ, and thou shalt be saved* (Acts 16:31). Can his ability to believe come from himself? Isn't he dead in sin? Don't waste your time wrangling about such questions, but learn that Jesus Christ has commanded men to believe. He has commissioned his disciples to cry, *Repent, for the kingdom of the heavens is at hand* (Matthew 4:17). And, *For the times of this ignorance, God overlooked, but he now commands all men everywhere* to *repent* (Acts 17:30).

He commands us to go and preach this word: *Believe on the Lord Jesus Christ, and thou shalt be saved.* But why command them? It's his will to do so, and that should be enough for you who call yourself his disciple. It was the same in Old Testament times when the Lord explained in a vision his way of dealing with a dead nation. There lay many dry bones in the valley, and Ezekiel was sent to prophesy to them.

What did the prophet say? *O ye dry bones, hear the word of the LORD* (Ezekiel 37:4). Was that his way of making them alive? Yes, he commanded them to hear – a thing which dry bones can't do. He issued his command to the dead, the dry, the helpless, and by the power of the command, life came. I pray you won't be disobedient to the gospel, because faith is a duty, or we wouldn't read about the obedience of faith. When Jesus Christ is about to bless, he challenges men's obedience by issuing his royal orders.

The same thing is true when we separate ourselves from our worldly life and join ourselves to believers. When God intends to bless his people and make them a blessing to those around them, he issues a command to accomplish this. We've been praying to the Lord that he would arise and display his magnificent power. His answer is, *Awake, awake, put on thy strength, O Zion* (Isaiah 52:1). We ask for the world to be brought to his feet, and his reply is, *All power is given unto me in heaven and in earth. Go ye therefore, and teach all nations, baptizing them* (Matthew 28:18-19).

> Christ's commands are not to be questioned, but obeyed.

The command is a vehicle of blessing to us. If we are to receive the blessing of converts multiplied and the church built up, Christ must give us the gift. It's completely his gift, as much as it was his to turn the water into wine. But first he tells us to go and proclaim his salvation to the ends of the earth. In that way, we will fill the waterpots with water. If we are obedient to his command, we will see how mightily he will be with us and how he will hear our prayers. That's the first principle I see here: Christ issues commands to those he will bless.

Secondly, Christ's commands are not to be questioned, but obeyed. The people want wine, and Christ commands the servants to fill the waterpots with water. If these servants had thought like the fault-finding critics of today, they would have stared at our Lord a long while, then objected boldly, "We don't want water. It's not the feast of purification; it's a wedding feast. We don't need water at a wedding. We want water when we're going up to the synagogue or to the temple, so we can purify our hands according to our custom, but we don't want water now. The hour, the occasion, and situation all call for wine." But Mary's advice to them was convincing: *Whatsoever he saith to you, do it.* In the same way, let's not question or criticize, but obey his command immediately.

Sometimes it might seem like Christ's command isn't applicable to our situation. The sinner, for instance, says, "Lord, save me. Conquer the sin in me."

Our Lord cries, "Believe." The sinner can't see how believing in Jesus will enable him to achieve victory over the sin that plagues him. At first, there doesn't appear to be any connection between the simple trusting of the Savior and the victory over a bad temper or getting rid of a bad habit like drunkenness, anger, greed, or lying. There is a connection, but remember, whether you can see the connection or not, it's not yours to reason why but to do what Jesus commands you to do. By submitting to the command, the miracle of mercy will be brought about. *Fill the waterpots with water,* even though what you want is wine.

Christ saw a connection between the water and the wine, even though you don't. He had a reason for the pots being filled with water, which you don't know yet. It's not for you to ask for an explanation but to yield obedience. You are to do what Jesus commands you the first time he asks, as he commands you, when he commands you, and because he commands you. If you do this, you will find that his commandments are not a burden, and a great reward results from keeping them.

Sometimes these commands may even seem to be trivial. They may look as if he toyed with us. The family was in need of wine. Jesus said, *Fill the waterpots with water.* The servants might have said, "He's clearly not taking this seriously; he's playing with us. We'd be better off going around to these poor people's friends and asking them to contribute another skin of wine. Our time would be better spent finding a shop where we could purchase more. But to send us to fill those huge waterpots that hold so much water seems like a waste of time and energy".

I know that sometimes the path of devotion seems as if it couldn't possibly deliver the desired result. We want to be doing something more. That something more might be wrong, but it looks like we could accomplish our plan more easily and directly, so we lust after this uncommanded and perhaps forbidden course. I know that many who possess a troubled conscience think that simply believing in Jesus is too small a price. The deceitful heart suggests a course, which looks to be more effective.

"Do some penance. Feel some bitterness. Weep a certain number of tears. Torment your mind, or break your heart," cries your carnal self.

Jesus simply commands, "Believe."

It appears to be too insignificant to be done, as if it couldn't possibly be that eternal life could be given by simply putting your trust in Jesus Christ. When Jesus Christ is about to give a blessing, he issues a command, which is not to be questioned, but to be obeyed at once. If you won't believe, you won't be eternally secure. But if you're willing and obedient, you will eat the good of the land. *Whatsoever he saith unto you, do it.*

The third principle is that whenever we get a command from Christ, it is always wise to carry it out wholeheartedly. He commanded them to *Fill the waterpots with water*, and they filled them *up to the brim*. You know there's one way of filling a waterpot, and then there's another way of filling it. It's full, and you can't heap it up, but you can still fill it up until it almost begins to run over. The liquid trembles as if

> Do not give people a half gospel; give them a brimming-over gospel.

it's going to spill over the edge in a crystal cascade. It's filling something to fullness.

In fulfilling Christ's commands, let's take it to the fullest extent. Let's fill them up to the brim. If his command is *Believe*, believe him with all your might and trust him with your whole heart. If it's *Preach the gospel*, preach it in season and out of season, and preach the whole gospel. Fill it up to the brim. Do not give people a half gospel; give them a brimming-over gospel. Fulfill his commands up to the very brim. If you are commanded to repent, ask to have a hearty and deep repentance. If you are commanded to believe, ask to have an intense, absolute, childlike dependence, so your faith will be full to the brim. If you are commanded to pray, pray mightily and fill the vessel of prayer up to the brim. If you are commanded to search the Scriptures for blessing, search them from end to end and fill the Bible-reading vessel up to the brim.

Christ's commands are never meant to be followed in a half-hearted manner. Let's throw our whole soul into whatever he commands us, even though we can't yet see the reason he's given us a certain task. Christ's commands should be fulfilled with enthusiasm and carried out to the extreme, if extreme is possible.

Christ's commands are never meant to be followed in a half-hearted manner.

The fourth principle is that our constant obedience to Christ is not in conflict with our dependence on him, but it's necessary to our dependence on him. Some people say, "You hold what you call revival services and try to arouse men by enthusiastic appeals and exciting sermons. Don't you see that God will do his own work? These efforts are just you trying to take the work out of God's hands. You should just trust in him and do nothing."

We see that you trust in him and do nothing. I'll go as far as saying that I'm not so sure that you do trust him, because I've been to your house, and you're about the most miserable, depressed, unbelieving person I know. Nine times out of ten you don't even know whether you are saved yourself. If you had such a wonderfully great faith, there is no doubt that your life would display the evidence of that faith. How many have been added to your church through your doing nothing this year? How many have been blessed in that church of yours, where you exercise this blessed faith without works? How many have been brought in? "Well, we don't have very many additions." No, and I don't think you're likely to. If you approach the Redeemer's kingdom with inaction, I don't think you're approaching it the way Jesus Christ approves of.

But we – who pursue working for Christ with all our heart and soul and using any means within our reach to bring men in to hear the gospel – feel the same as you do. We believe that we can't do anything at all apart from the Holy Spirit. And we trust in God, because our faith has produced more results than yours. I wouldn't be surprised if it turns out that your faith without works is dead, and that our faith having works with it has been living faith after all. *Even so faith, if it does not have works, is dead in and of itself. But someone may say, Thou hast faith, and I have works; show me thy faith without thy works, and I will show thee my faith by my works* (James 2:17-18).

I'll put it this way, Jesus Christ said, *Fill the waterpots with water.* The religious servant says, "My Lord, I fully believe that you can make wine for these people without any water, so I will leave it in your capable hands, and I will bring no water. I'm not going to interfere with the work of God. I'm quite sure that you don't want our help, gracious Lord. You can make these waterpots fill with wine without us bringing a single bucket of water, so we won't rob you of the glory of it. We'll just stand back and wait for you. When the wine is made, we'll drink some of it and bless your name. Meanwhile we ask that you excuse us, because carrying buckets is heavy work, and many would be needed to fill all those waterpots. We would be interfering with God's work, so we'll just stand back and watch."

Don't you think that servants who talked like that would prove by their very words that they had no faith in Jesus at all? We won't go as far as to say that it would prove their unbelief, but we will say that it looks very much like it.

Look at the servant in this wedding account. As soon as Jesus commanded, *Fill the waterpots with water,* he probably said, "I don't see the connection between fetching this water and providing the feast with wine, but I'm off to the well. Hand me a couple of pails. Come along, brother. Come along and help me fill the baths."

Off they go. And soon they come back with the water and pour it into the waterpots until they're full up to the brim. Those seem to me to be the believing servants who obey the command, not necessarily understanding it but expecting that Jesus Christ knows the way to work his own miracle. By our enthusiastic obedience, we're not interfering with him. Far from it. We're proving our faith in him if we work for him as he commands us to work and trust in him alone with undivided faith.

The next principle is that our action alone isn't enough. We know this, but let me remind you once again. We have these waterpots, and they are full and couldn't be fuller. As the servants filled the pots, the water ran over here and there. Once all six large waterpots are full of water, was there any wine after all that work? Not a drop. It's water that they brought, nothing but water, and it's still water.

Suppose they took that water into the feast. The guests probably wouldn't have thought cold water was the appropriate liquid to serve at a wedding. They should have happily drunk water, but I am afraid they weren't educated in the school of total abstinence. They would have said to the master of the feast, "You gave us good wine, and water is a poor finish for the feast." I'm sure it wouldn't have been well received. Yet, it was still water, and nothing else but water, when the servants poured it into the pots.

After all that sinners can do, and all that saints can do, there's nothing in any human effort which can be used for the saving of a soul until Christ speaks the word of power. When Paul has planted and Apollos watered, there's no increase until God gives it. *I have planted, Apollos watered, but God gave the increase. So then neither is he that plants anything, neither he that waters, but God that gives the increase* (1 Corinthians 3:6-7).

> There is no power in anything you do until Jesus Christ displays his divine might. His presence is our power.

Preach the gospel; labor with souls; persuade, urge, and exhort. But there is no power in anything you do until Jesus Christ displays his divine might. His presence is our power. Blessed be his name, he will come. If we fill the waterpots with water, he will turn it into wine. He alone can do it, and the servants who show the most enthusiasm in filling up the waterpots are the first to confess that it's him alone who can perform the miracle.

The last principle here is that although human action in itself falls short of the desired end, it still has its place, and God has made that action necessary by his divine plan. Why did our Lord have these waterpots filled with water? It wasn't absolutely necessary in itself, but in order that the miracle might be clear to everyone present, it was necessary. Suppose he had said, "Go to those waterpots and draw out wine." Those who watched him might have said that there was already wine in the pots, and that no miracle was performed. When our Lord had them filled up with water, everyone knew there was no wine in the waterpots.

Elijah did the same thing to prove that there was no concealed fire upon the altar at Carmel. He commanded the people to go down to the sea, bring water, and pour it on the altar and on the victim until the trenches were filled. He said, "Do it a second time," and they did it a second time. Then he said, "Do it a third time," and they did it a third time. And no possibility of deception remained (1 Kings 18:19-37).

When the Lord Jesus commanded the servants to fill the waterpots with water, he eliminated all opportunities for him to be accused of trickery. For this reason, we see why it was necessary that the waterpots needed to be filled with water.

In addition to all this, the exercise was necessary, because it was so instructive to the servants. Did you notice that when the butler of the feast tasted the good wine, he didn't know where it came from? He couldn't figure it out, and he uttered an expression which showed his surprise, mingled with his ignorance. But it's written, *the servants who drew the water knew.*

When souls are converted in a church, it happens in much the same way with certain members, who are good people, but they don't know much about the conversion of sinners. They don't feel much joy in revivals. In fact, like the elder brother in the parable of the lost son, they're rather suspicious of these undisciplined characters being brought in (Luke 15:11-32). They consider themselves to be very respectable, and they would rather not have the dregs of society sitting in the pew with them. They feel awkward just being around them. They aren't truly aware of what's going on. *But the servants who drew the water knew.* That is to say, the enthusiastic believers who do the work and fill the waterpots know all about it.

Jesus commanded them to fill the vessels with water on purpose, so the men who drew the water would know that it was a miracle. I guarantee you, if you bring souls to Christ, you will know his power. It will make you leap for joy to hear the cry of the repentant and see the bright flash of delight that passes over the newborn believer's face when his sins are washed away, and he feels himself renewed. If you want to know Jesus Christ's miraculous power, you must go and just draw the water and fill the waterpots. Do the ordinary duties of Christian men and women. Do the things in which there is no power of themselves, but which Jesus Christ connects with his divine working. It will be for your instruction and your comfort that you had such work to do. The servants who drew the water knew.

How to Carry Out this Divine Command

First, use the abilities you have in the service of Christ. The waterpots stood there, six of them, and Jesus used what he found immediately available. Water was in the well, and our Lord used that too. Our Lord skillfully uses his own people and the abilities that they have, instead of angels or a new class of beings created just for the purpose. If you don't have golden chalices, fill your earthen vessels. If you can't consider yourselves to be goblets of finely worked silver, or if you couldn't compare yourselves to the best fine china, it doesn't matter. Fill whatever vessels you have.

> If you cannot, with Elijah, bring fire from heaven, and if you can't work miracles with the apostles, do what you can.

If you cannot, with Elijah, bring fire from heaven, and if you can't work miracles with the apostles, do what you can. If you don't have silver and gold, dedicate what you have to Christ. Bring water at his command, and it will be better than wine. The most common gifts can be made to serve Christ's purpose. In the same way that he took a few loaves and fishes and fed the crowd with them, he will take your six waterpots full of water and make wine.

The servants had improved what they had, because the waterpots were empty, but they filled them. Many in college are trying to improve their gifts and abilities. I think you're doing the right thing, but I've heard some people say, "The Lord Jesus doesn't want your learning." No, it's very likely that he doesn't, any more than he needed the water. But he certainly doesn't want your stupidity and your ignorance, and he doesn't want your rough, uncultivated ways of speaking. He didn't seek empty pitchers on this occasion. He wanted them full, and the servants did the right thing to fill them.

Today our Lord doesn't want empty heads in his ministers, or empty hearts, so fill your waterpots with water. Work, study, and learn all you can, and fill the waterpots with water. Somebody will say, "But how are such studies going to lead to the conversion of men? Conversion is like wine, and all these young fellows will learn to be like water." You're right. But still ask these students to fill the waterpots with water and expect the Lord Jesus to turn the water into wine. He can sanctify human knowledge in such a way that it's useful to presenting the knowledge of Jesus Christ. I hope we are beyond the time when people think that ignorance and rudeness are helpful to the kingdom of Christ. The great Teacher would have his people know all that they can and to know him and the Scriptures, so they can present him and proclaim his gospel. *Fill the waterpots with water.*

To apply this principle, let's all use the methods of blessing that God chooses. What are they? First, there is the reading of the Scriptures. Search the Scriptures all you can. Try to understand them. You might ask, "If I know the Bible, will I be saved?" No, you must know Christ by the Spirit. Still, *Fill the waterpots with water.* While you're studying the Scriptures you can expect the Savior to bless his own Word and turn the water into wine.

Then there's gathering with believers and hearing a gospel ministry. *Fill the waterpots with water.* You might say, "But I may hear thousands of sermons and still not be saved." I know that's true, but it's your job to fill this waterpot with water. And while you are listening to the gospel, God will bless it, because *faith comes by hearing, and the ear to hear by the word of God* (Romans 10:17). Be careful to use the methods which God appoints. Since our Lord has appointed to save men by the preaching of the Word, I pray that he will raise up those who will preach without ceasing in season and out of season, indoors and in the streets. But they won't be saved by our preaching. Preaching is the water. While we are preaching, God will bless it and turn the water into wine.

Let's distribute religious books and tracts. People may not be saved by reading them, but while they're reading them, God may remind them of his truth and convict their hearts. *Fill the waterpots with water.* Pass out tracts to the masses and scatter religious literature everywhere. *Fill the waterpots with water,* and the Lord will turn the water into wine.

Remember the prayer meeting. What a perfect way to grow in grace, because it provides access to power to accomplish all the works of the church. *Fill that waterpot with water.* In answer to prayer, Jesus will turn the water into wine.

Sunday school teachers, don't neglect your method of usefulness. *Fill the waterpots with water.* Work the Sunday school system with all your heart. You might say, "It won't save the children merely by getting them together and teaching them about Jesus. We can't give them new hearts." Who said that you could? *Fill the waterpots with water.* Jesus Christ knows how to turn it into wine, and he doesn't fail to do it when we are obedient to his commands.

> When you're trying to evangelize the community, don't attempt it in a half-hearted way, as if you didn't care if their souls were saved or not.

Use all the methods he provides, but make sure you use those resources enthusiastically. I return to this part of the text – *And they filled them up to the brim.* When you teach the young ones in the Sunday school, teach them well. *Fill them up to the brim.* When you preach, don't preach as if you were only half awake. Stir yourself up and fill your ministry to the brim. When you're trying to evangelize the community, don't attempt it in a half-hearted way, as if you didn't care if their souls were saved or not. *Fill them up to the brim.* Preach the gospel with all your might and beg for power from God. Fill every vessel to the brim. Whatever is worth doing is worth doing well. Nobody has ever served Christ too well. I've heard that in some church services there may be too much enthusiasm. In the service of Christ, you may have as much enthusiasm as you want if it's joined with wisdom. *Fill the waterpots with water,* and fill them to the brim. Pursue doing good with all your heart and soul and strength.

In order to further apply this principle, be sure to remember that when you've done all that you can do, a great deficiency remains in all that you have done. It's a good thing to come away from distributing tracts, teaching Sunday school, and preaching and go home, fall on your knees, and cry, "Lord, I've done all that you have commanded me, and yet there's nothing accomplished unless you give it your finishing touch. Lord, I've filled the waterpots, and even though I could only fill them with water, I've filled them to the brim. Lord, to the best of my ability, I've tried to win the souls of men for you. There can't be a soul saved, a child converted, or any glory brought to your name by what I've done in and of itself. But, my Master, speak the miracle-working word, and let the water which fills the vessels blush into wine. You can do it, even though I can't. I leave the harvest to you."

This leads me to the last application of the principle, which is to trust in your Lord to do the work. You see, there are two ways to fill waterpots. Suppose these people had never been commanded to fill the waterpots, and their doing it had no reference to Christ at all. Suppose it had been a creation of their own imagination, and they said, "These people have no wine, but they can have a bath if they want, so we'll fill the six waterpots with water." Nothing would have come from such a task. They would have had six waterpots full of water. An Eton school boy said, "The water would have been conscious of everyone staring at it and blushed," a truly poetic expression. But even if the water were conscious, it would have only seen the servants and would not have blushed. It would have reflected their faces on its glass-like surface, but nothing more would have happened.

Jesus Christ himself must come, and in power he must work the miracle. It was because he had commanded the servants to fill the water-pots with water that he was obligated to turn it into wine. Otherwise, he would have been making fools of them. They also might have turned around and said, "Why did you give us such a command?" If after we've filled the waterpots with water, Jesus doesn't work through us, we will have done what he commanded us.

But if we believe in him, I will boldly say that he is obligated to come. Because even though we're losers, and dreadful losers at that, if he didn't display his power, we'd all cry out, "I've labored in vain and spent my strength for nothing." Yet, we wouldn't be as much losers as he would be, because the world would have evidence that Christ's commands are empty, fruitless, and idle. They would declare that obedience to his Word brings no result. The world would say, "You've filled the waterpots with water, because he told you to do it. You expected him to turn the water into wine, but he didn't do it. Your faith is in vain. Your whole obedience is in vain. And he's not a fit Master to be served."

We might be losers, but he would be a greater loser still, because he would lose his glory. For my part, I don't believe that a good word for Christ is ever spoken in vain. I'm sure that no sermon with Christ in it is ever preached without result. Something will come of it, even if it's not tonight or tomorrow. When I've published a sermon and seen it in the book, before long I've been delighted to hear of souls saved through it. And when I've only preached a sermon, I've still thought something will come of it. I preached Christ. I put his saving truth into that sermon, and that seed can't die.

If it lies unread in the volume for years, like the grains of wheat in the mummy's hand, it will live and grow and bear fruit someday. I heard recently of a soul brought to Christ by a sermon I preached twenty-five years ago. I hear almost every week of souls brought to Christ by sermons preached at Park Street, Exeter Hall, and the Surrey Gardens. I believe God won't let a single faithful testimony fall to the ground.

Carry on brothers and sisters. Go on filling the waterpots with water. Don't think that you are doing much when you've done the most you can. Don't begin to congratulate yourselves on your past success. Everything must come from Christ, and it will come from Christ. Don't go to prayer meeting and say, "Paul may plant and Apollos may water, but . . ." That's not what that passage says. It says just the opposite: *I have planted, Apollos watered, but God gave the increase.* The increase is given by God when the planting and sowing are done correctly. The servants fill the waterpots, and the Master turns the water into wine.

The Lord grant us grace to be obedient to his command, especially to the command, *Believe and live!* And may we meet him in the marriage feast in heaven to drink of the new wine with him forever and ever. Amen and amen.

Chapter 11

Satan's Banquet

When the butler had tasted the water that was made wine and knew not where it was from (but the servants who drew the water knew), the butler called the bridegroom and said unto him, Every man at the beginning sets forth the good wine, and when they are well satisfied, then that which is worse; but thou hast kept the good wine until now. (John 2:9-10)

The governor of the feast said more than he intended to say; in other words, he spoke more truth in what he said than he imagined. This is the established rule all over the world: *Every man at the beginning sets forth the good wine, and when they are well satisfied, then that which is worse.* This is the way with men, and haven't scores of disappointed hearts complained about it? Let's look at friendship. First, we get the smooth tongue and words softer than butter, then the drawn sword. Ahithophel acted with love and kindness to David, but afterward he forsook his master and became the counsellor of his rebel son (2 Samuel 15:12-17:23). At first, Judas behaved with fair speech and kindness, but afterward he betrayed his Master and brought forth *that which is worse.*

Maybe you have found this true with many you thought were your friends. While everything was going favorably, the sun was shining, and the birds were singing, they served the good wine, but then there came a chilling frost. It nipped your flowers; the leaves fell from the trees; your streams were frosted with the ice, and then they served *that which is worse*. They abandoned you and fled. They left you when you needed them and taught you the hard lesson that *Cursed be the man that trusts in man and makes flesh his arm* (Jeremiah 17:5). This is how it works in the whole world, not only with men but with nature too.

Doesn't this world treat us the same way? In our youth, it serves us the best wine. We have sparkling eyes, music brings us pleasure, and the blood races through our veins. But give it a little time, and that which comes afterward is worse.

> *In the day when the keepers of the house shall tremble and the strong men shall bow themselves and the grinders cease because they are few and those that look out of the windows are darkened; and the doors outside shall be shut because the voice of the grinder is low, and he shall rise up at the voice of the bird and all the daughters of song shall be humbled; when they shall also be afraid of that which is high, and fears shall be in the way, and the almond tree shall flourish, and the grasshopper shall be a burden, and appetite shall fail: because man goes to the home of his age, and the mourners shall go about the streets.* (Ecclesiastes 12:3-5)

First there is the flowing cup of youth and afterward the stagnant waters of old age unless God blesses you with a fresh flood of his lovingkindness and tender mercy, so that as it happens to the Christian, your cup will run over and sparkle again with delight. Christian, don't trust in men. Don't depend on the things of this world that are passing away, because this is always the rule with men and with the world: *Every man at the beginning sets forth the good wine, and when they are well satisfied, then that which is worse.*

Don't depend on the things of this world that are passing away.

Consider two different houses of feasting. Look within the doors of the first – the devil's house. He is true to his nature. He brings out the good wine, and when men have drunk their fill, and their brains are dulled with drunkenness, he brings out that which is worse. Since we've taken a moment to look there and tremble, let's pay attention to the warning.

In the same way that wisdom has built her house with seven pillars, folly has its temple and its tavern of feasting into which it continually tempts those who are thoughtless. Look inside the banquet house and see four tables, the guests who sit at them, and the courses brought in. As the cups of wine are brought, they vanish one after another. You'll notice that the pattern is the same at all four tables. First the good wine and then that which is worse. I'll even take it one step further and say, that which is *worst of all*.

Satan's Table of Pleasure

The immoral ones sit at the first table to which I'll direct your attention, though I beg you to never sit down and drink at it. The table is covered over with gaudy crimson, and everything upon it is bright and glistening. Many sit at this table, but they don't know that they're the guests of hell, and at the end of the feast, they will find themselves in the depths of perdition. Can you picture the great master of the feast as he comes in? He has a superficial smile on his face. His garments aren't black; he wears a robe of many colors. His words drip with honey, and the sparkle of his eyes draws the unsuspecting. He brings in the cup, hands it to a young man, and says, "Here, young man, drink this. It's beautiful and appealing to the senses. It's the cup of pleasure."

This is the first cup at the banquet house of Satan. The young man takes it and sips the liquor. At first, it's a cautious sip. He takes just a small amount, and then he'll restrain himself. He doesn't intend to indulge fully in lust; he doesn't plan to plunge headlong into perdition. There's a flower on the edge of that cliff. He'll reach forward a little and pluck it, but it's not his intention to throw himself over the cliff and destroy himself. Not him! He thinks it will be easy to put the cup away after he's tasted its flavor. He has no plan to abandon himself to its intoxication. He takes a small sip. Oh, how sweet it is! It makes his blood tingle within him. He thinks, *What a fool I was, not to have tasted this before! Have I ever experienced joy like this? Who could have thought that bodies could experience such ecstasy as this?* He drinks again. This time he gulps the crimson liquid, and the wine spreads warmth throughout his body.

Oh, how blessed he is! Now he would say anything in praise of Bacchus or Venus or whatever shape Beelzebub chooses to assume. He sings the praise of sin. It's beautiful, it's pleasant; the deep punishment of lust seems as joyous as the delights of heaven. He drinks and drinks and drinks again, until his brain spins with the intoxication of his sinful pleasure. This is the first course.

Woe to the crown of pride, to the drunkards of Ephraim and to the open flower of the beauty of their glory which is upon the head of the fertile valley of those that are overcome with wine! (Isaiah 28:1). Drink, you drunkards of Ephraim. Place the crown of pride on your head and call us fools, because we reject your cup. Go ahead and drink with the prostitutes and eat with the lustful. You might think you're wise for doing so, but we know that after these things comes something worse. Your vine is the vine of Sodom and Gomorrah. Your grapes are bitter, and your wine is the poison of dragons and the cruel venom of deadly snakes.

Now with a smirk on his face, the subtle master of the feast rises from his seat. His victim has had enough of the best wine. He takes away that cup and brings in another, not quite so sparkling. Look into the liquor. It's not filled with the sparkling bubbles of ecstasy. It's all flat, dull, and tasteless. It's called the cup of overindulgence. The man has had enough of pleasure. Like a dog, he vomits and returns to his vomit time and time again.

Who suffers misery? Who has red eyes? Those who linger over their wine. I'm now speaking figuratively of wine as well as literally. The wine of lust brings the same red eyes. The immoral man soon discovers that all the rounds of pleasure end in a feeling of fullness. He says, "What! What more can I do? I've committed every act of wickedness that can be imagined, and I've drained every cup of pleasure. Give me something new! I have tried all forms of entertainment. They're all worthless. I've tried every kind of pleasure that I can think of. It's all over. Even celebrations have grown flat and dull. What do I do now?"

This is the devil's second course – the effect of overindulgence, the result of the previous excess. Thousands drink of the tasteless cup of overindulgence every day. Some new invention that allows them to kill time or a discovery that provides a new outlet for their sin would be a wonderful thing to them. If some man invented a new form of wickedness or a new method of lust, they would bless his name for giving them something fresh to excite them. That is the devil's second course.

Can you picture them partaking of it? Some of you reading this have been drinking deeply of lust and pleasure. If you were to speak from your heart, you would be obliged to say, "I've tried pleasure, and I don't find it to be pleasure. I have gone around and around, and I have to go around again. I am spell-bound to the sin, but I don't take pleasure in it like I once did. Anything that seemed good has now faded and turned bitter."

The feaster remains a little longer in the putrid sea of his empty pleasure, but another scene is opening. The master of the feast orders another liquor to be brought. This time the fiend presents a black goblet as his eyes flash with fierce damnation.

"Drink that, sir," he says.

The man sips it, pushes it away, and shrieks, "O God! How have I come to this?"

"You must drink, sir. He who sips the first cup must drink the second, and the third. Drink, even though it's like fire down your throat! Drink, even though it's like lava in your bowels! Drink! You must drink!" He who sins must suffer. He who is immoral in his youth has rottenness in his bones and wickedness at his core. He who rebels against the laws of God will reap the harvest in his own physical body here.

I could tell you some dreadful things about this third course. Satan's house has a front room full of everything that is enticing to the eye and tempting to the senses, but there's also a back room, and no one knows or has seen all of its horrors. Finally, there's a secret room, where he shovels out the creatures he has destroyed. Beneath this room, lies the blazing fire of hell, but the heat of that horrible pit is felt even above the floor boards.

A physician might explain the horrors some have suffered as the result of their sin better than I can, but let me tell the one who wastes his life on immorality about the poverty he will endure as a result of his sin of extravagant lifestyle. I will also tell him that the remorse he will have to live with is the result of his own iniquity, because eventually sin gives birth to misery. If we sow the seed, we must reap the harvest. The law of hell's house stands: first, the good wine; then that which is worse.

Finally, we arrive at the last course. You strong men who ignored and laughed at the warning, which I willingly delivered to you from one brother to another and with an affectionate heart, even though my language may have seemed harsh, come and drink from this last cup. In the end, the sinner has brought himself to the grave. His hopes and joys were like gold put into a bag full of holes, and they have vanished forever. Now he has come to the end. His sins torment him, and his misbehavior confuses him. He is captured like a bull in a net and can't escape. He dies and descends from physical disease to eternal damnation.

As for you, who are still restrained by a father who cares about you and a mother who watches out for you, I beg you to have nothing to do with the life of sin and foolishness.

Earthly language is insufficient to describe the horrors of that last horrific cup, which the immoral man must drink forever. Look at the cup. You can't see how deep it goes, but just look at its boiling surface. I hear the noise of gnashing of teeth and the wailing of souls in despair. As I look into that cup, I hear a voice coming up from its depths: These *shall go away into eternal punishment* (Matthew 25:46). *For Tophet is ordained of yesterday for the king of Babylon, it is also prepared; he has deepened and enlarged the pile of her fire and much wood; the breath of the LORD like a stream of brimstone kindles it* (Isaiah 30:33).

And what do you say to this last course of Satan? *Who among us shall dwell with the devouring fire? Who among us shall dwell with eternal flames?* (Isaiah 33:14). Immoral man, I beg you in the name of God to back away from this table! Don't be so careless with the cups you drink. Don't remain comfortable and secure in the peace you currently enjoy. Death is at the door, and at his heels is swift destruction.

As for you, who are still restrained by a father who cares about you and a mother who watches out for you, I beg you to have nothing to do with the life of sin and foolishness. Let the words of wisdom be written on your heart, and keep them in mind when you are tempted.

> *My son, attend unto my wisdom, and bow thine ear to my intelligence; that thou may keep council and that thy lips may conserve knowledge. For the lips of the strange woman drop as a honeycomb, and her mouth is smoother than oil, But her end is bitter as wormwood, sharp as a two-edged sword. Her feet go down to death, her steps uphold Sheol, lest thou should ponder the path of life, her ways are unstable; thou shalt not know them. Hear me now therefore, O ye sons, and do not depart from the words of my mouth. Remove thy way far from her, and do not come near the door of her house.* (Proverbs 5:1-8)

Satan's Table of Self-Righteousness

The next table is the one right in the middle of the room. Many of you thought you skipped the feast of hell completely, but there's a table for you too. It's covered with a fine white cloth, and everything on the table is clean and pleasant to look at. The wine doesn't look like the wine of Gomorrah; it seems to have no intoxication in it. It's like the ancient wine which they pressed straight from the grape into the cup with no fermentation. Do you see the men who sit at this table? How self-contented they are! This is the table of the self-righteous.

The Pharisee sits there. You may know him. He has his phylactery between his eyes. The hem of his garment is made exceedingly broad, and he is one of the best professors. *But they do all their works that they may be seen of men: they make broad their phylacteries and enlarge the borders of their garments and love the first place at feasts and the chief seats in the synagogues and greetings in the markets and to be called of men, Rabbi, Rabbi* (Matthew 23:5-7).

"Ah!" says Satan, as he draws the curtain to hide the table where the immoral men are carousing. "Be quiet. Don't make too much noise, so these self-inflated hypocrites don't realize what company they're in. Those self-righteous people are my guests as much as you." So Satan, like an angel of light, presents an ornate goblet which looks like the chalice of the table of communion. And what wine is that? It looks like the wine of the sacred Eucharist. But it's called the wine of self-satisfaction. If you look closely, you may see the bubbles of pride gathered around the rim.

The bubbles of pride transform into a growing froth. *God, I thank thee that I am not as other men are: extortioners, unjust, adulterers, or even as this publican* (Luke 18:11). You know that cup, my self-deceived hearers. If only you knew about the deadly hemlock that is mixed in.

Sin as other men do? Not you. You're not going to submit yourself to the righteousness of Christ. What do you need that for? You're as good as your neighbors. If you aren't saved, you should be, you think. You're generous, and you've never robbed anybody. You do good deeds for your neighbors, and you're as good as other people. Very good!

That's the first cup the devil serves, and the good wine makes you swell with self-important dignity. Then its fumes enter your heart and puff it up with an accursed pride. I see you sitting in the room so cleanly swept and so decorated in a presentable fashion. And I see the crowds of your admirers standing around the table, even many of God's own children who say, "If only I was half as good as he is." The very humility of your righteous admirers provides you with fuel for your pride.

Give it a little time, you smug hypocrite, because there's a second course to come. Satan looks with satisfaction at his guests, just like he did at his table of immoral men. "Ah!" he says, "I cheated those pleasure seekers with the cup of pleasure, because afterward I gave them the dull cup of excess. I've cheated you too. You think you're all fine, but I've deceived you twice." So he brings in a second cup. It's called the cup of discontent and unquietness of mind.

Many are required to drink this cup after all their self-satisfaction. Don't you find, you who are very good in your own opinion but have no interest in Christ, that when you sit quietly and begin to consider your deeds in the light of eternity, they don't line up, and you can't come up with a balance in your own favor after all, like you thought you could? Have you ever found that when you thought you were standing on a rock, the sand beneath your feet started to shift?

You've heard the Christian sing:

Bold shall I stand in that great day,
   For who aught to my charge shall lay?
While, thro' thy blood, absolv'd I am
   From sin's tremendous curse and shame.

(Ludwig von Zinzendorf)

And you've said, "Well, I can't sing that. I have been as good a church member as ever lived. I've never missed going to my church all these years, but I can't say I have a solid confidence." At one time, you had a hope grounded in self-satisfaction. But now the second course has been served, and you're not quite so content.

"Well," says another, "I've been to my chapel, and I've been baptized. I even made a profession of religion, but I never came to know the Lord in sincerity and in truth. At one time, I thought everything was fine with me, but I seem to be searching for something I can't find."

Now comes a shaking in the heart. It's not as delightful as one assumed – building on one's own righteousness. That's the second course. Wait a while, and perhaps in this world, but certainly in your hour of death, the devil will bring in the third cup of dismay, at the discovery of your lost condition. So many people who lived in a self-righteous manner all their lives have discovered that the thing they placed their hope in has failed them in the end.

> So many people who lived in a self-righteous manner all their lives have discovered that the thing they placed their hope in has failed them in the end.

I've heard of an army that was defeated in battle and attempted to make a retreat. With all their might, the soldiers fled to a certain river, where they expected to find a bridge, which they could cross and be in safety. But when they came to the stream, there was a shriek of terror, "The bridge is broken, the bridge is broken!" That cry was in vain. The army pursued them from behind, attacked, and forced them into the river until the river was filled with the bodies of drowned men.

This is also the fate of the self-righteous. You thought there was a bridge of ceremonies. You thought that baptism, confirmation, and the

Lord's Supper made up the solid arches of a bridge of good works and duties. But when it's time for you to die, you'll hear the cry, "The bridge is broken, the bridge is broken!" It will be impossible for you to turn around then. Death is close behind you and forces you onward. You discover what it is to perish while attempting to save yourself through your own good works.

This is the last course, the worst wine; your everlasting portion must be the same as that of the blatantly immoral man. As good as you thought you were, and as you saw no need for Christ in yourself, you must drink the cup of the wrath of God. The cup which is full of trembling. The wicked of the earth will wring every drop out of that cup and drink, and you must drink of it as deeply as they do. Oh, listen to my warning in time! Humble yourselves under the mighty hand of God, and *believe on the Lord Jesus Christ and thou shalt be saved.*

Satan's Table of Worldliness

Some of you have escaped condemnation so far, but there's a third table crowded with most honorable guests. I believe there have been more princes and kings, mayors and aldermen, and successful businessmen sitting at this table than at any other. It's called the table of worldliness.

The successful man says, "Well, I dislike the profligate. That's my oldest son. I've worked and saved my whole life, and my own son can't hold a job. He's running headlong into immorality. I'm glad the minister spoke so directly about that. As for me, I don't care about you self-righteous people even a little bit. To me, none of it makes any difference at all, and I don't care about religion even to the slightest degree. I like to know whether stocks rise or fall, or whether there's an opportunity of making a nice return, but that's about all I care about."

Your mind is on worldly things. I read about a friend of yours who was clothed in scarlet and fine linen. He feasted heartily every day. Do you know what became of him? You should remember it, because the same end awaits you. The end of your feast will be the same as his. If your God is this world and you depend upon it, you'll find that your way is full of bitterness.

Observe the table of the worldly man who lives for gain. Satan brings him a flowing cup and says, "Young man, you're just starting in business. You don't need to worry about honesty or about the outdated beliefs of religion. Focus on getting rich as fast as you can. Get money, honestly if you can. But if you can't get it honestly, get it any way you can." And he put the cup down. "There," he says, "is a foaming drink for you."

"Yes," says the young man, "I have abundance now. My hopes have all come true."

Here we see the first and best wine of the worldly man's feast, and many of you are tempted to envy this man. "Oh, I wish I had such prospects in business," says one, "I'm not half as sharp as he is. I couldn't deal how he does, because my religion wouldn't let me. He gets rich so fast. I wish I could make money like he does."

But there's a second course to come, the thick and nauseating cup of care. The man's got his money, but those who are rich fall into temptation and a snare. Wealth, ill-gotten, ill-used, or hoarded, brings a disease with it. It doesn't affect the gold and silver but infects the man's heart. A diseased heart is one of the most awful things a man can have. Pay attention to this money-lover and watch carefully what's important to him.

There's a poor old woman who lives near his gate. She earns just a few cents per week, but she says, "Bless the Lord, I have enough!" She never asks how she's supposed to live, how she will die, or how she will be buried. She sleeps soundly on the pillow of contentment and faith. Then there's this poor fool with mountains of gold, and he's miserable because he accidentally dropped a coin as he walked down the street, or because someone asked him to donate to his charity, and since his friend was present, he felt obliged to give. He may even complain, because his coat wears out too soon.

Next comes the cup of greed. Many have had to drink of that cup. May God save us from its fiery drops. Henry Ward Beecher, a great American preacher, once said:

> Covetousness breeds misery. The sight of houses better than our own, clothes beyond our means, jewels costlier than we may wear, transportation with the greatest luxury, and rare curiosities beyond our reach hatches the viper brood of covetous thoughts. They vex the poor who desire to be rich and torment

the rich who want to be richer. The covetous man pines to see pleasure and is sad in the presence of cheerfulness. The joy of the world is his sorrow, because all the happiness of others is not his. I do not wonder that God abhors him. He inspects his heart as he would a cave full of noisy birds or a nest of rattling reptiles and loathes the sight of its crawling tenants. To the covetous man life is a nightmare, and God lets him wrestle with it as best he may. Riches may build a palace in such a heart; pleasure might bring all its revelry there, and honor might display all its garlands – it would be like pleasures in a sepulcher and garlands on a tomb.

When a man becomes greedy, all he has is nothing to him. "More, more, more!" he cries like an animal in a frenzied state. "Drink, drink, drink!" and you give him drink, but his thirst increases. Like a blood-sucking leech, he cries, "Give, give, give!" Pride is a raving madness that pursues all the wealth the world has to offer but despises the plenty it already has. Some have died with a bag of gold in their hands and a sad expression on their faces, because they couldn't take it with them into their grave or carry it into another world.

> **When a man becomes greedy, all he has is nothing to him.**

Then comes the next course. In times past some terrible old preachers pictured the miser, the man who lived only to make gold, in the middle of hell. They imagined Mammon pouring melted gold down his throat. "There," say the mocking demons, "that's what you wanted. You've got it now. Drink, drink, drink!" I won't indulge in any such imaginations, but this much I know – he who lives for himself here will perish. He who sets his affections on things on earth has built his house upon the sand. And when the rain falls, and the floods come, the house falls with a great crash. *And every one that hears these words of mine and does not do them shall be likened unto a foolish man, who built his house upon the sand; and the rain descended, and the rivers came, and the winds blew and beat upon that house, and it fell; and great was the fall of it* (Matthew 7:26-27).

However, man serves the best wine first. He is respected and honored, but later he serves that which is worse, when his wealth is gone, and greed has consumed his mind. If you give yourself up to worldliness, this is the end that is sure to come.

Satan's Table for Secret Sinners

The fourth table is set in a very secluded corner in a very private part of Satan's palace. This table is set for secret sinners, and here the old rule is observed. In a dimly lit room, I see a young man, and Satan is the waiter. He steps in so noiselessly that no one hears him and brings in the first cup. Oh, how sweet it is! It's the cup of secret sin. *Stolen waters are sweet, and bread eaten in secret is pleasant* (Proverbs 9:17). How sweet that bite, eaten all alone! Was there ever one that tasted so delicious? That's the first.

After that, Satan brings in the wine of a guilty conscience. The man's eyes are opened. He says, "What have I done? What have I been doing?" He cries like Achan. "The first cup you brought me, I saw a sparkling wedge of gold and fine Babylonian clothing (Joshua 7:19-20). I thought, *Oh, I've got to have that.* But now my thought is *What can I do to hide this, and where will I put it? I must dig. I must dig as deep as hell, so I can hide it, or it will be discovered.*"

The grim master of the feast brings in a massive bowl filled with a black mixture. The secret sinner drinks and becomes confused. He constantly fears that his sin will become known. He has no peace and no happiness, and he is full of uneasy fear. He's afraid that he will be discovered. At night, he dreams that someone is after him. A voice whispers in his ear and tells him, "I know all about it. I will tell."

The secret sinner thinks his friends will find out about the sin, which he has committed in secret. He fears his father will know and his mother will know. Maybe his physician will tell the tale and blab about his wretched secret. There is no rest for this man, because he's always in dread of being found out. He's like the debtor who was afraid the deputies were after him because he owed a great deal of money. One day he happened to catch his sleeve on the top of a fence post and said, "Let me go. I'm in a hurry. I'll pay you tomorrow," imagining that someone had caught him.

A man places himself in this position by partnering with the hidden things of dishonesty and sin. He finds no rest, because he fears discovery. Finally, the last cup is served, the discovery which often comes during this life. You can be sure that your sin will become known – usually while you're still here in this life. *Behold, ye shall have sinned against the LORD, and be sure your sin will catch up with you* (Numbers 32:23). We witness frightful exhibitions in our police stations and courts of law, as men are made to drink that last black drink of discovery. The man who led religious meetings or the man who was honored as a saint is at last unmasked. And what does the judge and the world say of him? They say that he's a joke and an embarrassment.

But suppose he's crafty enough to pass through life without discovery, though I think it's almost impossible. What a cup he must drink when he finally stands before the throne of God! "Bring him forward, jailor! Dread keeper of the dungeon of hell, lead the prisoner forward." He comes, and the whole world is assembled. "Stand up, sir! Didn't you make a profession of religion? Didn't everybody think you were a saint?" The secret sinner is speechless.

Many in that vast crowd cry, "We thought he was a saint." The book is opened and his deeds are read. Transgression after transgression is laid bare. Do you hear that hiss? As they realize they've been betrayed, the righteous lift up their voices against the man who deceived them and dwelt among them as a wolf in sheep's clothing. How terrifying it must be to bear the ridicule of the universe! The good can bear the ridicule of the wicked, but for the wicked to bear the shame and everlasting contempt, which righteous anger will heap upon them, will be a frightful thing. The only thing worse is the eternal wrath of the Most High, which is the last cup of the devil's terrible feast that the secret sinner will be filled with for ever and ever.

If you are eating the fat and drinking the wine of hell's banquet, please pause and consider what your end will be. *For he that sows to his flesh shall of the flesh reap corruption, but he that sows in the Spirit shall of the Spirit reap eternal life* (Galatians 6:8).

The Savior's Table of Outward Cost

Now I'll walk you through the house of the Savior where his beloved feast. Come and sit with us at Christ's table of outward cost. He doesn't work in the same way as the prince of darkness. The first cup Christ brings to them is often a cup of bitterness. Jesus brings in the cup of poverty and affliction, and he makes his own children drink of it until they say, "You have made me drunk with bitterness." This is the way Christ begins – the worst wine is served first.

When a commanding officer starts off with a young recruit, he pays him and afterward comes the battle. But Christ never treats his recruits like this. They must count the cost, so they don't begin to build without being able to finish. He doesn't seek disciples who are dazzled with first appearances. He begins harshly with them. Many of his children have found that the first course of the Redeemer's table has been affliction, sorrow, poverty, and need.

> Many of his children have found that the first course of the Redeemer's table has been affliction, sorrow, poverty, and need.

In biblical times when the best of God's people were at the table, he served them the worst. They wandered around in sheepskins and goatskins; they were destitute, afflicted, and tormented. The world was not worthy of them, but they kept on drinking from these bitter cups for many days. Afterward he brought out sweeter cups for them, and you who have been troubled experienced the same thing. After the cup of affliction comes the cup of comfort, and how sweet is that!

I have had the privilege to drink the cup of comfort after sickness and pain, so I can testify to this. I said of my Master, *Thou hast kept the good wine until now*. It was so luscious that the taste of it took away every taste of bitterness and sorrow. I said, "Surely the bitterness of this sickness is past, for the Lord has revealed himself to me and given me his best wine."

But, beloved, the best wine comes last. God's people will find it to be true in their outward experiences. A poor saint's time to die arrives; the master has given him the cup of poverty, and his time of drinking from that cup comes to an end. He has had the cup of sickness, and he will no longer drink from that cup. He has had the cup of persecution, but now he's glorified together with his Master and sits upon his throne. The best things have come last in his outward circumstances.

Two martyrs were burned at the stake. One of them was lame and the other blind. When they were tied to the stake, the lame man took his crutch and threw it down and said to the other, "Cheer up, brother, this is the situation that will heal us. Within an hour, I won't be lame, and you won't be blind." The best things came last.

I've often thought that the child of God is very much like the crusaders. When the crusaders started off on their journey, they had to fight their way through many miles of enemies and march through danger at every turn. When the armies of the Duke of Bouillon came in sight of Jerusalem, they sprang from their horses, clapped their hands, and cried, "Jerusalem, Jerusalem, Jerusalem." They forgot about all their work, all the weariness of the journey, and all their wounds, because Jerusalem was in their sight. And how the saint will cry at last, "Jerusalem, Jerusalem," when all sorrow and poverty and sickness are past, and he is blessed with immortality. The bitter wine is taken away, and the best wine is brought out; the saint sees himself glorified forever with Christ Jesus.

The Savior's Table of Inward Experience

Now we'll sit down at the table of inward experience. The first cup that Christ brings to his children at that table is one so bitter that perhaps no words can describe it. It's the cup of conviction. It's a black cup, full of the most intense bitterness. The apostle Paul once drank a little from this cup. It was so strong that it made him blind for three days. The conviction of his sin overpowered him totally. All he had left was fasting and prayer. It was only when he drank from the next cup that the scales fell from his eyes.

> After you drank the cup of sorrow, Jesus came and showed you his hands and his side and said, "Sinner, I died for you and gave myself for you. Believe in me."

I have drunk from the cup of conviction, and I thought Jesus was unkind, but after a while he brought me the cup of his forgiving love filled

184

with the rich crimson of his precious blood. Oh, the taste of that wine remains in my mouth even until now. Do you remember? After you drank the cup of sorrow, Jesus came and showed you his hands and his side and said, "Sinner, I died for you and gave myself for you. Believe in me." Do you remember how you believed and sipped the cup? Do you remember how you continued in your belief and took a deeper drink and said, "Blessed be the name of God from this time forward and forever! Let the whole earth say, 'Amen,' *For he has broken the gates of brass and cut the bars of iron asunder,* and let the captives go free" (Psalm 107:16).

Since then the glorious Master has said to you, "Friend, come up higher!" And he has taken you to the best seats in the best rooms and given you sweeter things. I will allow the spouse in Solomon's Song to elaborate on our topic. She drank of the spiced wine of his pomegranate, and so have you in those high and happy moments when you had fellowship with the Father and with his Son, Jesus Christ. But linger here a while, because the best wine is yet to come.

You will soon come near the banks of the Jordan and drink of the old wine of the kingdom that has been barreled up since the foundation of the world. The vintage of the Savior's agony, the vintage of Gethsemane, the old wine of the kingdom, will soon be opened for you. You've come into the land and can taste the full flavor of the refined wines.

John Bunyan described the state which borders the valley of death. It was a land flowing with milk and honey, where the angels came to visit the saints and bring bundles of myrrh from the land of spices. Then the big step is taken, and the Lord puts his fingers upon your eyelids, and your soul joins him with his kiss. Where are you now? In a sea of love, life, bliss, and immortality, "O Jesus, Jesus, Jesus, *thou hast kept the good wine until now!* My Master! I've seen you on the Sabbath, but this is an everlasting Sabbath. I've met you in the congregation, but this is a congregation that will never break up. Oh, my Master, I've seen the promises, but this is the fulfilment. I have praised you for your many blessings, but this is something more than all the others. You gave me grace, but now you have given me glory. You once served as my shield, but now you are my sun. I am at your right hand, where there is fullness of joy forever. You have kept your best wine until now. Everything I had before was nothing compared with this."

The Savior's Table of Fellowship

Finally, God's children must sit at the table of fellowship. The first thing they must drink is the cup of fellowship with Christ in his sufferings. If you are going to join Christ at the table of fellowship, you must first drink of the wine of Calvary. Christian, your head must be crowned with thorns, and your hands must be pierced. I don't mean with nails, but spiritually you must be crucified with Christ. We must suffer with him, or we cannot reign with him. We must drink the wine which his Father gave him to drink, or we can't expect to come to the better part of the feast.

After drinking the wine of his sufferings and continuing to drink it, we must drink from the cup of his labors. We must be baptized with his baptism; we must labor after souls and function as one with him in the ambition of his heart – the salvation of sinners.

After that, he will give us the cup of his future blessings. Here we will drink the good wine of fellowship with Christ in his resurrection, in his triumphs, and in his victories, but the best wine comes last. Ornate mansions of fellowship, your gates have been opened to me, but I've only been able to glance inside them. The day is coming when those gates will turn on their diamond hinges and stand wide open for ever and ever, and I will enter into the king's palace and never leave.

Christian, you will soon see the King in his beauty. Your head will soon rest in his loving arms, and you will sit at his feet with Mary. You will do as the spouse in Solomon's Song did; you will kiss him with the kisses of your lips and know that his love is better than wine. I can picture you saying in the first moment of your life, "He has kept the best wine until now." When you see him face to face and enter into the closest fellowship with nothing to disturb or to distract you, you will say, "The best wine was kept until now."

One time a saint was dying, and another who sat with him said, "Farewell, brother, I will never see you again in the land of the living."

The dying man said, "Oh, I'll see you again in the land of the living that's up yonder, where I'm going. This is the land of the dying."

O brothers and sisters, if we never meet again in the land of the dying, let us rest in the hope that we will meet in the land of the living and drink the best wine at last.

Chapter 12

The Feast of the Lord

When the butler had tasted the water that was made wine and knew not where it was from (but the servants who drew the water knew), the butler called the bridegroom and said unto him, Every man at the beginning sets forth the good wine, and when they are well satisfied, then that which is worse; but thou hast kept the good wine until now. (John 2:9-10)

Satan's feast diminished in value as it proceeded and went from the bright crackling of the thorn under the pot to the blackness of darkness forever. *The laughter of the fool is as the crackling of thorns under a pot, and this also (the laughter or prosperity of the fool) is vanity* (Ecclesiastes 7:6). Then I showed how the rule of Christ's banquet is the very reverse. Christ always gives the best wine last. He saves the good things until the end of the feast. Sometimes the first cups at the table of Christ are even full of wormwood and gall and are exceeding bitter. But if we linger at the feast, the cups will grow sweeter and sweeter and sweeter, until at last, we enter into the city of our God and are compelled to say, *Thou hast kept the good wine until now.*

This is a great fact – Christ's feast increases in sweetness. When the Lord Jesus Christ first proclaimed a feast for the sons of men, the first cup he set on the table was a very small one. The cup contained just a few words of comfort. Remember the inscription on that ancient vessel, the first cup of comfort that was ever extended to the sons of men, "The seed of the woman will bruise the serpent's head."

> *And the LORD God said unto the serpent, Because thou hast done this, thou art cursed above all beasts and above every animal of the field; upon thy belly shalt thou go, and dust shalt thou eat all the days of thy life; and I will put enmity between thee and the woman and between thy seed and her seed; that seed shall bruise thy head, and thou shalt bruise his heel.* (Genesis 3:14-15)

These words provided just a little sweetness to them. But there is much to us, because we can understand it better. God's Spirit helped some of them understand it, but even in its revelation of it, there seemed to be just a little promise. As the world went on, greater cups of precious wine were brought out. The patriarchs and ancient saints drank of these, but all the wine they ever had under the Old Testament dispensation was just a small taste of that which we drink.

He who is least in the kingdom of heaven is more highly favored than he who is first under the Old Testament dispensation. Our fathers ate manna, but we eat the bread that came down from heaven. They drank water in the wilderness, but we drink living water, which if a man drinks, he will never thirst. It's true they had much sweetness. The cups of the ancient tabernacle had precious wine in them. The outward symbol contained signs and shadows of things to come, but we must remember that today we drink of the wine which prophets and kings desired to drink but died without a taste of it. They imagined its sweetness. By faith, they could foresee what it would be. But we are allowed to sit at the table and drink freely of the refined wines which God has given to us in this mountain where he has made a feast of rich things for all people.

But, beloved, the text still stands true; there is better wine to come. In our privileges, we are superior to the patriarchs, kings, and prophets. God has given us a brighter and clearer day than they had. Theirs was like the morning twilight, compared with the midday sun which we enjoy. But don't think that we've come to the best wine yet. There are more extraordinary banquets for God's church to come; who knows how long before the best of the precious wine is opened?

Don't you know that the King of heaven is coming again upon this earth? Jesus Christ, who came and poured out his heart for us on Calvary, is coming again to flood the earth with glory. He came once with a sin offering in his hand. When he returns, he will bring the cup of salvation and of thanksgiving. He will call upon the name of the Lord and joyously take for himself the throne of his father David. You and I, if we are alive and remain, will bring that cup to our lips, and if we die we can take comfort in the fact that we will not be left behind, *for the trumpet shall sound, and the dead shall be raised without corruption, and we shall be changed* (1 Corinthians 15:52). We will drink of the millennial wine which Christ our Savior has reserved for the end. Christians, you can't even comprehend what the golden goblets will be like which you will drink from during the thousand years of the Redeemer's triumph.

> ## Don't you know that the King of heaven is coming again upon this earth?

You can't begin to describe the wine, sparkling and red, which will come from the vintage of the hills of glory when he, whose garments are red with treading the wine press, descends on that great day and stands upon the earth. The very thought of this cheered Job. *For I know that my redeemer lives and that he shall rise at the latter day over the dust; and afterward from this, my stricken skin and from my own flesh, I must see God: whom I shall see for myself, and my eyes shall behold, and not another, though my kidneys be consumed within me* (Job 19:25-27). Let this cause you to rejoice, Christian: the good wine is kept for that time.

Christ Keeps His Good Wine for Last

How true this is of some of God's people. Some of God's most faithful servants have their names on the breastplate of the great High Priest; they are purchased with his blood and very dear to his soul but haven't known for their whole lives what it's like to get out of the depths of poverty. They have lived from hand to mouth without knowing from day to day where their next meal would come from. Many of God's people lie on beds of affliction, and some of God's most precious diamonds lie on the dunghill of disease. You can go to any hospital and see the victims of all kinds of diseases, and you will find God's dear ones on their death beds.

Some of God's other servants spend their days in toil. The human body and soul need a little rest and a little of the food of knowledge, but these servants have had so little instruction that they can't get mental food ready for themselves. If they read, they can barely understand. They are so bound to constant work that it makes their lives bitter and hinders them from knowledge. They work from morning to night with barely a moment's rest. When death finally releases them, and they leave this world, they will say, *thou hast kept the good wine until now.*

What a change for her who limped along those many Sabbath days to the sanctuary. She will no longer go up to the Lord's house limping and lame, but *then the lame one shall leap as a hart* (Isaiah 35:6). And like Miriam, she will dance with the daughters of Israel (Exodus 15:20-21). You may have had to suffer sickness and sorrow and pain, blindness and deafness, and a thousand of this world's ills, but what a change when you find them all gone. No racking pains, no unmet need, no anxiety. You won't have to beg for sunlight to fill your hopes or weep because your health is failing through your constant work. You will see the light of God brighter than the light of the sun and rejoice in the beams that proceed from his presence. You will have no more sickness. Immortality will cover and swallow them up; that which was sown in weakness will be raised in power, and that which was sown full of pain, sorrow, and agony will be raised full of exquisite delights, no longer capable of anguish but quivering with unspeakable joy and bliss.

You will no longer be poor but richer than the miser's dream; you will no longer have to labor, but you will rest peacefully on your beds as each one of you walks in uprightness. You will no longer suffer from neglect, contempt, and persecution, but you will be glorified with Christ in the day when he comes to be admired by those who love him. For these, the best wine has indeed been kept until the last. They've never had any good wine in the eyes of men, but secretly they drank many times from the bottle of Jesus. He often put his gracious cup to their lips, and they've been like the ewe lamb that belonged to the man in Nathan's parable (2 Samuel 12:1-7). They drank from Christ's own cup on the earth, but the satisfying drink they will receive in the end will be even sweeter.

I put these first, as especially feeling the change, because we can see such a dramatic difference, but it will also be true of the most favored of God's children. All of them will say, *Thou hast kept the good wine until now.* Of all the men whom I might envy, I think the first would be the apostle Paul. What a man! How favored, gifted, and blessed! Paul could talk of revelations and visions from on high. He heard things which were unlawful for a man to utter and saw what few eyes have ever seen. He was caught up into the third heaven (2 Corinthians 12:2).

What thirst-quenching drinks of joy the apostle Paul must have had! He looked into the deep things of God and soared into the heights of heaven. There may have never been a man more favored by God. Paul had his mind expanded and filled with the wisdom and revelation of the knowledge of the Most High, but if you asked the apostle Paul if he believed there's anything better to come, he would have said, *For now we see as through a mirror, in darkness, but then we shall see face to face; now I know in part, but then I shall know even as I also am known* (1 Corinthians 13:12). He was clearly expecting something more than he had received, and he was not disappointed. There was a heaven far above all the spiritual blessings Paul received in this life and especially when compared to the depressions of his spirit when he said, *O wretched man that I am! who shall deliver me from the body of this death?* (Romans 7:24).

There are children of God who have all that they need of this world's goods, and they seem to be free from earthly care with enough faith to trust God with their future. Their faith is firm and strong, and they love their Redeemer. They are engaged in work they enjoy, which the Holy Spirit rewards with great success. Their days follow steadily one after another like the waves of the still calm sea. God is with them, and they are greatly blessed. *And he shall be like a tree planted by the rivers of water, that brings forth its fruit in its season; his leaf also shall not wither; and whatever he does shall prosper* (Psalm 1:3). Whatever they do, the Lord their God is with them, and in whatever land they put their feet, they are like Joshua. That land is given to them as an inheritance forever.

But even these people will see greater things than they can imagine. As fulfilling and satisfying as the room is where they now feast, the Master will say to them, "Come up higher." They will know more, enjoy more, feel more, do more, and possess more. They will be closer to Christ. They will have richer enjoyments and more fulfilling work than they've had, and they will know that their Master *hast kept the good wine until now.*

In every one of the many aspects of Christian life, we will say that Christ has kept the good wine until then. Here on earth, the believer enters into rest by faith, as the Christian enjoys rest even in the wilderness. The promise is fulfilled. *They shall dwell safely in the wilderness and sleep in the woods* (Ezekiel 34:25). God gives sleep to his beloved. There's a peace that passes all understanding, which we can enjoy even in this land of turmoil, strife, and alarms. *And the peace of God, which passes all understanding, shall keep your hearts and minds through Christ Jesus* (Philippians 4:7). The world cannot understand this peace.

> A holy calm within the heart,
>> The pledge of glorious rest.
> Which for the church of God remains,
>> The end of cares, the end of pains.

(Joseph Stennett)

But as much as we may drink from the cup of peace, the good wine is kept until a future time. The peace we drink today is sprinkled with some drops of bitter. The cares of this world will come, and doubts will arise. No matter how we live in this world, we can't escape anxiety and distress. Thorns in the flesh must come, but *there remains therefore a rest for the people of God* (Hebrews 4:9). What good wine that will be. God has a sun without a spot, a sky without a cloud, a day without a night, a sea without a wave, and a world without a tear. Happy are they who have passed through this world, bathing their weary souls in seas of heavenly rest, and have ceased from their own works, as God did from his.

Another aspect of heaven is that it's a place of holy company. In this world, we've had some good wine of sweet company. We can list the many precious sons of Zion with whom we've taken sweet counsel. The righteous haven't all faded from among men, for some of you can remember people who were very dear to you in the days of your youth – men and women to whom you would go to for wise counsel. Their words were sweet balm to you in the days of your sorrow when they comforted and consoled you. You have friends whom you look up to with some degree of respect, and they regard you with intense affection.

> All the fellowship with the saints that we've had here is nothing compared to what we will enjoy in the world to come.

Some men are comforters to your soul. When you talk to them, you feel that their heart answers your heart, and you can enjoy sweet fellowship with them. But, beloved, the good wine is kept for last. All the fellowship with the saints that we've had here is nothing compared to what we will enjoy in the world to come. How sweet it is for us to remember that in heaven we will enjoy the company of the best men, the noblest men, the most mighty men, the most honorable, and the most renowned.

We will sit with Moses and talk with him about his life of wonders. We will walk with Joseph and hear from him about the grace that protected him in his hour of danger. We may have the privilege of sitting next to David and hearing him tell about the perils and the deliverances through which he passed. The saints of heaven make up one body of believers, and they aren't divided into separate classes. We'll be allowed to walk through all the glorious ranks and partake of fellowship with all of them, and we have no reason to doubt that we will be able to know them all. In heaven, we will know even as we are known; we will know each other perfectly, and that makes us long to be there. We long to be away from this poor church here that is full of strife, divisions, bickering, jealousy, and animosity. We will get away from the society of men who are full of diseases, although they have much grace, and enter into a place where there will be no disease and no quick tempers. Our words will not cause offense, hurt feelings, or strife, and we will walk in the midst of them all and see love beaming from every eye and feel the deep affection flowing from every heart. That will be the best wine. Aren't you longing to drink of it?

> Then all the chosen seed
> Shall meet around the throne,
> Shall bless the conduct of His grace,
> And make His wonders known.

> (Isaac Watts)

Now, let's look at the point of knowledge. We know very well the things on earth that make us happy. Jesus Christ taught us many things that give us joy and gladness, but this world is full of ignorance. Through grace we've entered into the school of the gospel, and we've learned some sweet truths, much like the boy who is beginning to write. We had to make many ugly lines and marks, and we still haven't learned to write with the sweet flowing hand of joy, but the Lord has taught us some great truths to fill our heart with joy. The great doctrine of election, the knowledge of our redemption, and the fact of our security in Christ are great but simple doctrines that filled our hearts with bliss. But, brethren, the best wine is kept for last. When the Lord Jesus Christ takes the book, breaks its seal, and permits us to read, we will rejoice indeed, because the best wine will be at our lips. These old barrels of knowledge contain the richest wine, and Christ will open them; we will drink as much as we desire. We cannot know all things now, because we couldn't bear many things. Therefore, Christ holds them back.

> There shall you see and hear and know
> All you desired or wished below,
> And every power find sweet employ
> In that eternal world of joy.

> (Isaac Watts)

If you want, you can look at heaven as a place of manifestations and joys, but now this world can also be a place of manifestation to the believer with times when the Lord Jesus says to his beloved, *Come, my beloved, let us go forth into the field; let us lodge in the villages. Let us get up early to the vineyards; let us see if the vines flourish, whether the tender flowers appear, if the pomegranates bud forth; there I will give thee my loves* (Song of Solomon 7:11-12). But human words fail to describe the fellowship of heaven.

When I begin to talk about the fellowship of heaven, I get overwhelmed and can't even begin to imagine it. My next thought is one of overwhelming gratitude, coupled with a kind of fear that this is too good for such an unworthy worm as I. John had the privilege to put his head on the Master's bosom, but that's nothing compared with the privilege of lying in his embrace forever, but we must wait until we get there. As someone said, "In five minutes you'll know more about heaven than I could tell you in all my life."

All we need is to see our Lord, fly into his arms, and feel his embrace. We will fall at his feet, and rather than weep for joy, we will dissolve in ecstasy. We will have arrived in that dear place, which he spoke of when he said, *Let not your heart be troubled; ye believe in God, believe also in me. In my Father's house are many dwelling places; if it were not so, I would have told you. I go to prepare a place for you* (John 14:1-3). Truly, he has kept the best wine for last.

Our Lord's Reason

The Lord could have given us the best wine first, but he doesn't act in the same way as the devil. He will always make a clear distinction between his dealings and the dealings of Satan.

God won't give us the best wine first, because that's not his good pleasure. *Fear not, little flock, for it is your Father's good pleasure to give you the kingdom* (Luke 12:32). That's the only reason why you'll get it at all, so the reason you don't receive it now is that it's not your Father's good pleasure for you to have it just yet.

Your Father doesn't give you the good wine now, because he's helping you develop an appetite for it. At the old feasts of the Romans, men used to drink bitter things and noxious mixtures to make them thirsty. In this world, God makes his children thirsty, so they'll take deeper drinks of heaven. I don't believe that heaven would be so sweet to me if I hadn't first lived on earth. Who knows best the pleasure of rest? Isn't it the laborer? Who understands best the joy of peace? Isn't it the man who has lived in a war-torn land? Who knows the sweetness of joy the most? Isn't it the man who has passed through a world of sorrow? Your appetites are sharpened by these trials. God is preparing you to receive the fullness of joy that is in his presence forever.

The Lord is fitting you for the best wine, so he can be glorified by the trial of your faith. If it was within my power to go to heaven tonight, I would prefer to wait on my Father's time for I suspect there is more for me to suffer here. I believe we will bless God in heaven for all we've suffered here. When it's over, how sweet it will be to talk about it. When you and I meet each other in the streets of heaven, we will talk about how God delivered us, but we won't be able to talk in the same way as some of the tried saints, because some of us have only had a few trials, tribulations, and conflicts.

What sweet stories some will tell. I would like to sit next to Jonah and hear about how he went down to the bottom of the mountains. *I descended to the roots of the mountains; the earth put her bars about me for ever; yet thou hast brought up my life out of the grave, O LORD my God* (Jonah 2:6). I often think about what a great deal we'll get out of Jeremiah in eternity. He took such plunges into the sea of sorrow. And David, the sweet Psalmist, so full of experience, will never come to the end of talking about what the Lord has done for him.

And I think when you and I get to heaven, we will have plenty to talk about. When a poor woman was in great doubt and fear about whether she could be saved at all, she prayed, "Lord, if you will save me, I can only promise you one thing. If you will take me to heaven, you will never hear the end of it. I will praise you for eternity, and I will tell the angels that you saved me."

If we didn't have to pass through these trials and troubles and these soul conflicts, we would have little to talk about in heaven. I have no doubt that the babes in paradise are as happy as the rest, but I don't wish to be a babe in paradise. I praise God I didn't go to heaven when I was an infant, because I'll have more to praise God for when I look back on a life filled with mercies, trials, and sustaining grace. I think these are some of God's reasons.

The Lesson We Are to Learn

What is the lesson that we are supposed to learn from Christ keeping the best wine until last? Going home the other night, I noticed the difference between my horse's pace in coming here and going home. I thought to myself, *Ah! The horse goes well, because he's going home.* Then the thought struck me: *How well a Christian should go, because he's going home.* If we were going from home, every rough stone in the road might hinder us and we might need a good deal of whip to make us go.

But with every step going home, we may be knee-deep in trouble, but it's all on the road. We may be ankle-deep in fear, but it's going home. I may stumble, but I always stumble homewards. When all my afflictions and griefs throw me to the ground, they propel me toward heaven. The mariner doesn't mind the waves if every wave sends him closer to safety. He doesn't care how loud the wind howls if it blows him nearer to port. That's the Christian's happy destiny; he's going homeward. Let that cheer you and make you travel on joyfully, not needing the whip to urge you to do what you know you are supposed to do but continue forward with enthusiasm, because you are going toward home.

If we know the best things are yet to come, we don't need to be discontent. We can put up with a few of the bad things now, because they only seem to be bad. A traveller who is on a journey in a hurry and has to stop for the night at an inn may grumble a little at the lack of accommodations. But he doesn't say very much, because he is off tomorrow. He's only stopping a short time at the inn, and he says, "I'll get home tomorrow night." Then he thinks of the joys of home and doesn't care about the discomforts of his hard journey.

> You and I are travellers, and our journey will soon be over.

You and I are travellers, and our journey will soon be over. We may have been paid very little per week compared with our neighbor, but we'll be equal with him when we get to heaven. He may have had a large house with many rooms, while we only had one upper room. We may have a mansion as larger than his in paradise. We'll soon be at the end of this journey, and the state of the road won't matter, as long as we got there. We can put up with these few inconveniences along the way, because the best wine is coming. Let's pour out all the vinegar of murmuring; the best wine is yet to come.

> **If the Christian knows the best wine is yet to come, why should he envy the men of this world?**

If the Christian knows the best wine is yet to come, why should he envy the men of this world? David did. He was discontent when he saw the prosperity of the wicked, and you and I are often tempted to do the same thing. But do you know what we should say when we see the wicked prosper, or when we see them happy and full of the delights of their sinful pleasure? We should say, "My good wine is coming. I can accept that you'll have your turn, and my turn will come afterward. I can live without these things and lie with Lazarus at the gate while the dogs lick my sores. My turn is still to come when the angels carry me into Abraham's bosom, and your turn is coming too, when you lift up your eyes from hell in torment.

> There was a certain rich man who was clothed in purple and
> fine linen and fared sumptuously every day; and there was
> a certain beggar named Lazarus, who was laid at his gate,
> full of sores and desiring to be fed with the crumbs which
> fell from the rich man's table: moreover the dogs came and
> licked his sores. And it came to pass that the beggar died and
> was carried by the angels into Abraham's bosom; the rich
> man also died and was buried; and in Hades he lifted up
> his eyes, being in torments, and saw Abraham afar off and
> Lazarus in his bosom. (Luke 16:19-23)

We could learn a thousand lessons from this – that the best wine is kept for last. Take care that you also keep your good wine for last. The further you travel down the road make every effort to bring to your Savior a more acceptable sacrifice. Your faith was small years ago; bring out the good wine now. Make every effort to increase your faith, for your

Master is better to you every day, and you will see that he is the best of all Masters and friends. Do your best to be better to your Master every day, and be more invested in his cause, more active to work for him, more kind to his people, and more diligent in prayer. Make sure that as you grow in years, you also grow in grace, which is your sanctification. Do this, so when the Master finally gives you the best wine, you may also give him the best wine and praise him loudly when the battle is over and the whirlwind dies away into the everlasting peace of paradise.

Now I'm aware that I've totally failed in my attempt to bring forth this good wine. *But as it is written, That which eye has not seen nor ear heard neither has entered into the heart of man is that which God has prepared for those that love him. But God has revealed this unto us by his Spirit, for the Spirit searches all things, even the deep things of God* (1 Corinthians 2:9-10).

If I told you that your ear would have heard it, the text wouldn't have been true. Since I've unintentionally proven the truth of this Scripture, I can't be very sorry, because I testified to the truth of my Master's word. I'll just say this: the nearer you live to Christ, the nearer you will be to heaven. I've never seen heaven anywhere but close to Calvary.

When I've seen my Savior crucified, I've seen him glorified. When I've read my name written in his blood, I've seen my mansion which he has prepared for me. When I've seen my sins washed away, I've seen the white robe I'll wear forever. Live near to the Savior, and you won't be very far away from heaven. Remember that it's not far to heaven – it's only one gentle sigh, and we're there. We talk about it as a land very far away, but it's close. We know that the spiritual realm is all around us, and heaven is close to us. We can't tell where it is, but we know that it's not a far-off land. It's so near that, quicker than we thought, we'll be there, set free from our cares and sorrows, and blessed forever.

Chapter 13

The Beginning of Miracles

This beginning of the signs Jesus did in Cana of Galilee and manifested forth his glory, and his disciples believed on him. (John 2:11)

At this time, I won't consider the relation of this miracle to total abstinence from alcohol. The wine that Jesus made was good wine, and it was made from water. We aren't likely to find anything like it in this country, where the wine is seldom made from the pure juice of grapes, and it's not known who made it, or what it's made of. What we call wine is a very different liquid from what our Lord produced. We use our Christian liberty to abstain from wine, and we believe that our Savior would approve of our avoiding that which makes our brother stumble. Those of us who abstain view our Master's action in this instance in a certain way, and we don't find it difficult to see wisdom and holiness in it. Even if we couldn't interpret what he did in this way, we wouldn't dare to question him. Where others criticize, we adore. Even this is more than I intended to say on this subject, because the purpose of my lesson is far removed from this controversy. I pursue a spiritual theme and pray for help from on high to handle it in a way that's pleasing to God.

We find the account of this miracle only in John. Neither Matthew, Mark, nor Luke writes a word about it. How was John aware of it?

Partly because he was present, but we believe the scenario with Mary, the mother of Jesus, came to him in another way. Remember our Lord's words to John from the cross: *Then he said to the disciple, Behold thy mother! And from that hour that disciple took her unto his own home* (John 19:27).

On that day in Cana, I believe no one heard what Jesus said to his mother but Mary herself. In his delicate manner he corrected her in private. But after Jesus' death and resurrection when John and Mary talked, she probably reminded him of the miracle and told him about her mistake. Christians gain precious treasures from the experiences of God's poor and tried servants. Those who entertain the widow and the fatherless will not go without reward. *The pure and undefiled religion before God and the Father is this, To visit the fatherless and widows in their tribulation and to keep thyself unspotted from this world* (James 1:27).

If my theory is correct, we witness the holy modesty of Mary, because she exposed her own fault and didn't forbid John to mention it. The Holy Spirit moved the evangelist to chronicle not only the miracle but the error of Mary, which was wise, because this is a conclusive argument against the false belief that the mother of Jesus can intercede for us with her Son and use her authority with him. It's clear from this account that our Lord tolerated no such idea, either in her mind or in ours.

Jesus said unto her, Woman, what have I to do with thee? My hour is not yet come (John 2:4). This verse removes any idea of our Lord's obligation to relationships according to the flesh. With all loving respect, he decidedly shut out all interference from Mary. His kingdom was to be according to the spirit and not after the flesh. It brings me great delight to believe that even though Mary fell into a natural mistake, she didn't for an instant remain in it, and she didn't hide it from John. She probably made a point to tell him so others would not fall into similar error by thinking of her in an unfitting manner.

Let's never forget that the mother of Jesus had a firm and practical faith in her Son, concerning whom angels and prophets had borne witness to her. She had seen him in his infancy and watched him as a child. It couldn't have been easy to believe in the divinity of one whom you held as an infant and fed at your breast. From the time of his marvelous birth, she believed in him, so when she received a gentle rebuke from him, her faith did not fail her. She calmly turned to the servants and told them to be ready to obey his commands, whatever they might be. She believed that he would do the kind and necessary thing.

Even from his statement, *My hour is not yet come*, she probably gathered that his hour to work was coming. Her faith was accompanied with imperfection, but it was of the right kind. It persevered under difficulty, and in the end, it was triumphant, because the wine he provided was of surpassing quality.

May we all have faith that will survive a rebuke. May we sing like Mary: *My spirit hath rejoiced in God my Saviour* (Luke 1:47 KJV). May Jesus be to us, as he was to her, a trusted and adored one. Our souls must learn to wait on him with confidence, and I will approach this subject from that perspective. My great desire is that his disciples will trust him more and more. John also said regarding the actions of our Lord, *These are written that ye might believe that Jesus is the Christ, the Son of God, and that believing ye might have life in his name* (John 20:31). My intention here is that my readers may believe in the Lord Jesus and be saved.

The Significance of this First Sign

The first sign wonder Christ performed was the turning of water into wine at the wedding at Cana of Galilee. Just like we can often determine a man's course by its beginning, and the beginning is often the key to all that follows, we can learn the whole intent of our Lord's miracles from this one.

This miracle displayed his self-denial. Just a few days earlier, our Lord had been in the wilderness, and after forty days' fasting he was hungry. He had the power to command the stones to become bread, but had he done so, the beginning of signs would have been a miracle performed out of his own necessity. Such a beginning wouldn't have kept with his life's course; it would have been far removed from the conclusion of his life when it was said of him, *He saved others; he cannot save himself* (Matthew 27:42).

He wouldn't make bread for himself, but he would make wine for others. The fact that he made wine and not bread makes the miracle even more remarkable. He didn't make bread, which is a necessity; he made wine for them, which is a luxury. We witness the sharp contrast between his refusal to help himself, even with a crust of bread, and his readiness to give to men not only what they might need for life but that which was only for their joy. When the wine ran out, the only danger was that the bride and bridegroom would be upset, and the wedding celebration ruined.

How greatly we should admire and love our divine Lord who has no selfishness within him.

Our Lord prevents this. He wouldn't allow the humble celebration of two villagers to come to an untimely end, especially since they had invited him and his disciples. He repaid their courtesy by his spontaneous gift. How greatly we should admire and love our divine Lord who has no selfishness within him. Each of us can cry, "He loved me and gave himself for me." He laid down his life for men and gave his all to others with no selfish purpose ever. He didn't reserve any measure or degree of power for himself; for others, he used that power without holding back. This beginning of miracles is a display of unselfish working, as consideration for others shone in that miracle like the sun in the heavens.

Next, this miracle was marked with benevolence. As the beginning of miracles, it set the theme for the rest, and we can rejoice that it is full of blessing. Moses began his work in Egypt with a miracle of judgment, when he threw down a rod, and it became a serpent and turned water into blood. But Jesus overcame the serpent with the rod of Scripture and turned water into wine. He didn't work plagues but healed our sicknesses.

> Thine hand no thunder bears,
> No terror clothes thy brow,
> No bolts to drive our guilty souls,
> To fiercer flames below.
>
> (Isaac Watts)

The mission of Jesus is a happy one, so it appropriately begins at a marriage feast and is intended to bring joy and gladness to heavy hearts by an act of royal generosity. In London, the gutters in the financial district have run with wine at the coronation of kings, and at this wedding in Cana, the waterpots are filled to the brim with it. All the miracles after this were blessings.

True, he withered a fruitless fig tree, but even that was an act of kindness because the tree drew men out of their way with false promises of fruit and disappointed hungry and fainting travellers. The lesson was a good thing to teach us a practical lesson regarding sincerity at the small expense of a withering, goodfor-nothing tree.

All our Lord's actions toward men are full of royal benevolence and grace. One day the Lamb will be angry and return as Judge; he will condemn the ungodly. But while this dispensation lasts, he is all mercy, love, kindness, and generosity. If you will come to him, you'll find that his heart will go out to you. He will freely bless you with life, rest, peace, and joy; he will bless you and remove the curse far from you.

This beginning of miracles was performed at a wedding to show great benevolence. Marriage was the last relic of paradise left among men, and Jesus was quick to honor it with his first miracle. Marriage is his Father's ordinance, because it was he who brought Eve to Adam, and our Lord worked in harmony with the Father. He symbolically touched the very springs of manhood and gave his approval to the ordinance by which the race is preserved. Jesus attended a wedding and gave his blessing, so we can know our family life is under his care. We've sometimes thought that it was almost proof of the divinity of Christianity – that there could be homes as happy as some of our homes by the presence of our dear Lord, whom we invited to our wedding feast, and who has never left us in all these happy years. It was a miracle that confirmed an institution filled with happiness to our race.

Next, it was a miracle of compassion. In each case, our Lord performed miracles to meet a need. The wine had run out at the wedding feast, and our Lord came on the scene exactly when the bridegroom was afraid he was going to be embarrassed. That need itself was a great blessing. If there had been sufficient wine for the feast, Jesus wouldn't have performed this miracle, and they would have never tasted the purest and best wine. The need made room for Jesus to come in and perform miracles of love. It's good to run short, so we are driven to the Lord by our necessity, and he can abundantly supply it. If you have no need, Christ won't come to you, but if you're in dire necessity, he will stretch out his hand to you. If your needs stand in front of you like huge, empty waterpots, or if your soul is as full of grief as those same pots were full with water to the brim, by his will Jesus can turn all the water into wine and your sorrow into singing.

Be glad to be weak, so the power of God may rest upon you. As for me, I'm more and more dependent on the Lord for every particle of strength. My deacons and elders know how many Sunday mornings, before coming into the pulpit, I've thanked God that it is so. I'm glad to be entirely dependent upon the Lord, and I'm thankful to experience such failure in my natural wine of ability, so my Lord has ample opportunity to come in and supply wine of strength and of a divine quality.

> We are likely to do our best work when we most feel our insufficiency and are driven to God for help.

We are likely to do our best work when we most feel our insufficiency and are driven to God for help. If we go blundering into our service, we will fail, but if we go trembling in humility by confidently looking to the Lord, we'll be more than conquerors. If we have a great need, if something essential has run out, or if we are despised for a failure, in faith let us expect the Lord Jesus to come to our deliverance. From this miracle I see that our Lord cares about a man's necessities and not his possessions. He sees our failures and needs and makes our distress the platform on which he demonstrates his glory by supplying all our needs.

Further, I cannot help noticing how unpretentious this miracle was. We're told that it was performed at Cana in Galilee. This is mentioned twice, so we'll pay attention to it. Our Lord didn't choose the high places of Jerusalem or any of the notable cities of Palestine as the scene of his first miracle. He went to a quiet village in Galilee of the Gentiles, a despised district, and there he performed his first miracle.

This miraculous act didn't take place on a spiritual and sacred occasion or before religious elites and scientists. Some seem to think that everything our Lord does must be done in churches or cathedrals. This miracle took place in a private home and not at a prayer meeting or a Bible study. It took place at the wedding feast of a couple of poor peasants who remain unnamed. See how Jesus voluntarily descends from his divine position to the commonplaces of life and blesses the secular side of our existence.

Those who gave that feast were people of little means, or the wine wouldn't have been so quickly exhausted. It's true that seven extra guests came to the wedding, but if the family had been wealthy, they would have had more than enough to satisfy seven extra guests. It was common for families to keep an open house for all the guests during the marriage week.

They were by no means a family of aristocrats or Israel's notables. Why didn't our Lord begin his miracles before the king, the governor, or at least in the presence of the high priest, the scribes, and doctors of the law? Our Lord chose not to make his first demonstration of power before the great and dignified. I find comfort in this fact: that he comes to common-place individuals is pure joy to me. You and I may not amount to much according to the standards of this world, but Jesus lowers himself to men of humble means. The Lord came to common places to visit his people, which is where he had worked amazing transformations, and many ordinary lives were made rich and full through his grace.

Jesus can come to you, even though you're only a laborer, a servant, or a poor tradesman. Our Lord loves the poor, and he frequently visits cottages. He doesn't seek out important events but makes his home with the lowly. He is full of humility.

This first of miracles was luxurious. At the wedding, he didn't multiply the bread. He dealt with a luxury and blessed them with the pure blood of the grape. When our Lord fed the multitudes in the wilderness, he could have given them each a scrap of bread to keep them from starving, but he never scrimps. He added fish to accompany their bread. Our Lord not only gives existence but happy existence, which is truly life. He doesn't give men the minimum to survive but gives to the degree that we call enjoyment.

At the wedding he turned good, wholesome water into a sweeter, richer, more nourishing beverage. We can't comprehend how truly good and sustaining that God-made drink was to those who were privileged to taste it. Our dear Master will bless all those who are his followers with a joy unspeakable and full of glory. They won't only have enough grace to live by and barely hope and serve, but they'll drink of a feast of purified wines. They'll have grace to sing with and rejoice with, grace to fill them with assurance and cause them to overflow with delight.

Just as you are, you can believe in Jesus for eternal life.

Our Beloved hasn't only brought us to the house of bread but to the banquet of wine. We have heaven here below. Jesus doesn't measure out grace by the drop, as chemists measure medicines. He gives liberally, his vessels are filled to the brim, and the quality is as extraordinary as the quantity. He gives the best of the best joys, delights, and happiness. My soul sits at a royal table filled with benefits.

The miracle was gracious! How free! How unconstrained! He wasn't pressured into doing it, and Mary wasn't permitted to interfere. The Lord knew what the need was without being told.

To obtain the supply of wine, nothing was required from men except that which was very simple and easy. Be quick, obedient servants to fetch water, and just draw it from the well and pour it into those large waterpots. That's all you have to do. The Lord Jesus doesn't come to us with hard conditions and demanding terms.

Don't think for a moment that you have to do or feel some fantastic thing to be saved. Just as you are, you can believe in Jesus for eternal life, have enough faith to do what the Lord asks you today, and to your own amazement, water will become wine. By his Spirit, the Lord can come and change your heart. He will renew your spirit, so where only a little natural thought had been, spiritual life and feeling will increase and grow. He'll accomplish the transformation without pressuring and persuading, because grace is free, and Jesus has a tender heart toward needy sinners.

The first miracle was prophetic. Our Lord began his signs at a wedding, and everything will end at a glorious marriage supper. The story of our Bible ends like all well told tales: they were married and lived happily ever after. Read the book of the Revelation for proof. Our Lord will come to celebrate a wedding between himself and his bride. He will provide all the wine they will drink at that high festival and give all the joy and happiness. He is the sun of heaven's day, and he is the glory of the glorified. He will ensure that throughout the millennial age and eternity, the joy of his chosen will never fail. They will find joy in God without measure and without bound.

Our Lord began with this special miracle to show us that he came here to transform all things, to fulfill the law and its types, to give his words substance and reality, and to take man and lift him up from a fallen creature into a heaven-born son and heir. Jesus has come to remove the chains of this planet and dress it in garments of glory and beauty. Soon we'll see new heavens and a new earth; the New Jerusalem will come down from heaven, prepared as a bride adorned for her husband. Jesus has come to elevate and to fulfill, and he gives an indication of this in this beginning of signs.

The Special Manifestation of the First Sign

This first sign Jesus performed in Cana of Galilee and manifested forth his glory. I believe there's a clear connection between the first chapter of this gospel and the passage we're looking at. In the first chapter, John said, *And the Word was made flesh and dwelt among us (and we beheld his glory, the glory as of the only begotten of the Father), full of grace and truth* (John 1:14). At the wedding was an unveiling of that grace and glory.

Jesus manifested forth his glory. He glorified the Father, because that was his objective, but he also demonstrated his own glory in the process, which was never said of any prophet or saint. Moses, Samuel, David, Isaiah – none of these ever demonstrated their own glory. They had no glory of their own. Here is one greater than a prophet. Here is one greater than the holiest of men. He manifested his own glory; it couldn't be any other way.

I feel the need to adore my Lord Jesus while I read these words, for he revealed his own glory as God and man. During all the years prior to that wedding at Cana, his glory had remained veiled. He had lived as an obedient boy and an industrious young carpenter in Nazareth, when his glory was like a spring that was shut up or a fountain that had been sealed. But now his glory flowed from him in the stream of this great miracle.

If you think about it, you'll see more clearly what glory it was. He was a man like other men, and yet he turned water into wine. He was a man with a mother, who was there, as if to remind us that he was born of woman. He was so truly God that he created an abundance of wine. *For in him dwells all the fullness of the Godhead bodily, and ye are complete in him, who is the head of all principality and power* (Colossians 2:9-10). He was only one among many wedding guests, accompanied by his six humble followers, but he performed the Creator's role. He didn't wear the high priest's garments, the Pharisee's phylacteries, or any other form of ornament indicating religious authority, but he worked greater wonders than they could even attempt. He was simply a man among men, but he was God among men. His wish became law in the world of matter, so water received the qualities of wine. Adore him and bow low before him who was a man, a real man, and yet performed acts that only Jehovah himself could work. Worship him who doesn't count it robbery to be equal with God but is also found among the guests at a lowly marriage, revealing his glory even there.

> Let this mind be in you, which was also in Christ Jesus, who, being in the form of God, thought it not robbery to be equal with God, but emptied himself, taking the form of a slave, made in the likeness of men, and being found in fashion as a man, he humbled himself and became obedient unto death, even the death of the cross. (Philippians 2:5-8)

Notice he revealed his glory by operating beyond the power of nature. Nature doesn't turn water into wine in an instant; if this happens, it must be by the direct hand of the Lord. Dewdrops can enter the berry of the grape and gradually be turned into refreshing juice, but it would require miraculous power for water to be taken from an ordinary waterpot and be transformed into wine while being carried to the table. Only God himself could do this, and since Jesus did it, he displayed his Godhead and showed that he had all power on earth. He can do as he wills, and by this one act of creation, or transformation, he clearly reveals the glory of his power.

He did this without any instrument. When Moses sweetened the bitter water, he used a piece of wood, which the Lord showed him.

> *When they came to Marah, they could not drink of the waters of Marah, for they were bitter; therefore the name of it was called Marah. Then the people murmured against Moses, saying, "What shall we drink?" And he cried unto the LORD; and the LORD showed him a tree, which when he cast it into the waters, the waters were made sweet.* (Exodus 15:23-25)

When Elisha restored the springs, he threw salt into the water.

> *And the men of the city said unto Elisha, Behold, the seat of this city is good, as my lord sees, but the water is evil, and the ground barren. Then he said, Bring me a new cruse and put salt in it. And they brought it to him. And he went forth to the springs of the waters and cast salt in there and said, Thus hath the LORD said, I have healed these waters; there shall be no death or barrenness in them.* (2 Kings 2:19-21)

We see no instrumentality in Cana. Whenever our Lord used visible means, he selected an instrument completely and clearly insufficient for the purpose if not in complete opposition to his original creation. For instance, when he healed the blind man, he used clay mixed with saliva and put it on his eyes. This would ordinarily blind a man, rather than open his eyes. At the wedding, however, our Lord used no instrument at all. He didn't even speak a word and say, "Water, blush into wine." No, he simply willed it, and it was done. How clearly he demonstrated his divine glory!

Jesus operated easily and majestically. In his method, he reminds us of the way of our great God. He simply says, *Fill the waterpots*, and the servants follow his instructions with enthusiasm. Then he instructed them to draw from the pots and take it to the master of the feast. As they carried it, the water turned into wine. Visibly, there was no effort or preparation like someone gathering up his strength to perform a great feat. The earth revolves, but the wheel of nature never grinds upon its axle. God acts by his laws in a perfectly natural and unconstrained manner. Creation and divine authority dwell in majestic silence which comes from omnipotence. Everything works effortlessly with God. With his own will, he can do all things for us and in a moment turn the waters of our grief into joy.

Our Lord displayed his glory by operating naturally and without drawing attention. I believe that if you or I could have worked this wonder, we would have said to the ruler of the feast, "Call all the guests together to bring to their attention that the wine has run out, but I'm about to create a new supply. See this huge waterpot. Come and see that I've had it filled with water, so you know that there's no wine in it. Watch closely while I work the transformation." Then you would have spoken aloud, so everyone would know what you were doing. Jesus did nothing of the kind. He hates display, and he won't have his kingdom come with observation. He shuns pomp, noise, and ceremony. It was God-like on our Lord's part to perform so great a work without appearing to do anything uncommon.

That he performed the miracle was certified by impartial witnesses. John, Philip, or all six might have said, "Master, we'll fill the waterpots with water." But he couldn't do that; he didn't even want a hint of collusion between the Master and his disciples. The ordinary servants had to fill the waterpots with water. Then the disciples would have been happy to carry the wine to the master of the feast saying, "Here's the wine, which our great and good Master made for you." No, the servants had to bring in the wine and say nothing at all about where it came from. The chief witness would be the master of the feast, and he would testify that what they brought was really the best quality wine. He was a gentleman who wasn't at all spiritually minded, but he had been to many such feasts and knew the customs and had a proverb ready to testify. He was evidently a man who could judge the quality of wine, so we can safely accept his verdict: *Thou hast kept the best wine until now.*

The less spiritual the man in this case, the better the witness to the reality of the miracle. If he had been a follower of Jesus, he might have been suspected of plotting with him and his disciples, but it's clear that he was a man from another mold altogether. God's work is fact, not fiction and appeals to faith, not imagination. God does his transforming work in such a way that he will have witnesses ready to testify to it. When Christ rose from the dead, appointed witnesses certified it. In the same way, his first miracle is certified beyond all question as real and true by the best of witnesses.

There was a special reason for this. If you come to Christ, he will not deceive you, and his blessings aren't dreams. If you trust in Jesus, the work he'll do for you will be as real as what he did at Cana. Even the ungodly will be unable to deny that God has made a change in you. When they see your new life, they'll say, "Here is something good, and something we've never seen in him before."

I pray that you would come and take Christ to be your all. And he will literally be all that you need. Trust him with your sin, and he'll bring real pardon. Trust him with your trouble, and he will give you perfect rest. Trust him with your evil nature, and he will renew you. Everyone at the wedding witnessed him turn water into wine of special quality. He can also transform your character and turn it into something that nature can never produce. The beauty of this work of grace is that it revealed the Lord Jesus by his own almighty power, transforming men, things, and facts into more magnificent ones than they were before or could ever have become. This is the unique beauty of the works of Christ. *And he that was seated upon the throne said, Behold, I make all things new* (Revelation 21:5). He presents the best last; he raises the poor from hunger to feasting and uplifts fallen humanity into something so glorious that it stands in his person near the throne of God. In all this, Christ is revealed, and his name is glorified.

Confirmation of Faith

The apostle John said, *And his disciples believed on him.* How did John know that the disciples believed on him? Because he was one of them, and he himself believed on him. The best witness is one who shared in the experience. When you experience a thing yourself, you have a full assurance of it. John knew that the other five disciples believed on Jesus by what they said to him and because their feelings coincided with his own. Let's make sure that we also share in the faith, which the marvels and the record of our Lord are designed to produce.

Note that the guests at that feast all shared in the wine, but the disciples at that feast had something far better. They had an increase of faith, which was far better than all the delicacies of a feast. Others ate and drank, but these men saw God in Christ Jesus manifesting his glory.

What was there in this miracle that would confirm their faith? Notice that I say, *confirm* their faith. It wasn't the origin of their faith, but it established it. Their faith had originated with the word of the Lord preached by John the Baptist. They had believed in Jesus as the Lamb of God which would take away the sin of the world. *The next day John saw Jesus coming unto him and said, Behold the Lamb of God, who takes away the sin of the world* (John 1:29).

They had also enjoyed personal fellowship with Jesus by following him and dwelling with him. These experiences strengthened their faith, and they began to taste the benefits of being associated with Jesus and seeing for themselves what Jesus was able to do. Because of all these things, their faith grew. His disciples had already believed, but this miracle confirmed the confidence they placed in him.

The miracle solidified the disciples' belief in Jesus, because one miracle proved the power to work every miracle. If Christ could turn water into wine by an act of his will, he could do anything and everything. If Jesus exercised a power beyond nature one time, we believe that he can do it again. There is no limit to his power, because he is God, and with God all things are possible. In this way, the first miracle confirmed their faith.

Next, it showed that their Master was prepared to meet unexpected difficulties. Nobody had foreseen that the wine would run out, and Jesus hadn't gone to the wedding prepared and primed, as we say among men. The demand came all of a sudden, and the supply came in the same way. The wine ran out, and he was ready to handle the situation. Doesn't this confirm your faith? Christ is always ready for every emergency. Something may happen tomorrow that you haven't planned for, but Christ will be ready for the unexpected. Between here and heaven you'll experience many unlikely events, but they won't be surprises to him. He has clear foresight, and when the trial comes, he will provide. *And Abraham called the name of that place The LORD Shall See (YHWH-jireh). Therefore it is said to this day, In the mount of the LORD it shall be seen* (Genesis 22:14).

> When we get Christ into our battle for God's truth, the victory is no longer doubtful. In the question of your salvation, faith brings the Savior into the situation, and you can be sure of eternal life.

Their faith was confirmed, because he demonstrated that he would allow nothing to fail with which he was connected. I like to be sure that Jesus is with me in everything I do, because then I know that he is in control of the outcome. Even though it wasn't the wedding of one of his relatives or disciples, he was still a guest, and he wouldn't allow it to be said that they ran short of provisions while he was there.

His connection with the feast may seem to have been remote, but it was a connection, and even slight connections are noticed by our Lord Jesus. If I can just touch the hem of his garment, blessing will flow from him to me. When I get into the same boat with Jesus, I know that if I drown, Jesus must drown too, because otherwise he would save me. So I know I'm safe. If I grasp the hand of Christ in my hand, or he grasps my hand in his hand, I'm linked with him, and no one can separate us. My life, my safety, and my success rests in that union. Because nothing he touches or that touches him will ever fail.

He is only one of the guests at a wedding, but because he's there, things must go well. I think this encouraged the disciples when they began to preach, for their confidence would be that Jesus was with them, and they must succeed. They were poor, uneducated men, and all the experts of the age were against them, but they said to themselves, "We have nothing to fear, because Jesus is in this situation, and he'll see us through." When we get Christ into our battle for God's truth, the victory is no longer doubtful. In the question of your salvation, faith brings the Savior into the situation, and you can be sure of eternal life.

It also showed them that he could make use of very limited resources. To make wine, the Lord only had water and six large waterpots, but he made better wine out of water than men can make out of grapes. Observe his vats and his winepresses – six waterpots of stone. What are you and I? Well, we're poor earthen vessels, and I'm afraid we're a little broken. There's barely anything in us, and that little bit is as weak as water. But the Lord can cause wine to flow from us, which will cheer the heart of God and man – words of faith which will please God and save man. The disciples would come to know themselves to be nothing but earthen vessels, but they would never forget that their Lord could work miracles with them.

Don't you think it confirmed their faith when they saw the majestic ease of his working? He didn't call for angels; he didn't deliver a long prayer or repeat a sacred incantation. He willed it, and the deed was done. The next time they faced a difficult situation, the disciples would believe that the Lord could intercede for them, and they could stand still and witness the salvation of God. In one way or another, the Lord would provide, and he would perform wonders without doing more than willing something to be. We will come out the winners in this arrangement, because God is with us. *What shall we then say to these things? If God is for us, who shall be against us?* (Romans 8:31).

It also showed them that they never needed to be anxious. Notice the expression here when you read this passage in the original Greek: Does it say, "His disciples believed him"? No. Is it "Believed *in* him"? No. "Believed *on* him"? That's what it says in the version we use, but the word *into* would be more correct. The Greek is *eis*, meaning his disciples believed into him. They believed so completely that they seemed to submerge themselves into Jesus. *Into him*; think about what that means. John, Andrew, Nathanael, and the others cast their entire lifetimes' worth of concerns upon Jesus and felt like they would never have another care. Jesus would see them through to the end, and they would trust him for everything.

At the wedding, Mary took matters into her own hands a little, but she was in error to do this. The disciples entered into Jesus through the open door of this confirming miracle, and they remained there. *Humble yourselves, therefore, under the mighty hand of God, that he may exalt you in due time, casting all your cares upon him, for he cares for you* (1 Peter 5:6-7).

They believed right into Jesus. It's one thing to believe in him and another thing to believe him. It's a restful thing to believe on him, but it's the best of all to believe right into him, so your very personality is swallowed up in Christ, and you feel the bliss of a living, loving, and lasting union with him. Those six men couldn't have produced a drop of wine for the wedding, but add their Master into the mix with them, and the seven of them could flood the streets with it if there had been a need to do so. As they entered into partnership with Jesus, their faith rose as the sun on a morning without clouds. Now they were sure, unwavering, and strong, because their weak and watery faith had gained the fullness and richness of generous wine.

> Jesus is able to transform you from what you are now into something better, fuller, grander, nobler, holier, and more God-like.

To any who are undecided, Jesus Christ will come and visit just as you are. He's willing to go to plain men's houses, even while they have a feast going on. Ask him to come to you just as you are.

I encourage you to experience how he is able to bless human joy. You might think that you'll go to Jesus next time you're in sorrow, but I say to you, come to him now while you are in joy. You who are successful in business, you who rejoice over a newborn child, you who are newly married, you who have passed an exam with honors, come to Jesus in your joy. Ask him to increase your happiness and elevate it until it touches the joy of the Lord. Jesus is able to transform you from what you are now into something better, fuller, grander, nobler, holier, and more God-like. I pray that he does it now! Believe in him, believe him, believe on him, believe into him, and it will be done. Amen.

Chapter 14

The Nobleman's Faith

So Jesus came again into Cana of Galilee, where he had made the water wine. And there was a certain nobleman whose son was sick at Capernaum. When he heard that Jesus was come out of Judaea into Galilee, he went unto him and besought him that he would come down and heal his son, for he was at the point of death. Then Jesus said unto him, Except ye see signs and wonders, ye will not believe. The nobleman said unto him, Sir, come down before my child dies. Jesus said unto him, Go; thy son lives. And the man believed the word that Jesus spoke unto him, and he went. And as he was now going down, his slaves met him and told him, saying, Thy son lives. Then he enquired of them the hour when he began to get better. And they said unto him, Yesterday at the seventh hour the fever left him. So the father knew that it was at the same hour in which Jesus said unto him, Thy son lives; and he believed, and his whole house. (John 4:46-53)

This text illustrates the rise and progress of faith as it works in the soul. I pray that we will be able to experience the track of faith, because we desire for such faith to rise in our hearts, make progress in our spirits, and become at least as strong in us as it was in this nobleman. The point is not to only hear about these things but to have them copied in our own souls. We want to get down to real business and make the things of God matters of downright fact in our own lives. Our interest isn't only to hear about this nobleman from Capernaum or anybody else but to see in our own souls the same work of grace that was seen in them. The same living Christ is here, and we need his help as much as this nobleman ever did. My prayer is that we seek it as he sought it and find it as he found it. In this way, the Holy Spirit will write it all over again, not within the pages of a book but on the fleshy tablets of our hearts. *Forasmuch as ye are manifestly declared to be the epistle of Christ ministered by us, written not with ink, but with the Spirit of the living God; not in tables of stone, but in fleshy tables of the heart* (2 Corinthians 3:3).

> It's a sad thing with some people that the more the Lord blesses them, the more bad choices they make. On the other hand, some people have hearts that turn to the Lord when he smites them.

First, let's observe that trouble led this nobleman to Jesus. If he had not experienced trial, he might not have sought out his God and Savior, but sorrow came to his house, and it was God's angel in disguise. You may be in the midst of a troubling situation right now, and if so, I pray that your affliction may be the black horse upon which mercy will ride to your door.

It's a sad thing with some people that the more the Lord blesses them, the more bad choices they make. On the other hand, some people have hearts that turn to the Lord when he smites them. When they drift into deep waters, when they barely have enough to eat, when sickness attacks their bodies, and especially when their children suffer, they begin to think of God and better things. Blessed is the discipline of our heavenly Father in such a case. It's beneficial if their tribulation bruises their heart to the point of repentance, and repentance leads them to seek and find forgiveness.

The particular form of trial which visited this nobleman was the sickness of his child. He had a son he loved who was sick with a deadly fever. The father appeared to have been a naturally kind and affectionate person, and his servants evidently cared a lot about him and the sickness of his son, which grieved him. We observe their eagerness as they came to meet him to tell him of his son's recovery.

The father's heart was gravely wounded, because his dear boy was at the point of death. No doubt he had tried all the remedies known at the time and had sent for every physician who could be found within miles of Capernaum. Then, having heard of Jesus of Nazareth, who turned water into wine at Cana and had done many mighty works at Jerusalem, the nobleman turned to Jesus with eager petition and desperate hope. He might never have thought of seeking Jesus if it hadn't been for his dying boy.

It often happens that children, though they're not angels, are used to do better work than angels could accomplish. They often sweetly lead their parents to God and heaven. They wrap themselves around our hearts, but if we see them sick or hurt, our sympathetic hearts are twisted with anguish, and we cry, "O God, spare my child! Lord, have mercy on my little one!" The first prayers that come from many hearts are inspired by grief for dearly loved little ones. Scripture says, *and a child shall shepherd them* (Isaiah 11:6).

Such was the case with this man; anxiety over his child brought him to Jesus. Someone may be reading this who isn't converted, but they are searching, because they're in great sorrow. They may know a dear little one who is wasting away, their hearts are crying to God that the precious life may be spared. Their hearts are ready to break because of the loss they so much dread. I pray fervently that our Lord turns this trouble into a path to grace.

Trial was the preface to the work of divine grace, and next is the saving part of it, the faith which was born in this nobleman's heart.

The Spark of Faith

As we approach this topic, I encourage you to pray, "I'm going to look and see if I have such a spark of faith. If I find it, I will cherish it and pray for the Holy Spirit to breathe softly on it, so it can grow to something more permanent and powerful."

The faith of this nobleman rested, at first, entirely on the report of others. He lived at Capernaum, down by the sea where news travelled fast that a great prophet had arisen who was working great wonders. Our nobleman had never seen Jesus or heard him speak, but he believed the report of others, and he was right to do so, because they were credible people. Many people are in the early stages of faith. They've heard friends say that the Lord Jesus receives sinners, and he pardons sin, calms the conscience, changes our sinful nature, hears prayer, and sustains his people who face trouble. They've heard all these things from reputable people whom they trust, and they believe them.

Are you saying to yourself right now, "I have no doubt that it's all true, but I wonder if it could ever be true to me? I'm in trouble right now. Will the Lord Jesus help me? I have a burden on my spirit. Will prayer to him relieve me?" You can't say that you know, from anything you've ever seen of him, that Jesus would bless you in this way, but you can conclude that he will from what friends have told you.

Faith often begins that way. Men believe the report, which is brought to them by people they know who have experienced the power of divine love. In this way, like the Samaritans, they believe because of the woman's report (John 4:7-28). As time passes, they will believe because they've heard, seen, tasted, and handled for themselves, but the beginning is good. This faith that comes from a report by others is a spark of true fire. Take care of it. May God grant you grace to pray about it, so spark can be fanned into a flame.

This faith was so small that it only concerned the healing of the sick child. The nobleman didn't know he needed healing in his own heart, and he didn't realize his own ignorance of Jesus and his own blindness to the Messiah. Perhaps he didn't know that he needed to be born again and didn't understand that the Savior could give him spiritual life and light. He had little knowledge of the Savior's spiritual power, so his faith had a very narrow range.

What he did believe was that the Lord Jesus could prevent his child from dying from the fever if he would come to his house. He had believed that much, which is how much faith he had, and he turned that faith into practice immediately. You don't know yet how great my Lord is and what wonderful things he does for those who put their trust in him, but you're saying, "Surely he could help me in my present trial and deliver me out of my present difficulty." So far, so good. Use what faith you have. Let me encourage you to bring your trial before the Lord. If you can't come to him for heavenly things, you may begin with the sorrows and trials of earth. If you can't come to him for an eternal blessing, you can come to him for help in your current situation, and he's ready to hear you. Even if your prayer is only about worldly things and nothing more than a purely natural prayer, pray it.

The Scriptures tell us that he hears the young ravens when they cry, and I'm sure they don't pray spiritual prayers. The ravens can only ask for worms and flies, but he hears them and feeds them. *He who gives the beast his food and to the sons of the ravens which cry unto him* (Psalm 147:9). Though you may only pray for a common mercy, you can pray with confidence if you have any faith in the gracious Lord. Even though that faith may only be a spark, I wouldn't blow it out. Jesus won't blow it out either, because he said that *a smoking flax he shall not quench* (Matthew 12:20). If you have any desire towards him and any degree of faith in him, let it live and lead you to the dear Master's feet.

The nobleman's faith was a little weak that he limited the power of Jesus to his local presence. For this reason, his prayer was, *Sir, come down before my child dies.* If he could only convince the Lord Jesus to enter the room where the sick child lay, he believed that Jesus would speak to the fever, and the fever would be eased. He had no idea that the Lord Jesus Christ could work at the distance of twenty-five miles. He had no concept that the word of the Lord could operate apart from his presence. Still, it was better to have that faith than none at all.

When children of God limit the Holy One of Israel, it's gross sin. But if those who are seeking the Lord through ignorance and weakness of faith limit him, it's far more excusable in them. The Lord Jesus treats it graciously and corrects it with a gentle rebuke. It's not the same thing for a beginner to be weak in his faith as it is for you who have enjoyed the experience of God's goodness to fall into mistrust of him.

I say to you in whom the Lord is beginning to work – if you don't have any more faith than to say, "The Lord Jesus could heal me if he was here, or the Lord would help me and answer my cry if he was here," it's better to have weak faith than to be unbelieving. Your narrow faith greatly limits him, so you can't expect him to do many mighty works for you, but he will bless you up to the measure of your faith.

In an act of undeserved sovereign grace, he may do far more than what you ask or even think, so I encourage you to treat your faith like a little baby. I would nurture and feed it until it can stand alone. Then I would hold out my finger to help it until its tottering steps become firm. We won't blame the baby when it can't run or leap, but we'll cherish it and encourage it to grow, and strength will come in due time. Our Lord Jesus Christ deserves complete faith from each one of us. Don't grieve him by being suspicious of his ability. Give him what faith you have and ask for more.

Even though it was only a spark, the nobleman's faith in the Lord Jesus Christ influenced this nobleman. It led him to take a considerable journey to find our Lord, for he had travelled from Capernaum up to the hills of Cana to plead with Jesus. And he went personally; this is even more remarkable, because he was a man of rank and position. I wonder if he was Chuza, Herod's steward, because we don't hear of any other noble family being on the side of Christ. We do hear of the wife of Chuza as among those who ministered to our Lord out of their abundance (Luke 8:3). We also hear of Manaen, the foster brother to Herod (Acts 13:1).

It may have been one of these, but we don't know; noblemen were scarce in the church in those days, as they are now. We would naturally expect to hear of such a person again. Since we see these two mentioned, we aren't being unreasonable to think that this nobleman may have been one of them.

As a rule, noblemen do not take journeys themselves when they have so many servants at their disposal, but this nobleman came in person to Christ and personally begged him to come and heal his son. If your faith is weak in some ways but strong enough in others to drive you personally to Christ and personally to pray to him, your faith is an acceptable faith. If it leads you to pray to our Lord with all your heart and beg him, then your faith is of the right kind. If it leads you to plead with Christ to have mercy on you, that faith saves the soul. It may be as little as a mustard seed, but its plea shows that there's penetrating power in it. It's true mustard. *If ye have faith as a grain of mustard seed, ye shall say unto this mountain, Remove from here to yonder place, and it shall remove; and nothing shall be impossible unto you* (Matthew 17:20).

Are you praying at this time because of sorrow? In the silence of your soul are you crying, "O God, could this be the day that I'll be helped out of my trouble and be saved?" If your faith leads you to prayer, it is the acknowledged child of grace, because true-born faith always cries. If your faith helps you grab hold of Jesus with a firm grip and say, "I won't let go unless you bless me," it may be small faith, but it is true faith. It's formed in your soul by the Spirit of God, and it will bring a blessing with it. You will be saved by this faith to our Lord's glory and to your own comfort.

I notice that this man's faith taught him how to pray in the right style. He begged Jesus to come down and heal his son, because he was at the point of death. He simply pleaded the misery of the case. He didn't point out that the boy was of noble birth; that would have been pointless with Jesus. He didn't argue that he should be healed, because he was a lovely child; that would have been a pitiful argument. He pleaded that the boy was at the point of death.

His extreme situation was his reason for urgency: the child was at death's door, so his father begged that mercy's door may open. When you are taught by grace to pray correctly, you will focus on the facts which reveal your own danger and distress and not those which would make you appear rich and righteous. Remember how David prayed, *O LORD, pardon my iniquity; for it is great* (Psalm 25:11). That's evangelical pleading. Most men would have said, "Lord, pardon mine iniquity, even though it was excusable and never reached the level of wickedness of my fellowmen." David knew better. His cry is, *pardon my iniquity; for it is great.*

Plead with God, poor sinner; emphasize the enormity of your necessity and the desperation of your situation. Let him know that you are at the point of death and that the situation you bring to him is a matter of life and death. Any hint of goodness that your pride tempts you to throw into the picture would spoil it. Plead with God for his mercy, which is the only attribute you can hope to receive while you are an unforgiven sinner. You can't ask the Lord to bless you because of anything you've done or anything you have, because you don't have anything. You would be wise to plead for your necessities. Cry, "O God, have mercy on me, because I need mercy!" State your child's case and say, "For he is at the point of death." This is the key which opens the door of mercy.

Come right away. Don't be like a horse or mule, which have no understanding, but come to Jesus while he gently draws you.

Are you converted yet? Is there any desire in you to come to the Lord Jesus Christ, even if it's only because a physical trouble has become a burden to you? A horse doesn't need a dozen spurs to make it run. The one which currently wounds your flank is sharp enough, and it's plunged in so deep that you can't help but feel it. Yield to it. Unless you need the whip as well as the spur to make you respond. If you are the Lord's chosen, you will have to come. The more quickly you do, the better will it be for you.

Come right away. Don't be like a horse or mule, which have no understanding, but come to Jesus while he gently draws you. Even though it's with such feeble faith that you fear it's really unbelief, draw near to him. Come just as you are, and look up to Jesus, and pray. In that prayer lies the hope, even the certainty of relief. The perfect heart of Jesus will hear your prayer and say, "Go in peace."

The Flame of Faith

This man's faith was true, as far as it went. That's a great thing to say. His only hope for his child's life was in this great Prophet from Nazareth, so he didn't intend to leave until his request was granted. At first, he didn't get the answer he wanted, but he quickly asked again. This showed that his faith had heart and strength in it. It was no whim or sudden impulse, because he was persuaded of Jesus' power to heal. What mercy to be delivered from empty faith. It's much better to have a little real faith than to hold to all sorts of empty religious practice and give the Lord Jesus no credit. Tell me, do you have any real practical faith in the Lord Jesus?

The nobleman's faith was true as far as it went, but the Lord tested it by saying, *Except ye see signs and wonders, ye will not believe.* I know that many of you believe that the Lord Jesus can save, but you have set in your mind how he must do it. You've read certain religious biographies, and you find that certain men were driven to despair and had horrible thoughts. You believe that you must experience similar horrors, or you'll be lost. You establish your own method of how you must be saved, or you won't be saved at all. Is this right? Is it wise? Do you intend to dictate your terms to the Lord?

Perhaps you've read or heard that certain well-known people were converted through special dreams or through remarkable blessings, and you say to yourself, "Something equally extraordinary must happen to me, or I won't believe in the Lord Jesus." You err in thinking like the nobleman. He expected the Savior to come down to his house and perform some act to reinforce his prophetic position. This nobleman is a New Testament version of Naaman in the Old Testament. You remember how *Naaman went away angry and said, Behold, I thought, He will surely come out to me and stand and call on the name of the LORD, his God, and strike his hand over the place and remove the leprosy* (2 Kings 5:11).

Naaman had planned it all out in his mind and had no doubt arranged a very proper and artistic performance. When the prophet simply said, *Go and wash in the Jordan seven times,* he couldn't receive a gospel that was so plain and simple. It was too commonplace, too free from ritual. In their preconceptions many people bind the Lord of mercy to a certain way of saving them, but our Lord won't be constrained. Why should he be?

He will save whom he wills, and he will save as he wills. His gospel is not, "Suffer so much horror and despair and live," but *Believe on the Lord Jesus Christ, and thou shalt be saved.* He comes to many and calls them by the soft whispers of his love. They trust him and enter into immediate rest. Without any extraordinary feeling, either horrible or ecstatic, they quietly exercise a childlike confidence in their crucified Lord and find eternal life. Why shouldn't it be this way with you? Why should you keep yourself out of comfort by laying down your own terms and demanding that the free Spirit should pay attention to it? Let him save you as he wills; throw away your foolish preconceived ideas.

Next, the nobleman's faith endured a reprimand. Picture the Master saying to this poor anguished father, *Except ye see signs and wonders, ye will not believe*. It was true, but it sounded harsh. The dear lips of Jesus are always like lilies dipped in sweet-smelling myrrh. Myrrh is bitter to the taste, and Jesus' words seemed to be a bitterness to the nobleman, but the father didn't give up, turn on his heel, and say, "He's treating me harshly." He said within himself, *to whom should I go?* So, he didn't go away.

He was like the woman for whom the Lord's lips dropped a far stronger morsel of myrrh, as he said, *It is not good to take the children's bread and to cast it to the little dogs* (Matthew 15:26). Yet she found a sweet fragrance in that myrrh and perfumed her prayer with it as she said, *Yes, Lord, yet the little dogs eat of the crumbs which fall from their masters' table* (Matthew 15:27). This nobleman responded to our Lord with greater persistence. He would not go away. May you have such faith in Christ that you won't leave him even when he rebukes you. Jesus is your only hope, so don't turn away from him.

Imitate John Bunyan when he said, "I was driven to such straits that I must of necessity go to Jesus. And if he had met me with a drawn sword in his hand, I would rather have thrown myself upon the edge of his sword than have gone away from him, for I knew him to be my last hope." O soul, cling to the Lord, whatever happens.

This man pleaded with passion. He cried, *Sir, come down before my child dies*. It was as if he had said, "Lord, don't question me just now about my faith. O Lord, I beg you, don't think of me at all but heal my dear child, or he will die! He was at the point of death when I left him. Come quickly and save him." His faith was limited, because he still asked Christ to come to his home and seemed to think it was necessary for our Lord to make the journey to Capernaum to cure his son. Notice how intense, eager, and persevering his pleading was. Even though his faith was limited, it excelled in force. Follow his example here: Pray, and pray again. Hold on, and hold out. Cry on, and cry out. Never give up until the Lord of love grants you an answer of peace.

The Flame of Faith

Jesus said unto him, Go; thy son lives. And the man believed the word that Jesus spoke unto him, and he went. The nobleman believed the word of Jesus to the exclusion of all his former preconceived ideas. He originally thought that Christ could only heal if he came down to Capernaum. Then he believed, even though Jesus remained where he was and only spoke the word. Will you believe the Lord Jesus Christ simply on his word? Will you trust him without making any rules of your own regarding how he will save you?

> Will you believe in Jesus Christ as he is revealed in the Scriptures? Will you believe that he can and will save you now if you simply trust?

If you are believing that dark convictions, vivid dreams, or strange sensations are necessary for your salvation, will you turn from such foolishness? Will you believe in Jesus Christ as he is revealed in the Scriptures? Will you believe that he can and will save you now if you simply trust? Haven't you heard about his passion and death on the cross for the guilty? Haven't you heard that all sin and iniquity will be forgiven if men believe in him? Don't you know that he who believes in him has everlasting life? Will you be done with your nonsense about, "Come down and save me," or "Make me feel this, and I will believe you"? Will you believe in him despite all your former thoughts, self-importance, and desires? Will you say, "I will trust my soul with Christ and believe that he can save me"? If you trust, you will be saved.

The next thing this man did to prove the sincerity of his faith was that he immediately obeyed Christ. Jesus said to him, *Go; thy son lives.* If the man had not believed what Jesus said, he would have lingered there and kept on pleading. But he believed. He was satisfied with the word of the Lord and went his way without another word. *Thy son lives* was enough for him.

When you've heard the gospel preached, many of you have said, "You tell us to believe in Christ, but we'll continue in prayer." That's not what the gospel commands you to do. I hear you say, "I'll continue to read my Bible and enjoy his abundant grace." Aren't you satisfied with his word? Won't you take that word and go your way? If you believe in him, you'll go your way in peace; you'll believe that he has saved you and act as if you know it to be true. You will rejoice in the fact that you are saved and not stop to criticize, question, and pursue all kinds of religious experiences and feelings.

You'll exclaim, "He tells me to believe him, and I believe him. He says, *He that believes in me has eternal life* (John 6:47). I do believe in him, and therefore I have everlasting life. I may not feel any strange emotion, but I have eternal life. Whether I see my salvation or not, I am saved. It is written, *Look unto me, and be ye saved, all the ends of the earth* (Isaiah 45:22). Lord, I have looked, and I am saved. My reason for believing it is that you have said it. I have done as you have commanded me, and you will keep your promise." This line of reasoning is what we owe the Lord Jesus. He deserves to be taken at his word and trusted with everything we are.

> **Look unto me, and be ye saved, all the ends of the earth (Isaiah 45:22).**

The nobleman's faith had burst into a flame; he no longer believed in a report about Jesus – he believed the actual word of Jesus. He didn't wait for a sign, but he heard the word, and on that word, he hung his confidence.

Jesus said unto him, Go; thy son lives. And he went, so he could find his son alive. May God the Holy Spirit bring you to this state at once, so you can say, "O Lord, I won't wait any longer for any sort of feeling or evidence or sign. I will place my everlasting trust on the word that your blood has sealed. I accept your promise, and because I believe it, I will go my way in peace."

I'll still say that this man's faith fell somewhat short of what it could have been. Even though he had come so far, he still had much farther to go. He expected less than he could have expected, so when he saw his servants, he asked them when the child began to improve.

He was overjoyed when they said, "The fever left him all at once. He recovered at the seventh hour." He looked for the ordinary course of nature and expected a gradual restoration to health, but here we see a miraculous work. He received far more than he ever expected.

Even when we trust the Lord, our understanding and belief is small. We measure his boundless treasure by our inadequate purses. However, the faith that saves is not always full grown. There's plenty of room for us to believe and expect more of our blessed Lord, and I pray that we would do so.

There's one thing I don't quite understand. Perhaps you can solve the mystery. The father travelled with a *peace* which comes from *confident assurance*. It was about twenty-five or thirty miles to Capernaum, and I have no doubt the good man started off as soon as the Master said, *Go; thy son lives*. He would immediately obey such a command and make progress on the road home.

But we read that the servants met him. Did they start as soon as the child was cured? If so, they might have met him about halfway. It was uphill, so maybe they travelled ten miles. That left fifteen, or even twenty, for the nobleman to travel. The servants said, *Yesterday at the seventh hour the fever left him.* The seventh hour was about one o'clock in the afternoon, and that day was yesterday. I know the day closed at sunset, but nobody would talk about yesterday without a night between. Did he take fifteen or sixteen hours for that part of the journey? If so, he didn't travel with any excessive speed. That twenty-five miles was a good day's journey for a camel, because the roads were horrible, but it seems that the happy father moved with the ease of a believer, rather than with the hurry of an anxious parent.

A nobleman's usual progress through the villages was slow, and he didn't alter his usual pace, because he wouldn't hurry now that he believed, and his mind was at peace. He was confident that his son was all right, so the fever of anxiety left the father, just as the fever of illness had left his child. Anxious minds, even when they believe, are in a hurry to see. But this good man was so sure, he wouldn't allow parental love to make him act like a shadow of doubt remained. It is written, *He that believes shall not make haste* (Isaiah 28:16). This nobleman continued his journey in such a manner as a member of the royal household would be expected to travel, accompanied by a fitting entourage, so everyone saw that his mind was at ease about his son. It's encouraging to see this type of peace. It's fitting of a solid faith.

I want you all, when you believe in Jesus Christ, to believe right up to the hilt. Don't give him a half measure of faith, but give him a complete faith. Whether it's regarding a child or yourself, believe fully. His Word alone brings tranquility to the soul. Rest in the Lord and wait patiently for him. Even when amazing joy doesn't flash through your spirit, God has said, *He that believes in me has eternal life.* So you have everlasting life. If you don't jump to your feet and dance for joy, you may sit still and sing within your soul, because God has visited his believing servant. Continue to wait for more excellent joys to come, but meanwhile, trust and do not be afraid. Are you ready to exercise a substantial, restful confidence in Jesus?

The Full Blaze of Faith

As he travelled home, his servants met him with good news. In the peaceful confidence of his faith, he was overjoyed when they said, *Thy son lives.* The message flowed over him like an echo of Jesus' words.

"I heard that," he said, "yesterday, at the seventh hour, Jesus said, *Thy son lives.* It's a new day, and now my servants greet me with the same words, *Thy son lives.*" To hear the same words again must have astonished him.

As I'm preaching the Word, I often notice how the very words strike you, when God blesses them. People say to me, "You said the very same thing we were talking about earlier. You described what was said even including our thoughts. You mentioned exact expressions we used in our conversation. Surely God was speaking through you."

Yes, it's often so. Christ's words find many echoes from the mouths of his devoted servants. The Lord provides words as well as deeds. He makes men say the right words without knowing why they say them. God is so graciously omnipresent that all things reveal him when they are commanded to do so.

The nobleman's faith is confirmed by the answer to his prayers. His experience has come to the aid of his faith. He believes more confidently than he did before. The Lord's word has been proven to him, so he knows and is persuaded that he is Lord and God. The faith of a sinner coming to Christ is one thing. The faith of a man who has already come to Christ and obtained the blessing is another and stronger matter. The first faith, the simpler faith, is that which saves. But the more mature faith is that which brings comfort, joy, and strength into the spirit.

When the nobleman spoke to his servants, his confidence grew with each detail. He knew that his prayer had been heard. *Then he enquired of them the hour when he began to get better. And they said unto him, Yesterday at the seventh hour the fever left him. So the father knew that it was at the same hour in which Jesus said unto him, Thy son lives.* The more he studied the case, the more wonderful it became. The details only confirmed his confidence, and with every detail, he rose to a clearer and firmer faith.

Some of us have experienced many of these types of confirmations. Doubters attempt to argue with us about the simplicities of the gospel. They want to fight with us on their own ground of speculative reasoning, which is hardly fair to us. Our own ground is a completely different kind; we aren't strangers to the business of faith but experts in it, so critics should give some consideration to our personal experience of the faithfulness of the Lord our God.

> We know and are sure, because we've seen, heard, tasted, and handled the good Word of the Lord.

We have a thousand treasured memories of happy details, which we can't tell you. We don't call you swine, but at the same time we refuse to throw our pearls before you. *Give not that which is holy unto the dogs, neither cast ye your pearls before swine, lest they trample them under their feet and turn again and rend you* (Matthew 7:6).

We've experienced many things, but we can't repeat them, because they're too precious to us. For these reasons, we aren't able to speak of the very reasons our own hearts find the most convincing, but we have other arguments that we choose to discuss in open court. Don't be surprised about how unshakable we seem, for you can't even begin to comprehend how intensely sure we are. It's impossible for you to argue us out of our secret understanding; you might as well try to argue our eyes out of their sockets. We know and are sure, because we've seen, heard, tasted, and handled the good Word of the Lord. Certain things are so intertwined with our lives that we are anchored by them.

"Coincidences," you say.

Say what you please, but they aren't coincidences to us! Our soul has cried out time after time, "This is the finger of God." A man who has been helped out of very severe trouble can't forget his deliverer.

You reply, "You were fortunate to get out of it." This seems like a very thoughtless remark!

If you had been where I've been and experienced what I've experienced, you would agree that the Lord stretched out his hand and saved his servant. You would have the same intense conviction that God was there, working out salvation. I know that I can't create those convictions in you by telling you my story. If you're determined not to believe, you won't accept my testimony. You'll think I'm deluded, even though I'm no more likely to be deluded than you are. However, whether you're inclined to believe or disbelieve, I have absolutely no such hesitation. I am forced to believe, because the more carefully I examine my life, the more I'm convinced that God must have been at work with me and for me.

At the same exact moment that Christ said, *Thy son lives*, the nobleman's son lived. The same words Jesus spoke to the father were also spoken by the servants who had been thirty miles away. Therefore, the father knew that something more than human had crossed his path. Do you doubt it? Besides, his dear son, whom he found healthy and well, was strong proof. You couldn't argue the happy father out of a faith which had brought him such joy. His child was at the point of death until he received the word of the Lord Jesus in faith, and then the fever fled. The father had to believe. Would you want him to doubt?

Strengthened in his faith by his experience after he believed the simple word of Jesus, the good man saw that word fulfilled, and he believed in Jesus in the fullest sense. He believed for his body and his soul, for all that he was and all that he had. That day he became a disciple of the Lord Jesus. He followed him, not only as a Healer, Prophet, or Savior, but as his Lord and his God. His hope, his trust, and his confidence were fixed on Jesus as the true Messiah.

What came next was so natural and joyous that I pray it would be true for all of you – his family also believed. When he got home, his wife met him. Can you imagine the delight that sparkled in that woman's eyes! "Our son is well," she must have said. "He's like he was never sick. He didn't need to lie in bed for weeks to recover his strength after the fever weakened him. The fever is gone, and the boy is well. My dear husband, what a wonderful Being this must be who heard your prayers and spoke our child into health from such a distance! I believe in him, husband. I believe in him." I'm sure she would have spoken like that. The same processes which had been working in her husband had been working in her.

Think of the little boy. Picture him as he greeted his father with joy. His father told him all about the fever, his trip to see the wonderful Prophet at Cana, and how he said, *Thy son lives.* The little boy cried, "Father, I believe in Jesus. He is the Son of God." Nobody would doubt the child's faith. He wasn't too young to be healed, and he wasn't too young to believe. He had enjoyed a special experience, more personal than that of his father and mother. He had felt the power of Jesus. It was no surprise that he believed.

The father rejoiced to find that he wouldn't be a solitary believer, because his wife and boy also confessed their faith. But we aren't at the end of the matter. The servants who observed this miraculous work must have exclaimed, "Master, we believe in Jesus, too. We watched the child recover, and the power which healed him must have been from God." They all followed their master's faith in Jesus.

An old nurse might have said, "I sat up with the boy all night. I wouldn't go to sleep, because I was afraid that if I fell asleep, I might find him dead when I awoke. I watched him, and at the seventh hour I saw a beautiful change come over him, and the fever left him." She shouted, "Glory be to Jesus! I never saw or heard of anything like it. This was the finger of God." All the other servants thought the same thing. It was a happy household. Not only was the child cured, but the whole household was cured.

The father didn't know that when he went to find Jesus, he himself needed to be saved. The mother also probably thought only of her son. But now salvation had come to the whole family, and the fever of sin and unbelief was removed with the other fever.

May the Lord work such an amazing act in all our houses. If any of you are crushed under a burden of grief and surrender your burden to Jesus, I trust you will be so relieved that when you tell your wife of it, she will believe in Jesus too. I pray that your dear children believe in Jesus while still a child, and that all who belong to your circle of friends and family also belong to the divine Lord. Grant your servant's desire for your glory's sake! Amen.

Chapter 15

Characteristics of Faith

Then Jesus said unto him, Except ye see signs and wonders, ye will not believe. (John 4:48)

In his letter to Theophilus, Luke speaks *of all that Jesus began both to do and teach*, as if there was a connection between his doings and his teachings (Acts 1:1). In fact, there was a very intimate connection. His teachings were the explanation of his doings, and his doings were the confirmation of his teachings. Jesus Christ never had a reason to say, "Do as I say, but not as I do." His words and his actions were in perfect harmony with one another.

You could be sure that he was honest in what he said, because what he did reinforced that conviction in your mind. You saw that what he taught you must be true, because he spoke with authority, and that authority was proven and demonstrated by the miracles he performed. O brothers and sisters, when our biographies are finally written, I pray that they aren't a compilation of sayings, but a history of the things we said and the things we did – that the Holy Spirit dwelled in us so richly that the things we did didn't clash with the things we said. It's one thing to preach, but another thing to practice. Unless preaching and practice go together, the preacher condemns himself, and his lack of practice may condemn many through his leading them astray. If you make a profession of being God's servant, live up to that profession. If you think it's necessary to exhort others to a godly life, make sure you set the example. You have no right to teach if you haven't learned the lesson, which you attempt to teach others.

Three Stages of Faith

There was a nobleman living at Capernaum who heard a rumor that a celebrated prophet and preacher was going through the cities of Galilee and Judea. He understood that this mighty preacher didn't merely capture every hearer by his eloquence but won the hearts of men by extraordinary miracles, which he worked as a confirmation of his mission. He stored these things in his heart and never suspected that they would ever be of any practical benefit to him. Then his son got sick – perhaps his only son. The sickness, instead of subsiding, gradually worsened. Fever breathed its hot breath into the child and seemed to dry up all the moisture in his body and drain the color from his face.

The father consulted every physician within his reach. They each looked at the child and pronounced him hopeless; there was no cure. The child was at the point of death; the arrow of death had sunk into his flesh, and it had nearly penetrated his heart. This boy wasn't near death; he was right at the brink of it.

Then the father recalled the stories he had heard regarding the cures performed by Jesus of Nazareth. It was enough to make him employ every resource available to him to test the truth of what he had heard.

Jesus Christ had come to Cana again, which was a journey of about fifteen or twenty miles. The father travelled as fast as he could and arrived at the place where Jesus was. His faith had progressed to such a stage that, as soon as he saw the Master, he began to cry, *Sir, come down before my child dies.* Instead of giving him an answer which would comfort him, the Master rebuked him for the littleness of his faith and told him, *Except ye see signs and wonders, ye will not believe.* The man disregarded the rebuke, because he possessed a desire which had absorbed all the powers of his soul. His mind was so consumed with one burden that he was oblivious to everything else.

Sir, come down before my child dies. His faith had now arrived at a stage where he pleaded in prayer and begged the Lord to come and heal his son. The Master looked at him with eyes full of indescribable compassion and said to him, *Go; thy son lives.* The father went his way cheerfully, quickly, and trusting in the word which hadn't yet been confirmed.

He had come to the second stage of his faith. He left the seeking stage and entered into the relying stage. He no longer cried and pleaded for a thing he didn't have. He trusted and believed that the thing had been given to him, even though he hadn't seen the gift yet. As he journeyed home, his servants met him on the road. With joyful excitement, they say, *Thy son lives.* He asked about the time the fever left him. They explained that at about the seventh hour the fever left.

Then he came to the third stage. He returned home and saw his child perfectly restored. The child sprang into his arms and covered him with kisses. When he had held him up again and again to confirm that he was really the little one who lay so sick and pale, he gained even a greater victory. His faith had grown from reliance up to full assurance, and then his whole house believed with him.

I have given you just these outlines of the narrative, so you can clearly see the three stages of faith. Now, we'll examine each in more detail.

Seeking Faith

When faith begins in the soul, it's small like a grain of mustard seed. God's people aren't born giants; they start off as babies. Since they are babies in grace themselves, their spiritual maturity is in its infancy also. Faith is like a little child when God first gives it. To use another example, it's not a fire but a spark. This spark seems like it can easily go out, but when it's fanned and kept alive until it bursts into flame, it will be comparable to the heat of Nebuchadnezzar's furnace.

> God's people aren't born giants; they start off as babies.

When the nobleman was given faith, he had it in a small amount. It was seeking faith; that's the first stage of faith. Notice that this seeking faith prompted action. As soon as God gives a man seeking faith, that man is no longer at a standstill regarding spiritual things. He doesn't fold his arms with the wicked Antinomian and cry, "If I'm supposed to be saved, I'll be saved, and I'll sit still. If I'm supposed to be damned, I'll be damned." A person with seeking faith is no longer careless and indifferent, as he had been. He's got seeking faith, and that faith makes him place a priority on spiritual growth and leads him to search the Word and be diligent in the use of every God-given blessing for the soul. If there's a sermon to be heard, he will walk five miles; seeking faith puts wings on his feet – that would be a congregation where God is blessing souls. If he enters, the man will probably have to stand in the crowd, but seeking faith gives him strength to bear the discomfort of his position and say, "If only I can hear the Word." See how he leans forward, so he doesn't even lose a syllable, because he says, "Perhaps, the sentence I lose could be the one I need the most." He becomes one of the most enthusiastic men who attend that place of worship. Seeking faith gives a man activity.

More than all this, seeking faith, though it's weak in some things, gives a man great power in prayer. This nobleman was very enthusiastic when he pleaded, *Sir, come down before my child dies.* When seeking faith enters into the soul, it makes a man pray. He is no longer content to mutter a few words when he rises in the morning and when he's half asleep at night. Instead, he steals a quarter of an hour from his business if he can, so he can cry to God in secret. He doesn't have the faith yet which gives him the ability to say, "My sins are forgiven." He has enough faith to know that Christ can forgive his sins, but what he wants is to know that his sins are really cast behind Jehovah's back. Sometimes prayer is not convenient, but seeking faith will make a man pray in an attic or a hayloft, or while he's working or walking down the street. Satan may throw a thousand obstacles in his path, but seeking faith will compel a man to knock at mercy's door.

Seeking faith doesn't give you peace; it doesn't put you where there is no condemnation, but it is the type of faith that, if it grows, it will become faith that gives peace. It only needs to be nourished, cherished, and exercised. The little one will become mighty when seeking faith grows into a higher degree of development. You who knock at mercy's gate will enter in and find a welcome at Jesus' table.

In this man's case, seeking faith didn't only make him enthusiastic in prayer but persistent in it. He asked once, and the only answer he received seemed to be a scolding. He didn't turn away discouraged and say, "He scolded me." No. He said, *Sir, come down before my child dies.* I can't tell you how he said it, but I have no doubt it was expressed in soul-moving terms. I picture him with tears in his eyes, possibly on his knees, and his hands locked together in a position of pleading. His behavior would seem to say, "I can't let go of you until you come and save my child. Please come. Is there anything I can say that would persuade you? Let my fatherly affection be my best argument. If my words aren't convincing enough, let the tears of my eyes speak in place of the words of my tongue. *Come down before my child dies.*"

Seeking faith will make a man pray mighty prayers. I've heard a seeker plead with God with all the power that Jacob displayed at Jabbok's brook, when he wrestled with God (Genesis 32:22-31). I've seen the sinner, under the motivation of his distressed soul, seem to grab hold of the pillars of the gate of mercy and rock them back and forth, as though he would pull them up from their deep foundations, rather than go away

> **If you've been bringing your cold prayers before God, it's no wonder that you don't have any peace.**

without entering in. I have seen men pull, fight, and wrestle, rather than fail to enter the kingdom of heaven. He knew that the kingdom of heaven suffered violence, and the violent would take it by force. *From the days of John the Baptist until now, life is given unto the kingdom of the heavens, and the valiant take hold of it* (Matthew 11:12).

If you've been bringing your cold prayers before God, it's no wonder that you don't have any peace. Heat them up to red-hot in the furnace of desire, or don't assume that they'll ever burn their way up to heaven. You who coolly say in sterile orthodoxy, "God be merciful to me a sinner," will never find mercy. It's the man who cries in the burning anguish of heart-felt emotion, "God be merciful to me a sinner; save me or I will perish," that God hears. It's the man who's entire soul is in every word that wins his way through the gates of heaven. Once it's given, seeking faith can make a man do this. I'm sure some of you have come this far already.

Seeking faith can do a lot, but it makes many mistakes. The problem with seeking faith is that it knows too little. We see that this poor man said, "Sir, come down, come down." Well, he didn't need to come down. The Lord can work the miracle without coming down, but our poor friend didn't think the Master could save his son, unless he came, looked at him, put his hand upon him, and, perhaps, lay upon the child like Elijah did. *Then he went up and lay upon the child and put his mouth upon his mouth and his eyes upon his eyes and his hands upon his hands; thus he stretched himself upon the child; and the flesh of the child waxed warm* (2 Kings 4:34). "Oh, come down," he said.

It's the same way with you who have been dictating to God how he should save you. You want him to send you some powerful convictions, and then you think you might believe. Or you want to have a dream or vision or hear a voice speak to you and say, "Son, your sins are forgiven." That's your error. Your seeking faith is strong enough to make you pray, but it's not strong enough to overcome your own silly ideas. You want to see signs and wonders, or you won't believe. O nobleman, if Jesus chooses to speak the word and heal your son, won't that satisfy you just as well as his coming down? "Oh, I never thought of that," he says. So, poor sinner, if Jesus chooses to give you peace right now, isn't that better than another month without it? If you are able to simply trust in Christ and find peace, won't that be as good a salvation as if you had to go through fire and water?

Here's the weakness of your faith. There is good in it, because it makes you pray. There is also some negative in it, because it makes you unwisely dictate to the Almighty how he must bless you. This causes you to deny his sovereignty and leads you to ignorantly dictate to him how he will save you.

Saving Faith

Now we'll consider the second stage of faith. The Master stretched out his hand and said, *Go; thy son lives.* Can you picture the face of that nobleman? His furrowed brow seemed to relax in a moment. Those eyes were full of tears, but they're tears of joy. He clapped his hands. His heart was ready to burst with gratitude, and his whole soul was full of confidence. The conversation may have sounded like this:

"Why are you so happy, sir?"

"My child is cured," he says.

"But you haven't seen him cured."

"But my Lord said he was, and I believe him."

"But what if when you get home, you find your faith to be a delusion and your child a corpse?"

"No," he says, "I believe in that man. Once, I believed him and sought him. Now, I believe him and have found him."

"But you have no evidence that your child is healed."

"I don't want any," he says, "The naked word of that prophet from God is enough for me. He spoke it, and I know it's true. He told me to go home. My son lives. I'm on my way, and I'm at peace."

When your faith gets to the second stage where you'll be able to take Christ at his word, then you'll begin to know the happiness of believing. It's at this time that your faith saves your soul. Take Christ at his word, poor sinner. *Believe on the Lord Jesus Christ, and thou shalt be saved.*

One might say, "I don't feel any evidence." Don't believe it any less because of that.

Another says, "I don't feel joy in my heart." Believe it. Even if your heart is full of sorrow, joy will come afterwards. It's a heroic faith that believes Christ in the face of a thousand contradictions.

When the Lord gives you that faith, you can say, "I won't be swayed by flesh and blood. He who said to me, *Believe and be saved*, gave me grace to believe, so I'm confident that I'm saved. I committed my soul, sink or swim, to the love, blood, and power of Christ. Even though my conscience doesn't reassure my soul, and doubts and fears plague me, I will honor my Master by believing his Word."

It's an honorable thing when a man has a follower, and that follower believes him without question. The man proposes an opinion, which is in direct contradiction to the collective opinion of the universe. When he stands up and presents it to the people, they hiss, boo, and scorn him. But that man has one disciple who says, "I believe what my Master has said is true." There is something nobler about the man who gives that type of devotion.

He seems to say, "Now, I'm master of at least one heart." When faced with everything that stands in conflict with the ways of this world, you stand with Christ and believe his words; you show greater devotion than cherubim and seraphim before the throne. Dare to believe. Trust Christ, and you will be saved. In this stage of faith a man begins to enjoy quietness and peace of mind.

I am not certain about how many miles lie between Cana and Capernaum, but several excellent expositors say it's fifteen or twenty miles. It wouldn't have taken this good man long to get home to his son. During the seventh hour, the Master said, *Thy son lives,* but he didn't meet his servants until the next day. We know this because they say, *Yesterday at the seventh hour the fever left him.* What do you conclude from that? I believe that the nobleman was so sure his child was alive and well that he was in no extreme hurry to return. He didn't rush home immediately, as if he had to find another doctor if Jesus hadn't succeeded. He went on his way leisurely and calmly, confident in the truth of what Jesus had said to him. In the book of Isaiah, God said, *He that believeth shall not make haste* (Isaiah 28:16). In this case it was true, for the man took his time. It took him twelve hours or more before he reached his home, even though it was probably only fifteen miles for him to travel.

He who accepts the naked word of Christ to be the foundation of his hope stands on a rock while all other ground is sinking sand. *Therefore, whosoever hears these words of mine and does them, I will liken him unto a prudent man, who built his house upon the rock* (Matthew 7:24). Brothers and sisters, some of you have come this far, and you're now taking Christ at his word. Before long you will get to the third and best stage of faith. But even if it takes a long time, stand firmly, believe your Lord and Master, and trust him.

If he doesn't take you into his banqueting house, still trust him. If he locks you up in the castle or in the dungeon, trust him. Say, "Even if he puts me to death, I will trust him." If he lets the arrows of affliction pierce and remain in your flesh, trust him. If he breaks you to pieces with his right hand, trust him. And in time, your righteousness will shine as a light and your glory like a lamp that burns brightly.

Full Assurance of Faith

So, we come to the third and best stage of faith. The servants met the nobleman and informed him that his son was healed. He arrived home, embraced his child, and saw him perfectly restored. And then the text says, *He believed, and his whole house.*

But notice in the fiftieth verse, it says that he believed: *And the man believed the word that Jesus spoke unto him.* Some expositors have been greatly puzzled by this, because they didn't know when this man actually believed. Calvin said this man only had faith which relied on Christ for a single thing at first. He believed the word Christ had spoken and, afterward he had a faith which took Christ into his soul to become his disciple and trust him as the Messiah.

I think this is a beautiful illustration of faith in its highest state. He found out his son was healed at the very hour when Jesus said he would be, and he believed with full assurance of faith. His mind was so rid of all its doubt that he believed in Jesus of Nazareth as the Christ of God. He was sure he was a prophet sent from God, and any hint of doubt no longer occupied his soul.

I know many people who want to get to this state, but they want to get there all at once. They're like a man who wants to get up a ladder without climbing the lowest rungs. They say, "If I had the full assurance of faith, I would believe I'm a child of God." No. Believe; trust in Christ's naked word, and then you'll come to feel in your soul the testimony of the Spirit that you are born of God. Assurance is like a flower. You must plant the bulb first, the naked, unrefined bulb of faith. Plant it in the ground, and soon you'll have the flower. The shriveled seed of a little faith springs up, and then you have the ripe ear of corn – or the full assurance of faith.

Notice that when this man came to full assurance of faith, his house believed too. A text is often quoted, but I don't think I've heard it quoted correctly yet. (Some people don't know any more about authors than what they've heard quoted, and some don't know any more of the Bible than what they've heard quoted, too.) The passage says, *And they said, Believe on the Lord Jesus Christ, and thou shalt be saved.* What have the last three words done that they should be cut off? The entire verse reads, *And they said, Believe on the Lord Jesus Christ, and thou shalt be saved, and thy house* (Acts 16:31). Those three words seem to be as precious as the first.

Does the father's faith save the family? Yes and No! Yes, it does in some ways: the father's faith makes him pray for his family; God hears his prayer, and the family is saved. No, the father's faith can't be a substitute for the faith of his children; they must believe also. But when a man believes, there is hope that his children will be saved. There is a promise in those words, and the father shouldn't rest or be satisfied until he sees all his children saved. If he does, he hasn't believed right yet. Many men only believe for themselves. I prefer, if I get a promise, to believe it as broadly as it's given.

Why shouldn't my faith be as broad as the promise? So, here it stands, *And they said, Believe on the Lord Jesus Christ, and thou shalt be saved, and thy house.* I have a claim on God for my little ones. When I go before God in prayer, I can plead, "Lord, I believe, and you have said I will be saved, and my house. You have saved me, but you haven't fulfilled your promise until you've saved my house, too."

I know it's sometimes thought that we who believe that infant baptism is heresy neglect our children. But there couldn't be a greater slander. We think we're doing our children the greatest service that we can possibly do them when we teach them that they aren't made members of Christ's church the day they're christened, but that they must be born again. We teach them that the new birth must be in them, and they can consciously realize it.

The new birth is not a thing we can do for them when they're babies by sprinkling a handful of water in their faces. We think our children are far more likely to be converted than those who are brought up in the delusion taught to them in catechism: "In my baptism, I was made a member of Christ, a child of God, an inheritor of the kingdom of heaven." The Pope of Rome never uttered a sentence more unholy than that. He never said a syllable more contradictory to the whole intent of God's Word.

Children are not saved by baptism, and neither are grown-up people. *Believe on the Lord Jesus Christ, and thou shalt be saved, and thy house* (Acts 16:31). Baptism doesn't co-act or co-work in our salvation. Salvation is a work of grace, received by faith and faith alone. Baptized or unbaptized, if you don't believe, you are lost. But if you remain unbaptized and believe, you are saved, and our children who sadly die in their infancy without any unholy or superstitious ritual are still saved.

> Children are not saved by baptism, and neither are grown-up people . . . Baptized or unbaptized, if you don't believe, you are lost.

Three Diseases Which Affect Faith

In the first stage, the power of seeking faith is found in its ability to drive a man to prayer. But when seeking begins, we are likely to suspend prayerfulness. The devil whispers in a man's ear, "Don't pray, it's of no use. You know you'll be shut out of heaven!" Or, when the man thinks he has got an answer to prayer, Satan says, "You don't need to pray any more. You've got what you asked for." Or, after a month of crying, he receives a blessing, and then Satan whispers, "You're a fool for lingering at Mercy's gate! Get gone! Leave! That gate is nailed up and locked tight. You will never be heard."

My friends, if you're subject to this disease while seeking Christ, I beg you to cry against it, labor against it, and never cease to pray. As long as you can cry to God for mercy, mercy will never withdraw itself from you.

Don't let Satan push you back from the closet door; push in no matter what he does. Cease to pray, and you seal your own damnation. Abandon secret petitions to God, and you abandon Christ and heaven. Continue in prayer, and even though the blessing seems slow to come, it will come. In God's own time, it will become clear to you.

The disease which is most likely to fall upon those in the second stage of faith, those who trust Christ completely, is the disease of wanting to see signs and wonders in order to believe. In the early stage of my ministry, in the midst of a rural population, I often met people who thought they were Christians because, as they imagined, they had seen signs and wonders. Since then, I've heard the most ridiculous stories from enthusiastic and sincere people explaining the reasons they thought they were saved.

One explanation went something like this:

"I believe my sins have been removed."

"Why?"

"Well, sir, I was down in the back garden, and I saw a great cloud. I thought, now God can make that cloud go away if he pleases, and it went away. I thought the cloud and my sins were both gone, and I haven't had a doubt since then."

I thought, *Well, you have good reason to doubt, because that's totally absurd.*

If I told you the dreams and fantasies that some people get into their heads, you might smile, and that might not be a good thing. Men make up many worthless stories, strange imaginations, in order to convince themselves that they are secure in Christ.

Dear friends, if you don't have a better reason to believe you are in Christ than a dream or a vision, it's time for you to begin again. I grant you, there have been some who have been alarmed, convinced, and perhaps converted, by strange freaks of their imagination. But if you rely on these as being pledges from God and look at these as evidence that you're saved, you will be resting on a delusion. You may as well try to build a castle in the air or a house on the sand.

No, he who believes Christ, believes Christ because he says it and because it's written in the Word. He doesn't believe it, because he dreamed it or because he heard a voice or because he thought he saw an angel in the sky.

We must be done with this desire to see signs and wonders. If they come, be thankful. If they don't come, simply trust in the Word which says, *All manner of sin and blasphemy shall be forgiven unto men* (Matthew 12:31). I don't say this to hurt anyone's tender conscience, a conscience which may have found a little comfort in such unique wonders. I only say this, so you won't be deceived. I warn you, so you don't place any confidence on anything you think you've seen or dreamed or heard. You would do well to heed these words like a light which shines in a dark place. Trust in the Lord. Wait patiently for him. Place all your confidence where he put all your sins – on Christ Jesus alone – and you will be saved with or without any of these signs and wonders.

> **Trust in the Lord. Wait patiently for him. Place all your confidence where he put all your sins – on Christ Jesus alone.**

I'm afraid some Christians have fallen into the same error of wanting to see signs and wonders. They've been meeting together in special prayer meetings to pray for revival. Because people haven't dropped over in a fainting fit, screamed, or made noise, they think the revival hasn't come. If only we had eyes to see God's gifts in the way God chooses to give them. We don't want a wild, boisterous revival; we want the revival in its goodness, but not in that particular shape. If the Lord sends it in another, we'll be all the more glad to be without these exceptional works in the flesh.

Where the Spirit works in the soul, we're always glad to see true conversion. And if he chooses to work in the body, we'll be glad to see it. If men's hearts are renewed, what does it matter if they don't scream out? If their consciences are revived, what does it matter if they don't fall into a fit. If they find Christ, who is going to be upset if they don't lie for five or six weeks motionless and senseless. Take the revival without the signs and wonders. For my part, I have no craving for them. Let me see God's work done in God's own way, a true and thorough revival, but we can dispense with the signs and wonders. They are certainly not required by the faithful, and they will only be the laughing-stock of the faithless.

The third disease, which lies in the way of our attaining the highest degree of faith or full assurance, is lack of observation. The nobleman in our text made careful inquiries about the day and hour when his son was healed, and that questioning gave him his assurance. However, we fail to see God's hand as much as we should.

When it rained, our good puritanical forefathers said that God had unstopped the bottles of heaven. When it rains today, we think the clouds have become heavy with moisture. If the Puritans had cut a field of hay, they prayed to the Lord that he would command the sun to shine. Perhaps we are too wise for our own good. We consider it hardly worthwhile to pray about such things and think they'll just come in the course of nature. These Puritans believed God was in every storm and in every cloud of dust. They used to speak of a God who was present in everything, but we speak of such things as laws of nature, as if laws were ever anything if there wasn't someone to carry them out and some secret power to set the whole machinery in motion.

> Be on the alert for these three diseases: ceasing from prayer, waiting to see signs and wonders, and failing to see and recognize the obvious working of the hand of God.

We don't receive assurance, because we don't look for God enough. If you actively watched for God's blessings and goodness every day, if you noticed the answers to your prayers, if you just made mental notes of God's many mercies toward you, you would become like this nobleman who was led to full assurance of faith, because he noticed that the very hour when Jesus spoke was the same hour the healing came. Be watchful, Christian. He who looks for blessings will never lack a blessing to look at.

Be on the alert for these three diseases: ceasing from prayer, waiting to see signs and wonders, and failing to see and recognize the obvious working of the hand of God.

Three Questions About Your Faith

If you say, "I have faith," I pray that it's so. Many men have said they have gold but don't have it. Many think themselves rich, but they are naked, poor, and miserable. *Because thou sayest, I am rich and increased with goods and have need of nothing and knowest not that thou art wretched and miserable and poor and blind and naked* (Revelation 3:17).

Does your faith make you pray? Not the praying of the man who babbles like a parrot the prayers he has memorized, but do you cry the cry of a living child? Do you tell God your dreams and desires? Do you seek his face and ask for his mercy? If you live without prayer, you are a Christless soul; your faith is a delusion. And the confidence, which results from it, is a dream that will destroy you. Wake up out of your death-like slumbers, because as long as you are mute in prayer, God can't answer you. You will not live for God if you don't live in the prayer closet. He who is never on his knees on earth will never stand on his feet in heaven. He who never wrestles with the angel here will never be admitted into heaven by that angel above.

I know some of you reading this live prayerless lives. You have plenty of time to manage your finances, but you have none for your prayer closet. You've never had family prayer, but I won't even talk to you about that; you have neglected private prayer. You wake up so late in the morning that you are in a rush to keep your appointments; you kneel, it is true, but where's the prayer? And you never indulge your-selves in opportunities for extra prayer. You look at prayer as a sort of luxury – too decadent to indulge in often. He who has true faith in his heart is praying all day long. I don't mean that he's on his knees, but often when he's making business deals, in his shop, or taking care of his finances, his heart finds a little space or a vacuum for a moment, and it leaps into God's embrace. Then it's down again, refreshed to go about its business.

Those spoken prayers aren't merely filling the censer in the morning with incense, but they're adding little bits of cinnamon and frankincense all day long to always keep it fresh. That's the way to live, and that's the life of a true genuine believer. If your faith doesn't make you pray, get rid of it, and let God help you begin again.

You say, "I have faith." So I'll ask you a second question. Does that faith make you obedient? Jesus said to the nobleman, *Go; thy son lives,* and he went without a word. However much he might have desired to stay and listen to the Master, he obeyed. Does your faith make you obedient? In these days, we have specimens of Christians of the most sorry, sorry kind – men who don't have common honesty. I've heard from tradesmen that they know many men who aren't Christians but are just and upright men in their dealings. On the other hand, they know some professing Christians who aren't positively dishonest, but they aren't on time if they have a bill to pay. They aren't dependable. They aren't precise. In fact, sometimes you find Christians who take part in dirty deals and professors of religion who defile themselves with acts that many worldly men would hold with contempt. I speak as God's minister, too honest to alter a word to please any man that lives: you are no Christian if you can act in business with less than the dignity of an honest man. If God hasn't made you honest, he hasn't saved your soul.

If you continue being disobedient to the moral laws of God, if your life is inconsistent and sexually immoral, if your conversation is mixed up with things which even a worldly person might reject, the love of God isn't in you. I don't plead for perfection, but I do plead for honesty. If your religion hasn't made you careful and prayerful in everyday life and if you aren't a new creature in Christ Jesus, your faith is only an empty name, as sounding brass or a tinkling cymbal. *Though I speak with the tongues of men and of angels and have not charity, I am become as sounding brass or a tinkling cymbal* (1 Corinthians 13:1).

I will ask you one more question about your faith, and then I'll be done. You say, "I have faith." Has your faith led you to bless your household? In his own quaint way, Rowland Hill, an English preacher of the late eighteenth and early nineteenth centuries, once said that when a man became a Christian, his dog and his cat ought to be the better for it. And I think it was William Jay, an English Congregationalist preacher at the same time, who always said that when a man became a Christian, he was better in every relationship. He was a better husband, a better employer, and a better father than he was before, or his religion wasn't genuine. Have you ever thought, brothers and sisters, about blessing your household? Do I hear someone saying, "I keep my religion to myself!" Don't be concerned about it ever being stolen, then. You don't need to put it under lock and key, because there's not enough to tempt the devil himself to take it from you. A man who can keep his godliness to himself has so small a portion of it, I'm afraid it will be no benefit to himself and no blessing to other people.

> **A man who can keep his godliness to himself has so small a portion of it, I'm afraid it will be no benefit to himself and no blessing to other people.**

Strange to say, you do sometimes meet fathers who don't seem as if they have any interest in their children's salvation, any more than they have interest in poor children in the slums. They would like to see their boy succeed, and they'd like to see the girl married comfortably, but as to their being converted, it doesn't seem to cross their minds. The father occupies his seat in a church building and sits down with a community of Christians. And he hopes his children will turn out well. They have the benefit of his hope. When he dies, he will no doubt leave them his best wishes, and may they grow rich upon them! But it never seems to have burdened his soul, whether they will be saved or not. Throw away such a religion as that. Cast it on the dunghill. Hurl it to the dogs. Let it be buried like Koniah with the burial of a beast of burden. Throw it outside the camp like an unclean thing, for it is not the religion of God. *But if any provide not for his own and specially for those of his own house, he has denied the faith and is worse than an unbeliever* (1 Timothy 5:8).

Never be content, my brothers in Christ, until all your children are saved. Lay the promise before God. The promise is to you and to your children. The Greek word doesn't refer to infants but to children, grandchildren, and any descendants you may have, whether grown up or not. Don't cease to plead until not only your children but your great grandchildren are saved. I stand here today as proof that God keeps his promise. I can look back through four or five generations and see that God has heard the prayers of our grandfather's grandfather, who pleaded with God that his children might live for him to the last generation. God has never deserted his house but has been pleased to bring one at a time to fear and love his name.

Let it be the same with you. In asking this, you aren't asking for more than God is bound to give you. He can't refuse unless he turns away from his promise. He can't refuse to give you both your own and your children's souls as an answer to the prayer of your faith.

Someone might say, "But you don't know my children." No, but I know that if you're a Christian, they are children that God has promised to bless.

"Oh, but they're so unruly that they break my heart." Then pray for God to break their hearts, and they won't break your heart anymore.

"But they'll bring my grey hairs to the grave with sorrow." Pray for God to bring their eyes with sorrow to prayer and to supplication and to the cross. Then they won't bring you to the grave.

"But," you say, "my children have such hard hearts." Look at your own. You think they can't be saved? Look at yourself. He who saved you can save them. Go to him in prayer and say, *I will not let thee go except thou bless me* (Genesis 32:26). If your child is at the point of death, and maybe at the point of eternal damnation because of sin, still plead like the nobleman: "Lord, come down before my child dies and save me for your mercy's sake. You who dwells in the highest heavens will never refuse your people. We would never dream that you would forget your promise. In the name of all your people, we place our hand on your Word in all seriousness and ask you to keep your promise. You have said that your mercy is to the children's children of those who fear you and keep your commandments. You have said the promise is to us and to our children. Lord, you will not turn your back on your own covenant. We challenge your Word by holy faith and beg you to do as you said. Amen."

About the Author

Charles Haddon (C. H.) Spurgeon (1834-1892) was a British Baptist preacher. He started preaching at age 17 and quickly became famous. He is still known as the "Prince of Preachers," and frequently had more than 10,000 present to hear him preach at the Metropolitan Tabernacle in London. His sermons were printed in newspapers, translated into many languages, and published in many books.

Other Similar Titles

The Soul Winner, by Charles H. Spurgeon

As an individual, you may ask, How can I, an average person, do anything to reach the lost? Or if a pastor, you may be discouraged and feel ineffective with your congregation, much less the world. Or perhaps you don't yet have a heart for the lost. Whatever your excuse, it's time to change. Overcome yourself and learn to make a difference in your church and the world around you. It's time to become an effective soul winner for Christ.

As Christians, our main business is to win souls. But, in Spurgeon's own words, "like shoeing-smiths, we need to know a great many things. Just as the smith must know about horses and how to make shoes for them, so we must know about souls and how to win them for Christ." Learn about souls, and how to win them, from one of the most acclaimed soul winners of all time.

Available where books are sold.

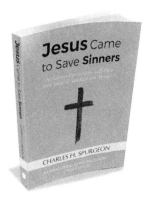

Jesus Came to Save Sinners, by Charles H. Spurgeon

This is a heart-level conversation with you, the reader. Every excuse, reason, and roadblock for not coming to Christ is examined and duly dealt with. If you think you may be too bad, or if perhaps you really are bad and you sin either openly or behind closed doors, you will discover that life in Christ is for you, too. You can reject the message of salvation by faith, or you can choose to live a life of sin after professing faith in Christ, but you cannot change the truth as it is, either for yourself or for others. As such, it behooves you and your family to embrace truth, claim it for your own, and be genuinely set free for now and eternity. Come and embrace this free gift of God, and live a victorious life for Him.

Available where books are sold.

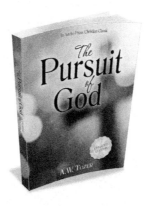

The Pursuit of God, by A. W. Tozer

To have found God and still to pursue Him is a paradox of love, scorned indeed by the too-easily-satisfied religious person, but justified in happy experience by the children of the burning heart. Saint Bernard of Clairvaux stated this holy paradox in a musical four-line poem that will be instantly understood by every worshipping soul:

> *We taste Thee, O Thou Living Bread,*
> *And long to feast upon Thee still:*
> *We drink of Thee, the Fountainhead*
> *And thirst our souls from Thee to fill.*

Come near to the holy men and women of the past and you will soon feel the heat of their desire after God. Let A. W. Tozer's pursuit of God spur you also into a genuine hunger and thirst to truly know God.

Available where books are sold.

Absolute Surrender, by Andrew Murray

"My God, I am willing that You would make me willing."

God waits to bless us in a way beyond what we expect. From the beginning, ear has not heard, neither has the eye seen, what God has prepared for those who wait for Him (Isaiah 64:4). God has prepared unheard of things, things you never can think of, blessings much more wonderful than you can imagine and mightier than you can conceive. They are divine blessings. Oh, come at once and say, "I give myself absolutely to God, to His will, to do only what God wants." God will enable you to carry out the surrender necessary, if you come to Him with a sincere heart.

Available where books are sold.

The Overcoming Life, by Dwight L. Moody

Are you an overcomer? Are you plagued by little sins that easily beset you? Even worse, are you failing in your Christian walk, but refuse to admit and address it? No Christian can afford to dismiss the call to be an overcomer. The earthly cost is minor; the eternal reward is beyond measure.

Dwight L. Moody is a master at unearthing what ails us. He uses stories and humor to bring to light the essential principles of successful Christian living. Each aspect of overcoming is looked at from a practical and understandable angle. The solution Moody presents for our problems is not religion, rules, or other outward corrections. Instead, he takes us to the heart of the matter and prescribes biblical, God-given remedies for every Christian's life. Get ready to embrace genuine victory for today and joy for eternity.

Available where books are sold.

Pilgrim's Progress, by John Bunyan

Often disguised as something that would help him, evil accompanies Christian on his journey to the Celestial City. As you walk with him, you'll begin to identify today's many religious pitfalls. These are presented by men such as Pliable, who turns back at the Slough of Despond; and Ignorance, who believes he's a true follower of Christ when he's really only trusting in himself. Each character represented in this allegory is intentionally and profoundly accurate in its depiction of what we see all around us, and unfortunately, what we too often see in ourselves. But while Christian is injured and nearly killed, he eventually prevails to the end. So can you.

The best part of this book is the Bible verses added to the text. The original Pilgrim's Progress listed the Bible verse references, but the verses themselves are so impactful when tied to the scenes in this allegory, that they are now included within the text of this book. The text is tweaked just enough to make it readable today, for the young and the old. Youngsters in particular will be drawn to the original illustrations included in this wonderful classic

Available where books are sold.

Printed in Great Britain
by Amazon

36792877R00155